Leave the Temple

Leave the Temple

Indian Paths to Human Liberation

Edited by
Felix Wilfred

WIPF & STOCK · Eugene, Oregon

Wipf and Stock Publishers
199 W 8th Ave, Suite 3
Eugene, OR 97401

Leave the Temple
Indian Paths to Human Liberation
By Wilfred, Felix
Copyright©1992 Orbis Books
ISBN 13: 978-1-60899-206-5
Publication date 11/5/2009
Previously published by Orbis Books, 1992

This limited edition licensed by special permission of Orbis Books.

Contents

A Note on Orthography   viii

Introduction   1
   Felix Wilfred

1. A Socio-Historical Perspective for Liberation Theology in India   9
   Walter Fernandes
   Pre-Independence Movements   10
   Alienation and Powerlessness   12
   Tribals and Alienation   12
   British Inputs and Destabilization   14
   Dalit Search for Alternatives   15
   Tribal Movements   16
   The Transition to Independence   17
   Religion, Status Quo, and Social Change   21
   Dalit Conversion and Social Mobility   22
   Major Trends in Post-Independence India   23
   Implications for Liberation Theology   29
   Conclusion   31
   References   32

2. Oppression and Liberation   35
   A Base for Theological Reflection on Indian Experience
   Yvon Ambroise
   Oppression in Indian Society   35
   Different Approaches to the Problem   41
   The Need and Urgency of Liberation Theology   44
   Conclusion   45
   References   45

3. *Bhakti* and Liberation Theology for India   47
   Walter Fernandes
   The Main Texts   48
   The First Stage of *Bhakti*: Brahmin-Kshatriya Competition   48
   The Second Stage of *Bhakti*: Brahminic Reaction   51

vi Contents

    The Third Stage of *Bhakti*: The Muslim Era   54
    The Fourth Stage of *Bhakti*: The British Era and the Freedom
        Movement   57
    Implications for an Indian Liberation Theology   59
    Conclusion   63
    References   64

4. DOMINANT TRENDS IN HINDU THOUGHT   66
Ignatius Puthiadam
    Background   67
    Modern Trends   69
    Moral Thought   71
    The Reinterpretation of Old Concepts   74
    Union with the Universal Spirit   75
    New Methods and Attitudes   76
    References   77

5. THEOLOGY OF LIBERATION AND GANDHIAN PRAXIS   79
A Social Spirituality for India
T. K. John
    Genesis of the Gandhian Praxis   80
    The Roots: Praxis in Early Hinduism   87
    Strategy for a New Society: *Satya* (Truth) in Praxis   89
    Sarvadharma Samabhavana: Religious Pluralism in Praxis   95
    Gandhian Praxis, the "Small Inner Voice," and Scripture   97
    The Task Ahead for Indian Theology   98
    References   99

6. THE LIBERATIVE PEDAGOGY OF JESUS   100
Lessons for an Indian Theology of Liberation
George M. Soares-Prabhu
    Teaching in Villages   101
    Teaching with Authority   104
    Teaching in Parables   108
    Lessons for an Indian Theology of Liberation   111
    References   114

7. INTERIORITY AND LIBERATION   116
Xavier Irudayaraj
    Two Approaches   117
    The *Upanishadic* Revolution   118
    Interiorization or Interiority   119
    The Way to Realization   120
    The Statement of Realization   120
    The *Jivanmukta* Model of Interiority and Service   121

  The Transcendence of Interiority 121
  Sannyasa: A Way of Life for Interiority 121
  Interiority in the Light of Liberation Theology 122
  Toward a Theology of Interiority and Liberation 123
  Conclusion 124
  References 124

8. **OUTSIDE THE GATE, SHARING THE INSULT** 125
  Samuel Rayan
  The Reality of Caste 125
  The Mind of Jesus 134
  The Task 142
  References 144

9. **TOWARD AN INDIAN THEOLOGY OF LIBERATION** 146
  Sebastian Kappen
  A Civilizational Crisis 146
  The Cry of the Poor and the Marginalized 147
  A Foundational Theology of Liberation 149
  Indian Christian Theology of Liberation 150
  From Theandric Practice to the Gospel 151
  From the Gospel to Theandric Practice 154
  References 157

10. **LIBERATION AS AN INTERRELIGIOUS PROJECT** 158
  Michael Amaladoss
  The Role of Religion in Society 160
  Religion in a Multireligious Society 162
  Conditions for Interreligious Collaboration 168
  Conclusions 172
  References 173

11. **LIBERATION IN INDIA AND THE CHURCH'S PARTICIPATION** 175
  Felix Wilfred
  Antyodaya (Awakening of the Least) and the Church 176
  Those Accompanying the Masses in Solidarity and the Church 181
  Questioning the Present Order 188
  An Ideological Framework for Indian Liberation and the
    Contribution of the Church 191
  Conclusion 195
  References 196

CONTRIBUTORS 199

A Note on Orthography

The problem of rendering non-Western systems of writing into Roman letters for English and other modern European languages is notoriously difficult. Joining many publishers who do not insert diacritical marks for words such as the Sanskrit *Śūnyatā*, this book also omits them.

Scholars and others who know languages such as Sanskrit, Pali, Arabic, or Japanese do not need the diacritical marks to identify words in their original written form. And persons who do not know these languages gain little from having the marks reproduced. We recognize that languages employing different orthographic systems have a richness and distinctiveness that *are* partially conveyed by the orthographics of diacritical marks. And while we do not wish to be part of flattening out the contours of our linguistically plural globe, the high cost of ensuring accuracy in using the diacritical marks does not justify reproducing them here.

Introduction

FELIX WILFRED

The best way to say what this book is all about is to begin with an Indian story.

There was a king who had passed an order that whenever he traveled, the bells of the temples on his way should be rung. This was an unquestioned practice for a long time. One day when the king was on his journey through a village, the temple bells did not ring, and at this, the king was enraged. He sent his minister to bring him the priest in charge of the temple. "Do you not know that you should ring the bell when I pass through the village?" asked the king. "Yes, Your Majesty, I am fully aware of it," replied the priest. "Then why did you not ring the bell?" asked the king. The priest answered, "Your Majesty, there are one hundred and thirty-nine reasons for not ringing the bell. But since I would not like to waste Your Majesty's time, let me give one reason and the most simple one: We do not have a bell in our temple!"

Ultimately liberation in India revolves around the most simple but crucial question of to be or not to be. To form an idea of what it is to struggle between life and death, one need only take a close look at the slums and pavements in the cities of Calcutta, Bombay, Delhi, Madras, where millions are consigned to the crucible of suffering, misery, and squalor, stripped of even the last bit of human dignity. Thousands in the innumerable villages of India succumb every day to starvation and malnutrition. The discriminated against women, the humiliated untouchables, the unemployed youth, the exploited tribals, the workers swindled of their rightful wages, the oppressed bonded laborers, forced rag-pickers (who are mostly children), the old and dying deprived of any medical care, those denied the possibility of any education (almost two thirds of the Indian masses is illiterate) — these victims are mute but eloquent witnesses of the range of oppression and injustice that plague every realm of life in India.

In the face of all this it becomes too evident why liberation is a pressing challenge in India today. It is a matter of delivering the lives of the masses of men, women, and children from death, destruction, and inhumanity. It is a question of survival of the least, the oppressed, and the voiceless.

But how can India be liberated? Where do the sources for its liberation lie? What direction does India follow in its project of liberation?

In the popular mind, India is so much identified with spirituality, meditation, gurus, and Yoga that any association of it with liberation and struggle may appear strange. It is often assumed that Indian religions are world-denying; they advocate passivity and resignation, and interpret everything fatalistically. From this, the conclusion is drawn that India must be pulled back from its other-worldly orientation, infused with a sense of history, and made to go through the process of modernization and secularization.

We must go beyond such stereotypes and view the whole situation and the prospects of liberation from within the experiences of India—past and present. The present task of liberation in India needs to be understood with reference to its millennial history, which has been characterized just as much by political revolutions, conflicts, wars, and movements against domination, injustice, and oppression as by flight into metaphysical speculations and relentless quest for the ultimate. Throughout the history of India various forces and movements of liberation have emerged in which religion has played no small role. It is enough to recall here that Buddhism was not only a spiritual movement; by upholding the equality of all and by questioning the hegemony of the Brahmins, it represented in Indian social history a great movement of liberation from the social stratification of caste.

Liberation, therefore, is not the monopoly of Christianity. To be effective in India, any praxis of liberation inspired by the gospel has to enter deeply into the past history of the liberation of its people and its present struggles. This entrance or immersion cannot fail to lead to a dialogue with the religious traditions of India.

In fact, the project of liberation is bringing the various religious traditions together in a new context with new challenges and tasks. Dialogue is becoming a constitutive part of the process of liberation, since this project stands in need of moral perspectives, spiritual foundations, and continuous clarification of vision.

However, we should not forget that religions can, in various ways, be forces of anti-liberation as well. This is not a mere possibility. History and experience testify that religions have legitimized slavery, the caste system, colonialism, patriarchy, and so on, and religious leaders have sided with the powers that be rather than with the poor, the marginalized, and the lowly. In India today, among other things, the fears of the minority religious groups and the apprehensions of the Hindu majority are being exploited by the political and economic vested interests. For religions, through dialogue and collaboration, to contribute to the liberation of the oppressed, it is important that each of them critically examines the role it has played and is playing in society, and that each of them reinterprets itself in the context of the present-day Indian situation. Herein lies also the importance of secular ideologies and movements that critically challenge the religions to play a liberative role in the society.

The present path of Indian liberation has to be understood against the background of a highly complex but at the same time very creative interaction between various religious and secular forces. And this encounter must be taken into account in evolving a theoretical framework for a genuine Indian theology of liberation.

Hinduism, the religion followed by the overwhelming majority of Indians, has been undergoing significant changes, particularly in what concerns society and the understanding of social responsibility. This is due to various factors: The movements of the marginalized from within the Hindu fold have continued to challenge the caste system, its oppressive structures and discriminatory practices. In the face of these challenges, Hinduism has been forced to rethink and reinterpret itself, developing in the process a sharper social consciousness. Further, the encounter with Christianity has brought about greater emphasis on history and awareness of the dimension of the personal. This new thrust is evident in Raja Rammohan Roy (1772-1833), a great religious and social reformer, considered to be the father of modern India; in Swami Vivekananda (1863-1902), who stressed the *karma marga*, or the way of action, and gave birth to the Ramakrishna movement; in Mahatma Gandhi (1869-1948), a saint in politics; and in Swami Agnivesh, who is today actively involved in liberating the bonded laborers.

In support of this new orientation, the traditional religious resources too were re-interpreted. For example, the *Bhagavadgita*, the most sacred of the Hindu scriptures, underwent a creative re-intepretation from the times of Lokamanya Tilak (1857-1920) in such a way as to include contemporary political and social concerns. Even more, the central Hindu *advaita* (non-duality) doctrine is given today a socially oriented interpretation. And this is of paramount importance for an Indian praxis, ethics and theology of liberation. For, in the classical advaitic approach attention was centered on the experience of the identity of the *atman* (one's self) with the Brahman or the Self; today, on the basis of the same experience, the other—individual and social—is being realized as one's very self. It is out of this experience of the other as one's own self ("You shall love your neighbor as yourself" [Mt. 22:39])—and therefore deeply involved in the collective self of the society—that one realizes advaitic identity or oneness with the Absolute.

Religious resources are not confined to the "great tradition" within Hinduism. The "little tradition" of popular religiosity with its strong emotional power and appeal has proved both in the past and in present times a rich source for liberation. *Bhakti*, although it also has a classical expression, is nevertheless predominantly a popular force of religiosity, albeit not the only one. The rich Indian source of popular religiosity is assuming today great importance in the struggle of the poor for liberation.

We cannot undermine the role played by the various secular ideologies oriented to the liberation of the downtrodden. This includes the anti-Brahmin ideologies of the *dalit* movements, the messianic ideologies of tribal movements, socialist movements, *sarvodaya*, and particularly Marxism. In more recent times Marxist ideology has been forced to reinterpret itself in relation to Indian society characterized by the caste system and its emphasis on the cultural, symbolic, and subjective dimensions of human life.

Various liberation groups and movements that draw inspiration both from religious and secular forces constitute a third force in the struggle of the poor for liberation. They operate on the basis of a critical interpretation of the Indian society, its past and present histories. They do not want to be identified or classified as belonging to a particular political party, ideology, or religious group. Their main concern is the defense of the dignity and rights of the people and their liberation, and therefore they are critical of religions and ideologies that are exploitative of the people or betray their interests. However, they do not underestimate the emancipative power of religion and ideologies.

These three forces, sometimes in dialogue and sometimes in conflict with one another, have led to the emergence of a new consciousness and set in motion a process of liberation in which the people themselves are the active subjects. As a result, the traditional and modern structures of injustice and oppression come increasingly under the critical scrutiny of the people. Institutions like parliamentary democracy, manipulated as they are by vested interests, have come to betray the cause of the people. Hence, there is an increasing struggle on the part of the people to arrive at people-oriented forms of governance in which they will have direct control over the exercise of power and the organization of the community. Similarly, there is a pressing demand that the power of science and technology, which today rests with those already powerful in the society, be shared with the people and directed toward the goal of equity and social justice.

To overcome the innumerable forms of oppression and enjoy integral freedom, people need to have a closer understanding of the nature of the evil operating in the society. The incisive Marxist tool of analysis has demonstrated itself a very useful instrument in unmasking the nature and mechanism of oppression and injustice in most societies. However, this analysis is found to be inadequate to explain the functioning of Indian society with its specific aspect of the caste system. This is why the Indian Theological Association, in the final statement of its tenth annual meeting, which dealt with the theme of sociocultural analysis, stated:

> In our search for effective tools, the value of the Marxist analysis must be given due recognition as it has made valuable contribution to the understanding of our situation in India. While acknowledging the specific merits of Marxist analysis, we feel the need for a holistic analysis incorporating all aspects of reality including the dimension of transcendence (*Vidyajyoti* 1987, 249).

Being aware of the limitation of Marxist and other imported forms of analysis, one tends, in the context of Indian theology of liberation, to give greater importance to people's own resources of liberation and their own analysis of the situation. One could think, for example, of the stories, myths, and sagas that abound in the daily lives of the people. These often carry not only messages of freedom, quest for fullness, and the hope for a liberated life, but also contain elements for analyzing society. For example, the great Indian epics *Ramayana* and *Mahabharata*, which are very much alive in the hearts of the Indian masses, furnish the perspective and tools to view the society and to analyze it. The analysis of the people often takes place in the form of typology. Rama, for example, is the type of a righteous person in the society and Ravana the unrighteous. Rama struggles to overcome the evil one. Sakuni, another figure in the *Mahabharata* represents the villain. Any event taking place in society is interpreted by the people with reference to a similar situation in the epics; to every human type there is a corresponding character in the epics. Given this, a villager is able to analyze his village pinpointing who is Rama, who is Ravana, and so on.

Employing these traditional resources of the people, which resonate with their present life and experience, roots the liberation praxis in the culture and thereby makes it effective. The Indian praxis of liberation must go hand in hand with the holistic and integral vision of reality, characteristic of the traditional Indian culture and heritage. In this vision, the sociopolitical struggle for liberation is not simply a matter of the empirical order or of ethical concern. The Indian approach places the empirical and ethical concerns within the frame of the totality of reality, which comprises the divine, cosmic, and human dimensions.

Every form of oppression and enslavement, including the sociopolitical, is seen as a fragmentation that unsettles the whole reality, as a distortion of the divine, the human, and the cosmic. Therefore, liberation must be integral, for it concerns the reality in its totality, with its inextricably interrelated and mutually interpenetrating triple dimensions. In other words, liberation is a matter of commitment to *sat* — the real, truth — or respect before being. In fact, in Sanskrit the word *satya*, meaning "truth," stems from *sat*, which denotes being or reality in its totality.

Liberation therefore has to be practiced and understood as holistic, integral, and ontic. The struggle to overcome various sociopolitical oppressions should be intertwined with the quest for being, truth, and wholeness. This is not to water down the force of historical involvement but precisely to give it strength and force. Being or reality is characterized by *sakti*, dynamism, energy, and the most fundamental form of it is self-affirmation as being rather than nothing or non-reality. Every domination that seeks to negate or disregard the power within being violates reality inasmuch as it is deprived of the power by which it can express itself, evolve, and grow in harmonious relation to the whole.

The negation of power to individuals and groups for their self-determination and growth as humans in relation to the whole, therefore, is an assault on being, on truth rather than just a moral and ethical question of the historical and empirical order. Hence the harmonizing and balancing of power at the sociopolitical level is an inner demand of the nature of reality, for the well-being of the whole and all its parts. Such an ontic and holistic vision should underlie the choice of social, economic, and political systems and policies, as well as the choice of the technological means through which human beings relate themselves to nature and benefit by its gifts.

From this perspective, an Indian theology of liberation would be a theology that challenges liberation understood only in historical terms, as though the real being were dissolved within the historical or within the rational. This theology would aim at freedom and liberation in the horizon of the whole and the ontic. Hence the new openness in the Indian experience to the historical, the social, and the ethical is not at the price of its ontic approach, namely, an approach based on *sat* (the real, truth), nor at the cost of organic and holistic vision. The originality of the emerging Indian theology of liberation consists in maintaining a dialectical tension between the historical, ethical, and empirical on the one side, and the ontic and the holistic on the other. To that extent it represents a challenge both to the Latin American theology of liberation and to western theological currents, such as political theology with its overstretching of the category of history.

Yet another dimension of the emerging Indian theology of liberation needs to be highlighted. Authentic emancipatory praxis is seen in India as rooted in *anubhava*, a deep experience of being, truth, beauty, life, and freedom. *Anubhava* can energize individuals and groups to hold out against the threats to life. Poverty, oppression, and exploitation constitute *adharma* (non-righteousness), which is diametrically opposed to truth, life, and freedom. Liberation is commitment to *dharma*—righteousness. But genuine praxis of *dharma* is not possible without detachment, renunciation, emptiness, silence, in short, kenosis, which expresses itself in suffering without anger and malice; it has enormous liberative potential. Emptiness and detachment form the locus for the discovery of truth, the experience of freedom, and the praxis of liberation in truth, justice, and love.

Following such a path of liberation is nothing but experiencing the way of Jesus in his kenosis; it gives a social and political expression to the Sermon on the Mount, the *dharma* of Jesus. There is no liberation without kenosis, without readiness to renounce, to sacrifice, to lay down even one's life (Jn 10:17-18). The fullness of life is emptiness or *sunyata*. Only a praxis that is sustained by kenosis can be liberating and life-giving inasmuch as it lets truth arise on the horizon of our historical engagement. "The truth will make you free"(Jn 8:32).

In the light of the above, it becomes clear why Indian liberation theology cannot be a theology concerned solely about liberation from oppressive sociopolitical structures. Such a project will not yield fruit, will not move in the direction of greater humanization, unless it is accompanied simultaneously by a process of personal conversion, liberation, and transformation of the subject. Indian theology will bring to bear upon sociopolitical liberation the strength of its traditional religious heritage relating to the inner liberation of the self. The symbiosis of these concerns will be the hallmark of an Indian liberation theology.

Finally a word about the title of the book. The phrase *Leave the Temple* is inspired by the verses of Rabindranath Tagore (1861-1941), a great modern poet of India and a man of deep spiritual insights. In a poem in *Gitanjali*, for which he was awarded the Nobel prize, he wrote:

> Leave this chanting and singing and telling of beads! Whom dost thou worship in this lonely corner of a temple with doors shut? Open thine eyes and see thy God is not before thee! He is there where the tiller is tilling the hard ground and where the pathmaker is breaking stones. He is with them in sun and in shower, and his garment is covered with dust. Put off thy holy mantle and even like him come down on the dusty soil (poem xi).

The scene the poet portrays is reminiscent of the words of Isaiah:

> When you come to appear before me,
>   who requires of you
>   this trampling of my court? . . .
> When you spread forth your hands,
>   I will hide my eyes from you;
> even though you make many prayers,
>   I will not listen . . .
> Wash yourselves; make yourselves clean;
> seek justice,
>   correct oppression,
> defend the fatherless,
>   plead for the widow (Is: 1:12-16).

The title also evokes the scene of Jesus driving out vendors from the Temple (Jn 2:13-17; Lk 19:45-46) and his call to worship God in "spirit and truth" (Jn 4:23-24).

More immediately, the title hopes to express the new orientation of historical commitment to the transformation of the world and solidarity with the least that has come about in the Hindu world, in part through its encounter with Christianity.

The title refers also to the deep Hindu conviction that the Divine is not confined to any one place, but is present in the entire reality—human, world, and nature. The searchlight that was focused traditionally on the interior self, the inner temple, in order to discover therein the ultimate reality, is today being turned also on the concrete historical and sociopolitical realities to discover in the heart of the struggles of human beings and their aspiration for justice, the unfathomable mystery of the Divine.

Gandhi was one of the most deeply religious persons who ever walked on our earth, and yet he was not known to have visited temples, shrines, and pilgrim-centers, which all abound in India. Gandhi symbolizes the new religious orientation of India, which draws inspiration from its ancient traditions. Accordingly, the Divine is not to be sought and meditated upon only in the temple of one's inner self or in the temples of stones, but to be encountered and contemplated within history through karma—liberative involvement.

This new orientation goes hand in hand with another experience. In the midst of the Indian situation of oppression something new is happening. As in the vision of Ezekiel (37:1-14) the dry bones in the Indian valley of misery and death are rising, stirred up by an invisible power, the spirit moving among them. This experience of the rising of the least could be called *antyodaya*. This term is the combination of two Sanskrit words. *Ant* means "last" or "least," and *udaya* means "rising." An Indian theology of liberation wants to reflect the experience of the rising Indian masses and their search for fullness of life, fellowship, truth, and freedom.

This book is exploratory in nature. It tries to interpret and reflect on the Indian situation of bondage and oppression, and attempts to open up avenues of liberation. The contributions reflect a wide spectrum of problems and concerns as perceived and interpreted by the different authors. In spite of all the differences, the reader will perceive a common thrust and convergence in method, content, and orientation.

Though the original manuscripts were written in English, the book was published first in German by Herder. Most of the articles have been revised for this English edition, which contains several that did not appear in the German edition.

I wish to thank Dr. Paul Knitter and the editorial staff of Orbis Books for their interest in bringing out an English edition. My sincere thanks go also to Fr. S. Nesamony, O.C.D., for his untiring and valuable assistance in editing this work.

REFERENCES

Vidyajyoti, 51, 1987.
Tagore, Rabindranath. 1918. *Gitanjali*, Macmillan, New Delhi/New York.

1

A Socio-Historical Perspective for Liberation Theology in India

WALTER FERNANDES

India today is a country of class and caste inequalities. Within this general division cumulative inequalities based on caste and sex discrimination are particularly conspicuous. Some groups accumulate almost hegemonic power and advantage based on urban-rural, class, caste, and sex-based differences. This section of the population can afford to live at western levels of consumption. On the other extreme, forty-eight percent of the country's 880 million people suffer from malnutrition, illiteracy, and ill health, and are victims of the same urban-rural, class, caste, and sex-based differences (de Souza 1986, 35-36).

Members of the former group are predominantly from the urban upper castes and classes, and the latter belong mostly to the rural lower classes and castes. On one extreme is the urban upper-class, upper-caste male, and on the other, the rural, poor, low-caste female. The former owns most of the assets, is politically powerful, has high social status, is culturally dominant, and has access to all the requirements for upward mobility. The latter has no assets, is politically powerless and culturally marginalized, has low social status, and is denied access to most services. In between are the middle castes and classes, whose ownership of assets, social status, and access to services depend more or less on their place in the continuum (Fernandes 1985, 7-12).

Accompanying these inequalities is religious revival, most of it controlled by reactionary forces. While the victims of socioeconomic inequalities struggle for change in the structures that marginalize them, those with a vested interest in the status quo use religion to counteract the forces of change.

On the other hand, those supporting change often use a purely secular language and even tend to discard religion as an exclusively reactionary and political tool; they rarely ask themselves why the masses are won over by the status quoist forces in the name of religion (Joshi 1989, 162-78). They see their efforts at change thwarted by the reactionary forces, who divert the attention of the poor from sociopolitical and economic exploitation by presenting efforts to change the unjust structures as proselytization or threat to religion (Fernandes and Lobo 1986, 306-9). Because social activists do not pay adequate attention to psychological and emotional components, and speak of religion as exclusively reactionary, they fall in the trap of the status quoists, who exploit the emotional component of religion to turn the poor against these agents of change (Fernandes 1988, 7-8).

The movements for liberation have to be viewed in the context of these inequalities and contradictions. We shall study the historical background of a few of these movements from the colonial period to the decades after the country's independence in 1947. An element of continuity is the link between religion and social change. Religion has historically been one of the major bases both in support of and against social change.

PRE-INDEPENDENCE MOVEMENTS

The very nature of colonial inputs ensured that there would be many liberation movements, though most of them would be coopted by the dominant sections at some stage or the other. The most successful movements have had to depend on religious legitimation in order to be effective. There have been low-caste and tribal movements—some violent, others peaceful.

THE *BHAKTI* MOVEMENT

The best-known caste movement in the last few centuries was *bhakti*. Its basic ideology is that no human group can be considered inferior or superior because of the work it does, as long as it is done out of devotion (*bhakti*) to God, before whom all are equal. This movement for social change with religious legitimation began in the fourteenth century and had spread to most of India by the sixteenth century. Efforts were made by the dominant castes to coopt it and reform the system without changing it, but it remained to a great extent an effort of the untouchables to free themselves from caste repression. This movement was the last chance Indian caste society had to reform itself within the Hindu fold. Its impact was still being felt in the nineteenth century (Harrison 1960, 64).

Colonialism played into the hands of the upper castes. Colonial rule is essentially an effort by a foreign power to control the local population through the indigenous upper classes by integrating them into the foreign-controlled hierarchy as intermediaries. At a moment when the impact of the *bhakti* movement was still being felt and the low castes had an equal opportunity of asserting themselves, the British strengthened the upper castes, whom they needed as their collaborators. The leaders of the latter were provided with opportunities of further strengthening themselves through access to western education and to administrative posts in the colonial system.

These colonial inputs dealt a decisive blow to the low castes and the aspirations symbolized by the *bhakti* movement. Any hope they had of change in the caste system within the Hindu fold disappeared. They would have to find other avenues of liberation.

LAND OWNERSHIP AND CRISIS

Other British interaction with local structures laid the foundation for further changes. Though colonialism was legitimized in the name of the "civilizing mission" of the European in the "barbarian continents of Asia and Africa," in reality it was a mode of transferring resources from the colony to the metropolitan country for the benefit of the industrial revolution of the colonizing nation and for creating within the colony a market for finished industrial products. To ensure this, the colonial administration had to depend on the traditional feudal system for tax collection, thus further strengthening it. When the local structures did not suit the above objectives, they had to be destroyed and a new legal system created to suit colonial needs (Sarkar 1983).

One system that had to be destroyed was communal ownership of property. Traditionally the relationship between castes was based on *jajmani*, or division of labor. Some castes divided this land between the families who cultivated it as trustees of the whole group. All the others were service castes rendering services as priests, barbers, tailors, sweepers, and so forth. Though the type of services rendered were linked to their caste, in reality each individual family was linked to a certain number of families in the landowning caste. At the time of the harvest, each landowning family was bound by custom and law to distribute grain to all the service caste families linked to it, the quantity depending not on the amount of work put in but on the status of the caste to which each family belonged (Anant 1972, 16-18).

British entrepreneurs wanted to appropriate land in India for tea plantations and mines. At the same time Indian farmers had to be forced to divert land from staple food to commercial crops, such as jute and indigo, which were required as raw material by British industry. The landholding pattern and legislation had to be changed to suit this purpose. Communal ownership had to be abolished and landlordism established. This was done through the *Permanent Settlement 1793*, which turned land in most of eastern and parts of southern and western India into the private property of the highest bidder at auction. These *zamindars* (landlords) became owners of that land subject to a fixed payment to the government (Sen 1979, 1-5).

In areas like Assam, the British entrepreneur also required a plantation-labor force. Policy there was rack-renting to force the peasants to surrender their land to the planters and become laborers on the land they once owned (Badgaiyan 1983, 83-86).

ALIENATION AND POWERLESSNESS

An immediate consequence of these policies was the weakening of the *jajmani* system. The service castes were freed from the landowning castes, to whom they had been tied till then. They were now free to become a mobile force available for work in British mines and plantations. The process was similar to the process in Europe at the beginning of the Industrial Revolution, where the freed serfs became available as a mobile labor force for factories. Because of the Industrial Revolution, they could get new jobs, though on extremely exploitative terms (de Boschere 1967, 222-25).

The difference in India, however, is that rack-renting of tenants by landlords discouraged investment in land and thus agricultural production stagnated (Sen 1979, 32-47). Further, industrial jobs were created because of the policy of deindustrialization. The extractive industries remained enclaves and did not develop the hinterland (Rothermund 1978, 2). The consequence for the service castes was freedom from the exploitative *jajmani* system without anything to take its place. *Jajmani* was an unjust system, which forced the low castes to retain their subordinate status with no possibility of freedom from the low status attached to their occupation. But it provided them with material security. Colonial intervention deprived them of this material security with no change in their social status.

A certain number of those who were thus freed were taken as indentured laborers to plantations in British colonies in the West Indies, East Africa, Mauritius, Sri Lanka, Malaysia, Fiji, and elsewhere. Indian merchants who followed these indentured laborers only added to their slavelike condition (Jayaraman 1975, 26-30). A very small percentage gained freedom by joining the British army (Robertson 1938, 59-64) or by commercializing products like liquor and other "low status" commodities the upper castes considered impure. Another small section sought freedom from caste oppression through religious conversion (Fernandes 1981). The rest were impoverished, often indebted, and forced to negotiate as individuals with individual farmers and accept employment that would eventually force them to become bonded laborers (Sarkar 1983, 34-35). Already a marginalized group, the untouchables were thus rendered more powerless by colonialism.

TRIBALS AND ALIENATION

The tribals, on the contrary, though not in the mainstream of India, were traditionally not as powerless as the untouchables. Although greatly diverse, they share a dependence on the land and forests for their very survival. Even today, tribals form around seventy percent of the forest dwellers in India. Traditionally their dependence on the forest was total. From it they got about eighty percent of their food, which included cereals and pulses harvested from shifting cultivation. They depended on the forests for fuel, timber and thatch for housing and furniture, agricultural implements, organic manure, fodder, medicinal herbs, and other needs (Fernandes, Menon, and Viegas 1988, 151-57).

To them land is not a purely economic asset, but a part of their spiritual as well as economic heritage. The importance tribals attach to the land that sustains them is much deeper than mere economic utility would indicate. All agree that the problems of land and tribals' rights on lands they cultivate are fundamental for a more efficient use of land resources (Reddy 1987, 14-15).

Given the extent of their dependence, tribals ensured that forests and land were treated as renewable resources that catered to the needs of their community and were preserved for posterity. Through an egalitarian community they served the needs of every family. They also had in-built social control mechanisms meant to discourage any family from appropriating to itself a larger share of the resource than was its due (Sharma 1978, 13-14). Conservation was ensured also by developing myths, traditions, and a whole culture geared to treating land and forest as community resources meant to be preserved for posterity and not as property to be destroyed at the owner's will (Fernandes, Menon, and Viegas 1988, 159-70). Many tribes, particularly those in northeastern India, supplemented this conservation-oriented culture with participatory political structures that ensured that no individual appropriated absolute power to himself and controlled a bigger share of the resource than was his due (Das 1986, 49). Briefly, land and forests were the very center of tribal life; tribals built their religious, cultural, social, economic, and political life around them. Consequently, any interference with these resources was bound to result in a total crisis in their whole society.

Such an intervention had begun already in the seventeenth century. In eastern India some of the tribal chiefs were jailed together with Hindu *rajas* (kings), thus exposing them to the luxurious life of the *rajas*. When they returned to their land, the tribal chiefs changed their traditional lifestyle; they brought non-tribal officials into their area and allotted them *jagirs* (territories) from which they were to collect tax and keep a part of this income for themselves (Kanjamala 1981, 55-56). When this income was inadequate, the chiefs handed other territories over to *thikedars* (merchants who supplied luxury goods) (de Sa 1975, 35-36). Often the *jagirdars* and *thikedars* behaved like landlords or even rulers and exploited the tribals by demanding tribute in the form of free labor. They did not, however, interfere with the internal self-government and the over-all socioeconomic system (Pathy 1988, 85-87).

In western India feudal intervention came through the conquest of tribal lands by Hindu kings, who brought Hindu *thikedars* and *jagirdars* with them (Chaubisa 1988, 38-41). As a result, alienation from tribal culture was greater in western than in eastern India. In the northeast the process of Hinduization, which had started in the sixteenth century, engulfed the Manipuri and Assamese tribals. By the mid-nineteenth century the thrust had begun toward the remaining northeastern tribes, which were attempting to maintain their identity against this onslaught (Downs 1983, 2).

Most tribals resented this interference with their culture, economy, and society. At times they resisted the external forces of exploitation. However, unlike in the British age when their resources became state property, in the feudal era there was relatively little interference with their informal economy and internal self-management. As a result, though they resented the intrusion, both external interference and tribal resistance remained within tolerable limits (de Sa 1975, 33-38).

BRITISH INPUTS AND DESTABILIZATION

The colonial need to provide capital and raw material to the factories in Europe and create captive markets for their finished products has to be situated in this context of the tribal informal economy based on an egalitarian community, word of mouth, mutual trust, and a barter system. Landlordism was the only ownership pattern the British recognized. At the *Permanent Settlement 1793*, therefore, the British recognized the *jagirdars* and *thikedars* as owners under the *zamindars*. In a society of illiterates based on word of mouth, they gave written *pattas* (land ownership documents) to the *zamindars*, who turned the tribals into tenants-at-will (Reddy 1987, 66-69). Administrative and legal systems were changed to suit colonial needs. The subordinate officials who ran this system had little understanding of the tribal society and less sympathy for it. They, as well as the police appointed by the British, supported the landlords (Singh 1983, 13). Besides, the landowning pattern introduced by the British was not production-oriented; it was geared to collecting tax for investment in Britain's Industrial Revolution. Consequently, what was till then a voluntary contribution to the chief and tax in kind was turned into monetary land tax.

Forced labor was extracted from the tribals for the maintenance of the landlord's family (Pathy 1988, 87). Tax collection was through rack-renting of the tenant-tiller or through sharecropping, in which an exorbitant share of the final produce went to taxes, for example, two-thirds of the crop. This discouraged the tenant both from producing more annually and from making any long-term investment in the land (Jetley 1977, 46-47).

Further, the British inputs came at a time when competition for land was increasing and more and more non-tribals were entering the area to occupy tribal land. The British policy of giving permanent tenure to the landlords through a written *patta*, and the absence of any such document in the hands of the tribals, resulted in massive land alienation. A survey in 1910 revealed that only ten percent of the tribals in Chotanagpur owned land (Kanjamala 1981, 59).

In addition, forest policy turned the tribal's life-support system into state property and a source of revenue for the colonial administration. Initially forest dwellers were given some rights. These were slowly turned into privileges and eventually into concessions (Fernandes 1988a, 84-94).

The net result of the land and forest policies was that a society, which was attempting to fight the inegalitarian tendencies coming in with nontribal rulers, was further marginalized. The foreign policies intensified inequalities.

A major consequence of the resulting tribal alienation from land and forests was their proletarization. As in the *jajmani* system, the crisis in the socioeconomic structures of the tribals provided British mines and plantations with the workers they required.

DALIT SEARCH FOR ALTERNATIVES

Eventually the powerless untouchables as well as the once self-reliant but now marginalized tribals began to search for alternatives. A small minority of the untouchables were integrated into the colonial system, in some cases because the commodities they produced, such as liquor, were commercialized for the first time. A few others, like the Mahars, were integrated into the British army (Robertson 1938, 59-64). Most of the remaining joined the proletariat and were either bonded or indentured.

A search for alternate coping mechanisms was inevitable. Given their powerlessness, an armed revolt was not easily possible among the untouchables, known today as *dalits* (the oppressed), and very few such revolts took place among them. Their search took the form of two types of cultural movements aimed at freedom from oppression (Shah 1985, 175). The first is reformative, that is, change within the Hindu system. It includes the *bhakti* movement, sanskritization, and the non-vedantic *dalit* movements in Maharashtra, Tamilnadu, and elsewhere. The initiative in a few of these movements came from the upper castes, but it was a response to pressure from below.

The second type of movement includes alternatives outside the Hindu fold. In some cases these took the form of conversion to Christianity, Islam, Sikhism, and other religions that preached equality (Sharma 1976, 219). The untouchable converts are often accused of being "rice Christians," persons who embraced Christianity "for a plate of rice," that is, material incentives. It is true that in many cases the missionary offered material inducements in order to attract *dalits* to Christianity. However, a deeper analysis of the conversion movements, made not from the missionary or upper-caste point of view but from that of the convert, shows that to the untouchable change of religion was not primarily a mode of economic improvement. It was, more than anything else, an effort to change social status, a search for freedom from caste oppression (Forrester 1980, 74).

In other cases the alternatives took the form of secular movements among the *dalits*. One can mention among them the Self-Respect Movement in Tamilnadu (Saravanan 1987, 228-43), Jotiba Phule's movement for social reform and equality in Maharashtra (Aggins and Lochan 1989, 142-50) and the *Sri Narayana Dharma Paripalana* among the Ezhavas of Kerala (Oddie 1977, 53-56). In many of these cases there was an element of change within Hinduism through sanskritization, acceptance of upper caste customs, culture, gods, and food habits. But their distinguishing feature was upward mobility through education, political organization, and other secular inputs.

TRIBAL MOVEMENTS

As for the tribals, their very independence, self-respect, and human dignity were closely linked with their forests and land. Consequently, loss of these resources jeopardized their family, cultural, religious, and social life. Their very identity was under attack.

Protests against this marginalization and efforts to recover their lost identity were inevitable. Being a more cohesive group than the untouchables, there were more organized movements among them than among the *dalits*. Religious conversion was one such effort to recover the security and identity lost through colonial interventions. Given the total crisis in their life, they were prepared to go along with those who fought for their land rights since their identity was linked to this resource. Fr. Constans Lievens, a Belgian Jesuit, and a few others did this for them, and this resulted in mass conversions among the tribals in Chotanagpur in Bihar, beginning from the 1880s (de Sa 1975).

Apart from religious conversion, protests also took a violent form. Major rebellions in Chotanagpur included those of the Mundas and Oraons in 1820; the Kol rebellions of 1831-32; the Santal Rebellion of 1855-57, which cost at least ten thousand lives; the Munda revolt of 1860; and the revolt of the Oraons in 1890. In Andhra Pradesh in the south there have been many violent agitations of the tribals, beginning with the anti-*muttadar* (landowner) uprising of 1862 and ending with the *pithoori* conspiracy of Alluri Ramachandra Raju in the 1920s (Rao and Rao 1983, 313-14). In the western region there have been movements among the Warli, Bhil, and other tribals. One series of violent uprisings lasted from 1818 to 1846, and another from 1859 to 1880 (Mathur 1988, 31-41, 66-69).

While the intensity of these agitations and the efficacy of their organization differed, common to all of them was tribal impoverishment caused by land alienation and the forest policy.

The scene in every tribal area of the country during the British period was almost the same. Interference with the internal traditional affairs, oppression and inhuman treatment, alienation from the basic productive resources of land and forest were the order of the day. In all the cases of tribal insurgency or armed struggles during the period, the tribals chose rebellion or revolt as a last resort after having failed to attract the attention of the authorities through repeated appeals and even representation (Reddy 1987, 7).

Another common feature was the role religion played as a coping mechanism. Repression was great. The British, interested as they were in maintaining law and order for commercial purposes, used their army in support of the *zamindars* to quell the uprisings. Initially, a religious revivalist movement followed the failure of every revolt.

Slowly, however, the tribals combined religious revival with socioeconomic rebellion. Such, for example, was the Birsa Munda movement in Chotanagpur toward the end of the century. In doctrine it was a combination of Munda religious systems, Christian beliefs, and the Hindu *Sadan* movement. The Mundas accepted the Hindu God Shiva as the *Mahadev Bonga* (the Great Spirit). The movement combined into one cohesive whole a quest for land, anger against *dikus* (foreigners, non-tribal exploiters), and hope for the future (Singh 1983, 18-20). Similar movements arose among the Warlis of Maharashtra, the Bhils of Rajasthan, and other tribes of western India (Chauhan and Chelawati 1978, 119-22). To a society in crisis, conversion was not a purely spiritual act but a coping mechanism and search for liberation. It was thus a social revolt with a religious legitimation.

THE TRANSITION TO INDEPENDENCE

Unlike the above rebellions of the oppressed, the freedom struggle was to a great extent an upper-class movement. It was led by the elite, which had been coopted into the British system and had strengthened itself as a result of colonial inputs but was disillusioned with the double standards of the foreign rulers. These people saw all the contradictions that were emerging in the Indian society as a result of foreign interventions. They used the popular demands of the earlier peasant, *dalit*, and tribal movements to get the masses on their side, thus consolidating their own hold over the masses (Sarkar 1983).

Religion and Society

Religion was an essential element in this consolidation, both because the popular resistance movements such as those of the *dalits* and tribals had found a religious legitimation for social protest and because the British had encouraged Hindu-Muslim, caste, and cultural cleavages as part of their divide-and-rule policy. The leadership of the freedom struggle came primarily from the Brahminic classes. The movement was funded by the new Indian capitalists belonging to the middle castes. The latter viewed their financial support of the freedom movement as an investment in the future, whose benefits they would reap after the country's independence. In order to gain control over the freedom movement they intensified the religious, cultural, and caste cleavages that had till then been sustained by the British for colonial ends. The foundation was thus laid for post-independence religious and inter-caste competition and clashes (Shankardass 1982).

The Brahminic class leaders of the movement had to find a rallying point to bring the masses together. This unity was essential because the British had presented India as a conglomeration of religions, castes, cultures, and languages that would be constantly at war but for the presence of the foreigner. The colonizer had also devalued Indian culture and presented it as barbarian and superstitious. The upper castes thus felt threatened by the British as well as by the missionary onslaught on the Hindu social system and caste structures.

The rallying point needed was found in religious revival. Intellectual debate was continuing on whether this onslaught could be contained through social reform, economic development, or religious revival. Till the end of the century pure social reform without any emotional component was attempted by Rammohan Roy and others who followed him. These reformers "believed that they could reconstruct Indian society by mechanically introducing western ideas and institutions" (Karunakaran 1970, 38). The impact of this school of thought was confined to the upper classes in a few states. They succeeded in getting the colonial government to pass some progressive laws, such as those against *sati* (burning of widows), despite British opposition to the measure. But the social base required for accepting these changes was missing and the movement remained marginal.

Simultaneously, religious revival was beginning in reaction to the devaluation of Indian culture by the colonialists. The Theosophical Society, for example, was founded in 1875 by a Russian noblewoman and an American colonel at a time when Indian economy was subjugated to British industry and political India was colonized by a foreign power convinced that it was the "superior race." Many upper-caste Indians, therefore, accepted as true the myth of the superiority of Indian spirituality over western materialism. They, therefore, believed that India could regain its self-respect through religious revival and going back to its heritage (King 1985).

CONVERGENCE OF INTERESTS

The freedom movement was forced to face the religious question and find legitimation in it. The British had visualized the Indian Association, which was founded in 1852 and became the Indian National Congress in

1885 as a safety valve. The religious and social reform movements functioned as a counterweight against this effort to coopt the Indian upper classes and eventually turned the Indian National Congress into a freedom movement.

Some, like M. G. Ranade (1842-1901), gave primary importance to social reform with a religious basis. Others, like Dayananda Saraswati (1824-83), even while demanding religious reform and reconversion to Hinduism of those converted to Christianity and Islam in the nineteenth century, gave adequate importance to social, particularly caste, reform. A few, like Aurobindo Ghosh (1872-1950), gave a religious legitimation to the political freedom and economic development of India. Aurobindo introduced the idea of the country as Mother Goddess and national freedom and economic development as *yajna* (ritual sacrifice) against the "delusion that a foreign and averse interest can be trusted to develop us to its own detriment" (Aurobindo's speeches, in de Bary 1966, 174-75).

A few others, like Vinayak Savarkar, Ramakrishna (1834-86), his disciple Vivekananda (1862-96), and Bal Gangadhar Tilak (1856-1920), Ranade's adversary in Maharashtra, gave importance almost exclusively to religious revival. Some of them certainly preached social reform. But it was secondary and subordinate to religio-cultural renaissance. For example, unlike Saraswati, who propagated the abolition of castes and raising the Shudra (low caste) to the level of the Brahmin, Ramakrishna only advocated the revalorization of Shudrahood, but not an end to caste stratification (Karunakaran 1970, 71).

At times only a thin line divided social reform from religious revival. Saraswati, for example, introduced the idea of *shuddhi*, the purification and reconversion of Christians and Muslims. He also spoke of *sangathan* (solidarity of Hindus against the foreigner) as well as Hindu exclusiveness. Saints of other religions could not be honored. Social reform was meant to sustain this *shuddhi* and *sangathan*. Ramakrishna, on the other hand, spoke of bringing all the religions together by going back to the Indian heritage and spreading it to the rest of the world. Thus he introduced proselytization into Hinduism for the first time. Also, Saraswati spread the idea of going back to the Indian heritage in order to purify Hinduism. He propagated return to vedic times when monotheism prevailed, castes were nonexistent, Hinduism was not divided into six schools of thought, and idolatry was unknown (de Bary 1966, 77-84). But this was only to reconvert those who had left Hinduism because of its unjust structures, not to proselytize.

Such revival made a major difference to the freedom movement since it was instrumental in involving the masses. Some, like Tilak, deliberately introduced Hindu festivals as part of this revival and used the gatherings to mobilize the masses. In other cases the masses were involved through the call to return to vedic times. In reality, the freedom fighters had to follow the path of religion because social questions affecting the Hindu community are all bound up with religious considerations. The social reformer in India had to fight against forces believed to be semi-divine.

The revival and reform movement had a definite Hindu orientation. What was upheld as the Indian culture to be revived was Brahminic and upper caste in character. Though the freedom movement had coopted other tribal, peasant, and *dalit* struggles in order to acquire a mass base, in reality the culture and economy of the subordinate classes was not accepted in the mainstream. The fundamental thought was that India had a single stream of (Hindu) culture and that the *dalits* and others should be raised to the Brahminic level or should be revalorized without really being accepted as equals. The religious minorities and socially powerless groups such as the *dalits* and tribals were excluded unless they were ready to be integrated into the single stream. In that sense, those who spoke primarily of religious reform laid the foundation of post-independence fundamentalist religious revival.

GANDHI AND THE MOVEMENT

It is in this context that Mahatma Gandhi arrived on the scene. Like Saraswati and Savarkar, who had given the call of "back to the Vedas," and Tilak, who had found in the *Bhagavadgita* the inspiration of political action as a religious deed, Gandhi too found an equally strong religious base in the same scriptures. He used the *Bhagavadgita* to preach active nonviolence. Unlike Ramakrishna, who went back to the Indian heritage to speak of Hinduism as the umbrella that brought all the traditions together, Gandhi spoke of the *Bhagavadgita* as proclaiming the equality of all religions. Active nonviolence to him was *satyagraha* — the fight for truth. In this case it was the fight for the transfer of political power to its true inheritors, Indians (Gandhi 1949, 149-51).

To achieve this it was crucial to counteract the two instruments through which the foreign ruler had forced Indians to submit to his power. First, through their divide-and-rule policy the British had set Indians against Indians and had forced all the classes to cooperate with them in order to safeguard their self-interest. Second, state violence had frightened Indians into submission. Against the physically violent foe it was essential to use the psychological violence of noncooperation. This required the awakening of all Indians, a mass movement compelling the people to act in a disciplined and nonviolent way. Cooperation among all the Indian classes, which was essential to ensure noncooperation with the British, required a sense of belonging and self-respect in every Indian. Equality of all the religions was an essential prerequisite to this feeling of belonging.

Similarly, like the "back to the Vedas" call of those who preceded him, Gandhi called his followers to go back to the pristine past of *Rama Rajya*, the rule of the mythical hero Rama, who symbolized justice and equality. In reality every call to go back to the past was an invitation to give birth to a future society unknown to history. This was true of the call to return to the vedic times as well as to *Rama Rajya*.

Perhaps Gandhi was conscious of the fact that his was a historic mission. But he also appealed to the past and often stated that the *RamRaj* should be established in India. To a large number of people in India this meant a call to reproduce the golden age of the Hindus, although Gandhi gave the same term his own definition which did not suit any historical period (Karunakaran 1970, 16-17).

This was the dilemma faced by those like Gandhi who were close to the masses as against the intellectuals who blindly accepted western standards or the revivalists who thought primarily in terms of Hindu religion and culture. Leaders like Gandhi had to reconcile the triple conflict of religious revival versus social reform, conflict versus cooperation between religions, and violence versus nonviolence. In a culture in which outdated social norms claimed the support of religious sanctions, it was important to present reforms within the same religious framework. Gandhi, therefore, presented himself as a *Mahatma* — a man of God — and gave a new interpretation of nonviolent political action and equality of religions through the *Bhagavadgita*. He used *Rama Rajya* to speak of a new ideal state of justice, caste reforms, and equality of women (Gandhi 1957, 46-50). In doing this he ran the risk of identifying India with Hinduism and of being perceived as the leader of one religion alone; in fact, his aim was to become the unifying factor.

RELIGION, STATUS QUO, AND SOCIAL CHANGE

Religion is thus put to double use. It is used by the dominant sections to rally the masses around themselves. In that sense it could function as a reactionary element. In fact, religious revival was not limited to Hindus but was an equally strong force also among the Muslims. Among them too, it was a need of the upper classes, which were in competition with the Hindu leaders. The Muslim leaders also used religion to rally the masses around themselves. Consequently, religion became a divisive force that could be used by the upper classes to get popular support for their own leadership and against those with whom they competed for economic and political leadership (Hasan 1979). Fundamentalist religious revival was thus both a reactionary and divisive force in the hands of the status quoist forces, who only used it as an emotional rallying point to get a mass base.

Second, religion was used as a tool of sociopolitical change. For example, Gandhi turned it into a uniting factor, but with limited success. As long as the religious framework used was that of the ruling classes, it always ran the risk of being identified with one of the religious communities. But, as seen in the tribal movements, when popular religiosity or the framework of the subordinate classes was utilized, it became a rallying point for change among the oppressed. The conversion movements among the *dalits* have also shown the social change potential of religion.

At the same time, the freedom movement demonstrates the potential of the upper classes to coopt popular movements. This interaction between the ruling and subordinate classes also operates between the secular and religious frameworks. Crisis in the life of the subordinate classes begins as a result of secular interventions. The oppressed classes often find a religious response. However, because of the emotional component of religion, and since the subordinate sections are socially powerless, their movements can easily be coopted by the ruling classes.

DALIT CONVERSION AND SOCIAL MOBILITY

The interaction between the social (secular) and religious factors is seen in the post-independence developments in the country as a whole as well as in the church. To begin with the latter and limit ourselves to *dalit* conversions, the crisis in their life began as a result of British economic interventions. But they sought a religious response of conversion as a mode of upward social mobility. This interaction was inevitable because of the close link between their cultural, economic, religious, and social life. In that sense conversion was not merely a religious act but also a search for a new social identity.

However, their search was hampered by secular forces within the church community. Missionaries had thought of their conversion as a purely religious act; they did not understand and respond to their social aspirations. The Christian community itself was dominated by persons from the upper castes whose families had been converted in the sixteenth century or earlier. On the Konkan coast (Mangalore-Goa-Bombay), Catholics owe their baptism to the Portuguese, who had a vested interest in keeping the caste system unchanged. They needed the cooperation of the upper castes in order to make colonial rule acceptable. Hence, they had to get the Brahmins and other upper castes into the church without changing the system. The upper castes remained major landowners and continued to control churches just as they had done with the temples earlier. The lower castes, who were landless agricultural laborers, also changed their religion. But their social status did not change with their baptism. Caste and class division continued among Christians.

Similarly, the Syrian Christians of Kerala, who were according to tradition converted by the apostle St. Thomas, had adapted themselves to the Indian system and had been accepted as a high caste. In Tamilnadu several persons from the upper castes had been baptized by the De Nobili mission in the seventeenth and eighteenth centuries. They too were not prepared to change their social status. Consequently, when persons from lower castes joined the church, in order to prevent defections of the upper castes in the

Christian community, De Nobili and his followers opened separate missions for the Shudras. The latter were served by *Pandaraswamis*, while the upper castes were ministered to by the *Brahmanasanyasis* in church buildings reserved for them.

A new division was introduced among Christians with the *dalit* conversions. The eighteenth century Shudra converts called themselves upper castes and referred to the *dalits* as New Christians, continuing to treat these nineteenth-century converts as untouchables. Unlike the De Nobili Mission, which created two different sets of priests and churches for the high and low castes, the nineteenth-century missions in parts of Tamilnadu introduced segregation inside the church building. The two castes worshipped inside the same building, but the upper castes sat to the right and the others to the left, with a railing separating the two (Fernandes 1981, 30-33). This segregation has been abolished since the 1930s in some dioceses and since the 1950s in others. But discrimination against the New Christians continues in other forms. Briefly, the secular organization of the church, dominated by the upper castes, has gone against the social aspirations of those who were searching for a new identity through their religious conversion.

MAJOR TRENDS IN POST-INDEPENDENCE INDIA

A second set of interactions between socioeconomic inputs and religious revival is seen in the developments in the country as a whole. The pattern of development chosen at independence has resulted in an economy of shortages. There is, therefore, competition among various communities for scarce resources. In the context of these shortages and inequalities, there have been movements of the marginalized as well as of several relatively powerful sections. The fundamentalist religious revival is important because of the attempts of the dominant sections to counteract the demands of the oppressed by introducing the emotional factor. Some of the marginalized groups have used their culture and popular religiosity as rallying points as well.

THE PATTERN OF DEVELOPMENT

Three major patterns of development were presented at independence. Gandhi suggested that India evolve a village-based model of development and a technology that would first and foremost be at the service of the last person. The People's Plan accepted the need for technological advancement, but insisted that the means of production be controlled not by a few individuals or even the bureaucracy, but by the majority of the population through cooperatives. It suggested the development of appropriate technology to ensure control by the working class, resources used according to the needs of the majority, and assets and income controlled by those who produced the goods. Finally, the Bombay Plan, worked out mainly by industrialists, was based on capital accumulation and technology. It was based on the western model of sophisticated technology resulting in economic growth. It was assumed that the consequent higher production would ensure the growth of all the sectors, generate employment, distribute income to every class, and reduce inequalities. A modification was introduced according to the Soviet model of state ownership of the means of production. The industrialists who formulated this plan in 1945 suggested that key industries like steel be in the hands of the state. This ensured that the private sector that took control of consumer industries got raw materials at subsidized prices without itself investing in these long-gestation industries.

For all practical purposes, the five-year plans adopted the approach of the Bombay Plan, with several statements from the other two documents inserted without a clear commitment to their perspective. The growth of the GNP thus became the main criterion of national development. The thinking behind this approach was that technology had led to progress in the West. The deindustrialization and exploitation of the colonies abroad and the repression of workers at home during the Industrial Revolution were not given adequate importance. At the political level individual based democracy was introduced with the hope that it would move the country away from the caste system, which fixed a person's status in society according to his birth, and toward a society that encouraged social promotion based on an individual's achievement in life. It was assumed that modernization of Indian society would be the consequence of this process, and the removal of inequalities its end product. Community development through the *Panchayati raj* (village self-government) was introduced from the Gandhian approach in order to encourage the participation of every rural family for the improvement of its quality of life. Land reforms suggested by the People's Plan were promised but were not implemented except in a few states. Briefly, the strategy was not redistribution of wealth but increased demand through investment in basic industries and through mixed economy.

This strategy has borne fruit from many points of view. India has today become an important industrialized country. It has the third biggest pool of scientific personnel in the world, coming immediately after the United States and the USSR. The country's GNP has increased enormously during the last four decades. However, in this very growth lay the seeds of inequality.

All the five-year-plan documents have insisted that their objective is movement toward equality. The very first five-year plan insisted that the elimination of poverty cannot be achieved merely by redistributing existing wealth. Nor can a program aiming only at raising production remove existing inequalities. Only a simultaneous advance along both these lines can create conditions in which the community can put forth its best efforts for promoting development.

While the good intention of dealing with the dilemma between higher productivity and greater equality was recognized, in reality modernization was attempted without changing the unequal socioeconomic structures. Most rural as well as urban societies in which *Panchayati raj* was introduced were not egalitarian communities but conglomerations of unequal castes, classes, and power groups. Capital, land, and other productive assets were distributed unequally. Because of their access to education the upper classes had taken control of the administrative apparatus at independence in 1947, which did not herald change in the socioeconomic structures but only transfer of power from the British colonizer to the Indian bourgeoisie. Post-independence modernization further strengthened the capitalist and land-owning classes, which took control of the financial institutions and used modern technology to further increase the productivity of their already productive assets (Fernandes 1985, 16-20).

Maximizing the utilization of natural resources such as water, minerals, and forests was an important method of increasing production. Most of these resources are in the tribal areas, where they were a life-support system. The tribals had, therefore, developed a culture and sociopolitical structures geared to keeping a balance between human and environmental needs. In the modernization perspective, on the contrary, these resources are seen only as raw material to the industrialist, a source of revenue to the state, and a means of profit to the capitalist. The formal economy and the corporate sector, which have taken control of these resources, have power that the tribals and other powerless communities, which depend on these resources for their very survival, lack (Sharma 1978, 27-32).

In summary, the western pattern of development chosen by the five-year plans is resource-intensive. The overexploited natural resources are mainly in the tribal areas. But the classes that have access to education and to money have taken control of these resources and have depleted them. Forests, for example, have been reduced from an estimated twenty-two percent of the country's land mass at independence to around ten percent today. The result is the impoverishment of the tribals, particularly of women (Fernandes and Menon 1987, 97-105).

Displacement for development projects has had major impact. While the sixty million tribals form a little over seven and a half percent of the country's population, they are more than fifty percent of the more than fifteen million people displaced during the last four decades by major dams, mines, and wildlife sanctuaries. They are also a substantial number among those displaced by industries. Fewer than twenty-five percent of those displaced have been rehabilitated during the last three decades. The new skilled jobs created in the area are taken over by the classes that have had access to education. Consequently, the tribals who have been deprived of their life-support system are reduced to being unskilled and even bonded laborers at exploitative wages (Kebra 1987, 34-35).

What is said about the tribals is equally true about the *dalits*, who form fifteen percent of the country's population, the small and marginal farmers, and other weaker sections. The *dalits* depended on traditional skills that have been replaced by sophisticated technology. They have thus been deprived of their centuries-old knowledge systems without any alternative to these survival mechanisms. Agricultural policies and the Green Revolution have favored the big farmer at the cost of the small and marginal farmer. Consequently, large sections of these two classes have either been displaced or have been forced to migrate to the city slums where they are further exploited.

DOMINANT RELIGIOUS REVIVAL

In the context of these growing inequalities, there is a fundamentalist religious revival among the ruling as well as subordinate classes. But the two have different objectives. To begin with, dominant fundamentalist revival around secular demands can be seen from the fact that many leaders, who had till now presented themselves as secular, have begun to use religion overtly as a political tool, not covertly as in the past.

Second, though this revival is primarily of the Hindu types, it is not limited to that community. Every religion feels its impact. For example, most major religious groups have a political party or a quasipolitical organization to represent them. The Kerala Congress is considered a Christian party in that state, and *Akali Dal* represents the Sikhs in Punjab. The All India Muslim League is yet another political party. The quasipolitical parties include *Vishwa Hindu Parishad* (VHP), *Rashtriya Swayamsevak Sangh* (RSS), and others.

Third, many parties, like the *Shiv Sena* in Maharashtra, were founded around regional grievances but have today taken on emotional, religious overtones in order to get votes. Some parties that were considered secular, such as the Peasants' and Workers' Party (PWP), are seeking alliance with religion-oriented parties like the *Bharatiya Janata Party* (BJP), which is linked to the Hindu fundamentalist RSS. The BJP in its turn is invading secular domains such as the peasant movements in several states. This trend is also clear from the fact that many people involved in struggles for social transformation, who otherwise consider themselves radical or secular, take a purely emotional attitude when their caste, religion, or region is involved in a conflict.

Recent events thus give clear indications that the causes of religious fundamentalism are primarily political or economic, not religious. One can see it from the demands made in the name of religion. For example, the main grievance of the RSS is not that Hindu religion is devalued but that Hindus, who form eighty-five percent of the country's population, do not have political power proportionate to their numbers. Similarly, inter-caste riots are not to preserve ritual purity but to prevent the *dalits* from getting more economic benefits, such as education and jobs, which might erode the power and privileges of the ruling classes. This dynamic is seen also in the reaction to the women's movements. Although often given a religious interpretation, reaction is in fact aimed at maintaining a male-dominated society. Interreligious riots are the same. Most of them are not spontaneous; increasing stages of tension as well as the final attack are well organized. Studies have shown that the main targets of attack today are not religious places, as was the case three or four decades ago, but factories and shops. The purpose is to weaken the economic base of the leaders of the other community. Religious struggles today are not about religious rights, but secular demands. Religion is used as a rallying point by the leaders.

So, religion plays a role in social change, but it is controlled by the ruling classes. It is oriented toward the status quo and goes against women and the subordinate classes. This fundamentalist role religion plays in post-independence India has to be situated in the historical context of British policies, the freedom movement, and the post-independence pattern of development discussed above. The process allows the already powerful to strengthen themselves while the powerless classes become further marginalized. Given that the pattern of development is resource-intensive, it further impoverishes those who had earlier used the natural resources as a life-support system, those who had survived on their traditional knowledge systems, and other marginalized classes. An immediate consequence of such a monopoly of capital, technology, knowledge systems, natural resources, and political power by a small minority is an economy of shortages and competition for scarce resources. While the ruling classes compete for a bigger share of the economic benefits, the subordinate groups have to compete for the minimum required for survival as human beings.

These shortages and impoverishment have to be situated in the context of the aspirations roused during the freedom movement. The cry of national development and equality, *Rama Rajya*, was used by the leaders to create a mass movement. Disillusionment followed among the subordinate classes as inequalities increased. They demand a better life. Simultaneously, the leaders of the dominant sections compete for more economic and political benefits. They present these shortages as the result of too many privileges acquired by other religious communities or by the subordinate castes like the *dalits*. They thus turn what is a class conflict for economic benefits into a religious conflict and divide the subordinate classes.

One cannot claim, however, that economic and political demands are the only causes of the fundamentalist religious revival. They are predominant, but not exclusive. This revival has to be viewed also in the context of eight centuries of external domination of the Hindu society and devaluation of its culture, on the one hand, and of the external influences that have destabilized traditional socio-cultural systems on the other. We have already discussed the first aspect while analyzing the freedom movement. We have only to add that the dominant sections of Hindu society now feel that a new society based on Hindu ethos can be rebuilt and that Hindus can acquire economic and political power. In other words, it is the awakening of a society dominated by external—perceived as initially Muslim and later Christian—colonizers for eight centuries. Similar revival is occurring in other countries colonized for centuries by European countries perceived as Christian: Iran, Saudi Arabia, and most other Muslim countries of West Asia; Buddhist countries like Sri Lanka, Burma, Thailand; and in many other "non-Christian" former colonies. In that sense revival belongs to a definite historical moment.

The second aspect, the destabilization of Indian society, is an offshoot of the first. The traditional Indian (Hindu) ethos was integrationist, built around a society limited to a relatively small group—a few villages and the local sub-caste. Besides, it was an unequal society. Into this society the concept of a nation-state was introduced, together with the value of modernization that had developed in a totally different (western) social and historical situation. The objective of modernization was precisely to change this traditional value system. A new political system, technology, and economic organization were introduced to suit the needs of this modern state and economy. The reaction to the destabilization that set in is the search for a new identity by the Hindu community.

Briefly, while the socioeconomic and political needs of the leaders are crucial to understanding recent fundamentalist religious revival, the emotional side of religion and the community's search for a new identity after centuries of subordination have to be borne in mind.

RELIGION AND THE SUBORDINATE CLASSES

One can see from the above that religion is used by the ruling class to maintain the status quo and keep itself in power. From that point of view, it is a reactionary force and, as such, anti-poor. It has sustained the present type of modernization, which is favorable to the achieving society and strengthens inegalitarian tendencies.

The reaction of the marginalized sections is a search for alternatives, to be more exact, a search for autonomy, which is linked to a new economy. Among the *dalits* this autonomy takes the form of a new type of literature. Many women's movements search for autonomy through a new historiography and theology. Tribal struggles for autonomy have taken the form of *Jharkhand* (forest state) in Chotanagpur in eastern India, nationalist uprisings in the northeast, and others elsewhere. Common to all is the search for a new value system required for their identity, and a struggle for control over their resources. All of them also try to develop a new leadership from their own ranks to lead them in this struggle for a new economy.

The new movements focus on aspects that have been looked down upon or the value systems that have been imposed on them by the ruling classes. A few of them would reject religion as exclusively reactionary. But most tribals would use popular religiosity and traditional culture as a rallying point in their struggles, which are predominantly for land and forests.

Crucial to the search for a new identity is the demythologization of many traditions considered sacred by the ruling classes and revalorization of the cultural and religious system looked down upon till now and considered superstitious. *Dalit* literature and theology would fall under this category. Many women's groups today consider it essential to challenge not merely the male-dominated economy but also the societal reproductive systems of education and religion. Since male domination is perpetuated through religious legitimation, they believe an equally strong religious base is required to change the value system in favor of the poor.

This is a struggle for humanization. The classes that have for centuries been treated as untouchables or as inferior demand their human rights. Consequently, unlike the upper classes, they do not focus only on material benefits. The subordinate classes view even their impoverishment as a symbol of the subhuman status that enables the ruling classes to treat them as tools for their own enrichment. They, therefore, demand through their literature, leadership, theology, and historiography, recognition as human beings who are creative and can make their own decisions.

Popular religiosity and culture have functioned as rallying points in this effort. In these movements religion plays the role of welding the oppressed as a group not by discarding popular religiosity as the ruling classes have traditionally done, but by using it to revive their identity, improve their self-image, and reinforce their sense of being human, and affirm their right to self-respect and to control over their resources and productive assets.

Thus religion plays a double role in social change. In the hands of the ruling classes it becomes a tool of oppression. With the oppressed it plays a prophetic role that enables them to reacquire their lost identity.

IMPLICATIONS FOR LIBERATION THEOLOGY

Within this double role of religion one can also see the option to be made in favor of liberation. Because of the use it has been put to by the ruling classes, many of those committed to the oppressed have made an option in favor of exclusively secular social change and have rejected religion as purely reactionary. Others, however, have understood from Indian history that the poor are conditioned by their religious value system, which presents their oppressive state as God-given. Consequently, they cannot respond to movements of social transformation unless they perceive also liberation from oppression as a religious value.

The latter approach must be taken if economic liberation is not to suffer for lack of emotional support. Granted that historically mainstream religion has been a legitimizing factor in the hands of the ruling classes. Nonetheless, the oppressed have been able to take up the protest and prophetic elements of religion and find in it emotional support for their mobilization for economic and political rights (Joshi 1989).

This has to be the basis of a liberation theology. It must begin with popular culture and religiosity, which express the people's aspirations rather than those of the ruling classes. The first attitude required in this approach is trust in the people that they can free themselves by relying on their own theology and culture. The temptation to reject religion as reactionary has to be replaced by an assumption that every religion has a prophetic role to play. While militants get inspiration from their religion, they have to identify its protest and prophetic aspects and adapt them to suit the needs of the exploited.

For this to be feasible, a second requirement is respect for religious pluralism. One cannot think of a Christian liberation theology for a country like India; it must be an *Indian* liberation theology.

Third, this effort has to be an interreligious enterprise. It must begin with the recognition that even popular religiosity in this country is conditioned by the Hindu ethos. At the same time, the pluralist aspect has to be recognized, the prophetic elements of Sikhism, Islam, and Christianity have to be identified and their commonalities analyzed. While dominant theology has been a divisive factor and a source of interreligious conflicts, the people belonging to different religious traditions are united at the level of popular religiosity and culture. It is true that dominant traditions often coopt popular religiosity too, and its leaders divide the people even at this level. This is an integral part of a historical process and has to be viewed within its dialectical dimensions.

Merely accepting popular religiosity is insufficient if it is done without the basis of involvement with the victims of inequality. The ruling classes often keep away from them the possibility of liberation by exploiting their need for emotional security through the divisive aspects of the dominant religion. While accepting the need for doctrinal aspects, greater importance must be attached to liberative action that unites the people and help evolve a theology from this involvement. In other words, one cannot transfer Latin American liberation theology to India; rather, one must reinvent liberation theology in this country according to the local situation and the condition of the exploited. The commonality with its Latin American counterpart is the process of humanization to replace the dehumanizing exploitation which the exploited internalize in the name of religion.

Fourth, one needs a historical perspective. Christian, particularly Latin American, liberation theology has to be situated in its proper context, and the present historical moment of India has to be understood and respected. The so-called Christian countries have passed through a totally different historical process. For several decades in the post-Napoleonic age West European Catholics went through a monarchic and feudal type of fundamentalist reaction based on papalism. This was in reaction to the French and other political revolutions that were considered anti-Catholic.

Thus Christians have had 150 years to deal with this fundamentalist phenomenon. During these centuries Christian Europe was also the colonizing continent. As such, the Christian countries were able to look at the world and even guide its destiny from a dominant position. Consequently, many in Christian countries have been able to go beyond this fundamentalist reaction without a feeling of threat.

On the other hand, most religions other than Christianity have been practiced by the colonized peoples. Colonialism has often been legitimized in the name of the West's civilizing and evangelizing mission. Buddhism, Hinduism, Islam, Sikhism, and other non-Christian religions have been despised, and Christianity declared superior to them. Their culture has been devalued.

In other words, at the moment when Christian countries were able to get away from the post-Napoleonic reactionary stage and feudalism, the colonized peoples were being forced into a defensive posture. Consequently, their independence movements were also accompanied by a conservative cultural and religious renaissance. This revival was reactionary in nature both because it was a reaction to colonial degradation of their culture, economy, and religion, and because the freedom struggle was led by an elite that had a vested interest in the status quo. In these countries, therefore, religion is in the hands of fundamentalist groups. The situation is thus similar to that in post-Napoleonic Europe. Because of the reactionary nature of religion in these countries, progressive elements among Hindus, Muslims, and others tend to reject any religious basis for social change.

The exceptions to this colonial history are the Philippines and Latin American countries where the colonialists also imposed their religion. Consequently, reaction in these countries could not take the form of total rejection of the religion of the outsider. There certainly was cultural revival, sometimes sustained or coopted by the new bourgeoisie and at other times a result of popular upsurge. But it was within a Christian ethos. Simultaneously, while most of Europe had reached the capitalist stage, the Philippines and Latin America had remained in the feudal age. Consequently, they had to focus more on the economic and political forces of exploitation. Since there was also a popular cultural revival, a liberation theology could evolve from it in support of their economic and political aspirations.

CONCLUSION

We have analyzed in this chapter the historical process through which various classes in India have been able to use theology in their own interest. While the mainstream religion has been reactionary, the exploited classes have used its protest and liberative aspects as tools of social transformation. That is where Christians in India can make a contribution to the emergence of an *Indian* liberation theology. Many Indian Christians have been able to learn from their Filipino and Latin American counterparts, who have the experience of being involved in the evolution of a liberation theology beginning with basic communities and popular culture and religiosity.

Christians have to work at two levels. First of all, they have to share with those from other religious traditions who are working for social transformation the experience of Christians in India and elsewhere in using popular religiosity and culture as a tool of protest. The objective of this interaction and alliance is to enable their non-Christian counterparts to go back to their own religious tradition and find in it the inspiration that is required for prophetic reflection and action for social transformation. To achieve this, all those involved in the struggle for social change have to better understand the ethos of popular religiosity and the need to combine the political and economic aspects with the religious in the search for an alternative.

Second, Christians with a social concern also have to play a prophetic role within their own communities. The country as a whole cannot be changed only by reforming the church. However, while working for change within the country as a whole, Christians also have to make a beginning with the justice dimension within their own communities. Caste, for example, is as strong among Christians as it is in the country as a whole. It is inconsistent for Christians to demand a change in the country as a whole if they close their eyes to the plight of those who came to the church in search of equality preached by Christ but continue to be treated as untouchables. The prophetic role has to be played both by working for social transformation with people of every religious persuasion and by Christians themselves. An Indian theology of liberation will emerge from this involvement and alliance.

REFERENCES

Aggins, B., and Rajiv Lochan. 1989. "Religion and Social Change: The Case of Jotiba Phule," *Social Action* 39.

Anant, Santokh Sing. 1972. *The Changing Concept of Caste in India*, Vikas Publications, New Delhi.

Badgaiyan, S. D. 1983. "Tribal Workers in Colonial Industry." In *Tribal Area Development*, ed. S. N. Mishra and Bhupinder Singh, Society for the Study of Region Disparities, New Delhi.

Bary, W. T. de. 1966. *Sources of Indian Tradition*, vol. 2. Free Press, New York.

Boschere, Guy de. 1967. *Autopsie De La Colonisation*, Editions Allin Michele, Paris.

Chaubisa, M. L. 1988. *Caste Tribe and Exploitaion: Exploration of Inequality at Village Level*, Himanshu Publications, Udaipur.

Chauhan, B. R., and D. S. Chelawati. 1978. "Bhil Gauri." In N. N. Vyas et al. eds., *Rajastan Bhils Manikyalal Verma*, Tribal Research and Training Institute, Udaipur.

Das, S. T. 1986. *Tribal Life of North-Eastern India: Habitat, Economy, Customs and Traditions*, Gian Publishing House, Delhi.

Downs, Frederick S. 1983. *Christianity in North India: Historical Perspectives*, Indian Society for Promoting Christian Knowledge, Delhi.
Fernandes, Walter. 1980. *The Indian Catholic Community: Its Peoples and Institutions in Interaction with the Indian Situation Today*, PMV Asia Australia Dossier 12-13, Brussels.
———. 1981. *Caste and Conversion Movements in India: Religion and Human Rights*, Indian Social Institute, New Delhi.
———. 1985. "Development and People's Participation: An Introduction." In Walter Fernandes, ed., *Development with People: Experiments with Participation and Non-Formal Education*, Indian Social Institute, New Delhi.
———. 1988. *The Role of Christians in National Integration*, Indian Social Institute, New Delhi.
———. 1988a. "The Draft Forest Policy 1987; The National Water Policy 1987," *Social Action* 38.
———, and R. G. Lobo. 1986. "Social Action Groups and the Search for Alternatives." In Walter Fernandes, ed., *Inequality, Its Bases and Search for Solutions: Dr. Alfred de Souza Memorial Essays*, Indian Social Institute, New Delhi.
———, and Geeta Menon. 1987. *Tribal Women and Forest Economy*, Indian Social Institute, New Delhi.
———, Geeta Menon, and Philip Viegas. 1988. *Forests, Environment and Tribal Economy: Deforestation, Impoverishment and Marginalisation in Orissa*, Indian Social Institute, New Delhi.
Forrester, D. B. 1980. *Caste and Christianity: Attitudes and Policies on Caste of Anglo-Saxon Protestant Missions in India*, Centre of South Asian Studies, University of London.
Gandhi, M. K. 1949. *Cent Per Cent Swadeshi*, Navjivan Publishing House, Ahmedabad.
———. 1957. *Christian Missions: Their Place in India*, Navjivan Publishing House, Ahmedabad.
Harrison, Selig. 1960. *India: The Most Dangerous Decade*, Princeton University Press, New Jersey.
Hasan, Mushirul. 1979. *Nationalism and Communal Politics in India*, Manohar, Delhi.
Jayaraman, R. 1975. *Caste Continuities in Ceylon: A Study of the Social Structure of Three Tea Plantations*, Popular Prakashan, Bombay.
Jetley, Surinder. 1977. *Modernising Indian Peasants: A Study of Six Villages in Eastern Uttar Pradesh*, Asian Educational Services, New Delhi.
Joshi, P. C. 1989. "Religion, Class Conflicts and Emancipation Movements: Some Reflections," *Social Action* 39.
Kanjamala, Augustine. 1981. *Religion and Modernisation of India: A Case Study of Northern Orissa*, Satprakashan, Indore.
Karunakaran, K. P. 1970. *Religion and Political Awakening in India*, Meenakshi Prakashan, Meerut.
Kebra, Govind Das. 1987. *Tribal Worker in an Industrial Setting*, Vohra Publishers and Distributors, Allahabad.
King, Ursula. 1985. *The Blue Mutiny*, University of Philadelphia, Philadelphia.
Mathur, L. P. 1988. *Resistance Movement of Tribals of India: A Case Study of the Bhils of Rajasthan in the 19th Century*, Himanshu Publications, Udaipur.
Oddie, G. A., ed. 1977. *Religion in South Asia: Religious Conversion and Revival*

Movements in South Asia in Medieval and Modern Times, Manohar, New Delhi.
Pathy, Jaganath. 1988. *Ethnic Minorities in Process of Development*, Rawat Publications, Jaipur.
Planning Commission. 1951. *First Five Year Plan*, Government of India, Shimla.
Rao, Kamala Manohar, and D.L. Prasad Rao. 1983. "Tribal Movements in Andhra Pradesh." In Singh, 1983.
Reddy, Prakash G. 1987. *Politics of Tribal Exploitation: A Study of Tribal Unrest in Andhra Pradesh*, Mittal Publications, New Delhi.
Robertson, Alexander. 1938. *The Mahar Folk: A Study of Untouchables in Maharastra*, Oxford University Press, Calcutta.
Rothermund, D. 1978. "The Coalfield: An Enclave in a Backward Region." In *Zamindars, Mines and Peasants Studies in the History of an Indian Coalfield and Its Rural Hinterland*, ed. Dietmar Rothermund and D. C. Wadhwa, Manoha, New Delhi.
Sa, Fidelis de. 1975. *Crisis in Chotanagpur*, Redemptorist Publications, Bangalore.
Saravanan, C. S. 1987. "Regionalism and the Dravida Kazhagam Phenomenon in Tamil Nadu," *Social Action* 37.
Sarkar, Sumit. 1983. *Modern India 1885-1947*, Macmillan, New Delhi.
Sen, Sunil. 1979. *Agrarian Relations in India 1793-1947,* People's Publishing House, New Delhi.
Shah, Gyansham. 1985. "Anti-Untouchability Movements." In *Caste, Caste Conflict and Reservation*, ed. I. P. Desai, et al., Ajanta Publications, Delhi.
Shankardass, Rani Dhavan. n.d. *The First Congress Raj*, Macmillan, New Delhi.
———. 1982. *The First Congress Raj*, Macmillan India, New Delhi.
Sharma, B. D. 1978. *Tribal Development: The Concept and Frame*, Prachi Prakashan, New Delhi.
Sharma, Ursula. 1976. "Status-Striving and Striving to Abolish Status: The Arya Samaj and the Low Castes," *Social Action* 26.
Singh, K. 1983. "The Gond Movements." In *Tribal Movements in India*, ed. K. S. Singh, Manohar, New Delhi.
Souza, Alfred de. 1986. *Relevance of Religion and Inter-Religious Dialogue in Modern Society*, Indian Social Institute, New Delhi.

2

Oppression and Liberation

A Base for Theological Reflection on Indian Experience

YVON AMBROISE

There is a story of two men fighting with each other about the color of a chameleon. One said it was green; the other said that it was red. They went to a man of God living under a tree to settle their dispute. He told them that neither of them was correct. He took a chameleon from his pocket, and it was white! Indian socio-cultural reality is like a chameleon, which is seen in many ways by different people. Contradictory views are expressed about Indian society today. For example, some consider it fast-developing, while others view it as an underdeveloping country.

This essay attempts to examine today's Indian society from a critical and analytical point of view. The perspective adopted is that of the poor, and consequently it includes a descriptive as well as an analytical picture of oppression in various spheres—economic, political, social, ideological, and religio-cultural. The essay also pinpoints the efforts taken to meet the situation of oppression chiefly by the church and voluntary organizations. In this way this study reflects on the sociological bases for building up a proper theology of liberation.

OPPRESSION IN INDIAN SOCIETY

When India achieved independence on August 15, 1947, two major problems were facing it, problems which continue today: 1) the formation of a modern nation-state, and 2) forging a national identity for all the people living within the geographical territory called India, one capable of leading them toward self-reliance in socioeconomic, political, and cultural fields. The burden of realizing these objectives fell on the shoulders of Pandit Jawaharlal Nehru.

The first issue, forming the modern national state, was met by the framing of the Constitution for a Democratic Republic. But that was not the end. Problems crept in because of the traditional concept of power, which was considered absolute and not something to be shared. Though there was a parliamentary democracy, the participation of the people in decision-making was only nominal, and the traditional feudal relations among the peasants remained very strong. Thus the very class that was oppressing and exploiting the peasants came to rule and govern them under the guise of democracy. Once political power was in the hands of the rural bourgeoisie, it was easy for them to oppress the poor with politico-legal means and all the machinery of the state, like the police and bureaucracy.

As for the second problem, forging a national identity and achieving self-reliance, India needed an ideological frame to unite all its peoples. In a pluralistic country with various cultures and ethnic groups, Jawaharlal Nehru formulated the overarching concept of a secular state. He intended to unite people under the ideology of building up one secular nation called India. Further, the ideology of development understood in terms of building up an industrially advanced India was to function as the driving force for the unity of the nation. But no ideology can have credibility unless social justice is meted out to the people. As the whole idea of development was based on capitalism and indeed the ruthless capitalism of the West, it brought along with it several in-built mechanisms of exploitation and oppression. Since profit and production for market are the goals of capitalism, the efforts taken by the state to develop the country did not profit the poor.

There were the five-year plans, intended to make concrete the dream of building up India as a powerful and self-reliant nation. Since the political class consisted of the landed rural bourgeoisie and the industrial urban bourgeoisie, the resources of the country were basically diverted through five-year plans to increase the resources or increase the productivity of the assets of these rich sections by providing them a basic infrastructure of development like irrigation, transport, communication, and electrical facilities. The campaign for the Green Revolution has historically proved to be beneficial only to the big landlords, thereby increasing the power of the rich group over the poor. In the 1980s the government declared several times that India had produced a fifteen to twenty million ton surplus of food grains. Yet side by side with this phenomenon of plenty and overproduction, millions of people, practically fifty percent of the population, live below the poverty line.

All this shows how an ideology of development devoid of social justice only increases the wealth of the few who were already rich and further pauperized the poor. Hence the credibility of this ideology as a unifying force for the nation has increasingly come into question. We can note several internal separatist tendencies demanding not only more regional autonomy based on language, ethnicity, and so forth, but also separate nationhood.

Why was social justice not built into the present system and its ideology of development? How does the mechanism of exploitation and oppression in every sphere of life deny social justice to the poor? Indeed, what is happening to the poor under the present economic, social, political, and cultural systems?

THE ECONOMIC SYSTEM

Despoiled and discriminated against as landless laborers, more than half of the Indian population lives in rural areas with total uncertainty about tomorrow (Shah 1983, 259). The monsoon rains playing hide and seek force the poor peasants to borrow from the landed rich for the necessities of daily life; they are slowly led into a debt-trap. In addition, the low wages they receive and the disproportionate expenses they incur for ceremonies and celebrations connected with birth, death, marriage, and so on, make them easy prey to money lenders. With exorbitant interest rates, sometimes as much as three hundred percent, the poor, landless peasants end up as bonded laborers (Das and Nailakant 1979, 238). For women this bondedness often means physical and sexual abuse by the affluent, who for a moment forget the untouchability they impose in other spheres of life. All these abuses are seen by the traditional leaders of the village as normal, and they use every means to sustain this status quo.

Special sections of people, like the tribals, who are very much attached to their tribal economy of land and forest, undergo the worst type of exploitation. Although India has the largest tribal population (ten percent of the total population) in the world, the tribals face extinction and extermination. The dominant forces of the industrialist class look upon the tribals as a problem for them, because the forest areas constitute major storehouses of natural resources and reservoirs of mineral wealth needed for modern industrial economy (Sethi and Kothari 1983, 203ff.).

The wealthy argue that national progress cannot be halted just because a few "primitive people" refuse to be uprooted from their peculiar way of life. The tribals are thus viewed and treated as objects, as subservient to the interests of the capitalist class that claims to be the vanguard of national development.

Middlemen thrive on the ignorance and economic vulnerability of the marginal farmers who are enticed to take loans at high interest rates. Once the harvest is made, middlemen appear on the scene, fix a low price for the farmer's produce, then sell it in the market at great profit for themselves. Lack of roads and means of transportation also force the marginal and small farmers to depend on these middlemen for the sale of their produce. Agricultural goods from the rural areas do not get a fair price from the government either. As prices are low during the harvest, and twice as high, if not more, at lean season and times of scarcity, the price fluctuations are manipulated to the advantage of the urban class and big landed groups. This creates an artificial scarcity in the market with soaring prices, and also encourages a black market, both of which hit the poor very hard.

Why does such a system operate to the disadvantage of the poor and oppress them? The question leads us back to the system inherited from feudalism: colonial capitalism and capitalism of the post-independence period. The landholding pattern had been in favor of the high castes in the pre-colonial period. This inequality was further reinforced by the British through *zamindari* and *riotwari* systems whereby the moneyed group claimed the arable land as their possession (Frykenberg 1977, 67ff.). Land emerged as a marketable commodity that could be sold or mortgaged. This led to the accumulation of land by the moneyed group. Alongside these economic changes, monetization invaded all spheres of life. Accumulation of money became an end; it determined social power, access to education, and social mobility.

The mirage of money and employment possibilities attracts many of the impoverished rural people to urban areas. Loss of land, social conflicts, natural disasters, cessation of earlier occupations—all these are factors accounting for the migration to urban areas. The poor, however, are allowed to be only at the periphery of the urban area (Refebure 1978, 36); they live in overcrowded slums in most inhuman and unhygenic conditions (Hiro 1979, 25). These huge reserves of the poor are used by the unscrupulous industrialist class as contract laborers and handy thugs for illicit trades, smuggling, crime, and so on. Many destitute women are lured or kidnapped to red-light areas. Children are exploited as cheap labor and employed in all sorts of jobs, often under conditions that are hazardous to their lives and harmful to their health. Women normally provide a menial work force, laboring in several houses for a meager sum. The dreams that the poor brought to the urban area become nightmares that continue in the lives of their children, born and brought up in the slums.

For the industrialist class of the urban areas, labor is the most critically needed commodity, for it is the only one that can create value and surplus value. The availability of an abundant labor supply is the best climate for commodity production. With only labor power at their disposal, the poor migrants from the villages form a huge reserve labor force. Because of this surplus labor force, the industrialist class can bargain the price of labor to their advantage with the result that the poor are left at the subsistence level (Sen 1979, 40). Further, to maintain this dependence, other exploitative mechanisms such as casual labor, contract labor, and other forms of injustice are built into the system and maintained by laws promulgated by the same class holding the reins of political power. The drive for profit and the desire to increase production lead to the installation of industries with little security measures for the working class. The Bhopal gas tragedy is a grim reminder of the cost of such unscrupulous industrial policies.

THE SOCIAL SYSTEM

The poor suffer not only economic but also social deprivation based on caste (Mandelbaum 1970, 358ff.). Human dignity is a rare commodity for the men and women of low castes, earlier called the untouchables. Mahatma Gandhi baptized them as *harijans*, meaning "people or children of God." But they preferred to be called *dalits*, which means "the oppressed." In the name of caste, inhuman treatments are meted out to the low castes. In many places, even today, they do not have the right to walk in the main streets of the village, to wear clothes above the waist in front of high castes, to have houses adjacent to those of high castes, to take water from the wells of high castes, and so on. Though conditions have changed in urban areas, these practices survive in several villages, especially in interior areas.

The caste system is further exacerbated by a superimposed class structure; the combination leads to increasing social conflicts. The class structure groups several high and intermediary castes. The low castes find themselves more and more in a disadvantaged position, as high castes form associations and use their social, economic, and political power against the low castes.

THE POLITICAL SYSTEM

Members of the rich class both in rural and urban areas seek to increase their political clout. They want to control the legal situation, without which they cannot continue their exploitation and oppression. Political power also gives them the leverage they need to manipulate the distribution of public resources to their own advantage.

The legislative, judiciary, and executive functions reflect very often the interests of the rich classes. The rich monopolize all these spheres, and consequently the poor are not only rendered powerless but also voiceless. Through politico-legal means, the rich classes are able to justify all the exploitation and oppression, while maintaining the facade of working for national development. Any struggle of the poor classes is violently put down and repressed under the cover of law and order.

The social activists who work among the poor also face repression and harassment. This repression has brought a new class of political prisoners into existence. Torture and deaths in prisons are also on the increase. The victims often do not have any chance of getting justice.

The electoral practice as it exists today is very much tied to caste and feudal loyalties, which enables the rich class to obtain the votes of the rural poor and come to power, often through intimidation, cooption, and future promises. The poor remain fragmented and divided, and this situation is turned by the rich to their own advantage.

THE IDEOLOGICAL SYSTEM

Such a complex system of exploitation and oppression cannot be maintained by violent means alone, which becomes very expensive and is not always effective. Hence the rich class formulates some legitimizing explanations for these exploitations and oppressions, and uses them as ideological tools to manipulate the poor (Drucker 1977, 140ff.). When such ideological explanations have full hegemony over the people, they accomplish in the society what guns, prisons, and torture fail to do; namely, they lead the poor to submit themselves voluntarily to the designs of the powerful.

The ideology of hard work in an unequal society explains that the rich are rich because of their hard work, while the poor remain so due to lack of hard work. Hence if the poor work hard—so goes the explanation—they too would become rich. This ideology serves the double purpose of making the poor work hard—to the profit of the rich—and of giving a positive image to the rich as good people. The religious ideology of karma, and the ideology of the blind acceptance of the present oppressive situation as the will of God, go against the interests of the oppressed. The belief that accepting patiently present sufferings and miseries in order to merit a better life in the next birth or life, fulfills the same function as a carrot held before the donkey to make it do all the slave labor. Further the ideological explanation of poverty as the result of laziness gives the poor a negative self-image. There are many such ideologies at work.

THE CULTURAL SYSTEM

The concept of culture has been the object of much discussion and debate in recent times. Without entering into this debate, we want to consider the cultural system as consisting of both internal and external elements. The internal element, or the core of culture, contains the values individuals profess and the meaning they offer to each person. The external element is the outward expression of culture in terms of symbols, traditions, customs, artifacts, and so on.

Values serve as the mobilizing forces or guiding principles in life. We acquire them from the society through a process of internalization. They come to us at various stages and through different means. Since culture is a powerful means for mobilizing the people, the rich and the elitist groups try to appropriate culture and permeate it with the values that support their interests and condition the poor to accept their poverty voluntarily. Through the system of values the rich manipulate the society to their advantage to such an extent that the poor may consider even the oppressive measures perpetrated against them as favors. To cite a few examples, caste-consciousness itself becomes an important value in deciding a person's social status. Both among the high castes and the low castes there are a number of subdivisions. These divisions are a great obstacle to people coming together on certain important issues on a class basis. Though caste seems to have undergone changes, it has only changed its face in the public sphere of life; in the private sphere it is strongly operative.

Women are particular victims of a certain value system offered by Indian society. The ideal woman, they are taught, lives fully the values of shyness, fearfulness, decency, obedience, service, dependency, and the like. These values keep women as a docile work force for men; control and exploitation of women is made easier.

Thus the cultural system, through its process of symbolic interaction, maintains a certain meaning system (Nisbet and Perrin 1977, 53) that is produced by the affluent and maintained by them through the cultural media. The poor have their own folklore and cultural media that are operative in their day-to-day life. Through these media the exploitative values are conveyed. Religious stories, myths, proverbs, popular stories, similies, and metaphors are some of the mechanisms of cultural media whereby the oppressive values, meanings, and attitudes are transmitted from generation to generation. The educational system itself is dominated by the rich and the middle class. It is geared to their interests, and it transmits values advantageous to them.

Culture gives identity, values, and meaning to social groups. When culture is manipulated by the rich, oppressive means become doubly powerful and get deeply rooted in a society.

DIFFERENT APPROACHES TO THE PROBLEM

The church has tried to respond to the oppression of the poor. The response was one of gradual evolution, from charity to people's organizations. This evolution and growth was influenced both by the emergence of a fresh consciousness within the church about the plight of the poor and by the various forces operating in society for its transformation. This growth in the response of the church had a qualitative impact on the faith consciousness of the people. Church efforts can be summarized in three approaches.

THE CHARITY APPROACH

During the colonial period in the nineteenth century, there were organized and institutionalized efforts to meet the needs of the poor and the marginalized in terms of charity. Several socioeconomic and political factors necessitated this response of the church. The incoming of capitalism began dismantling the feudal relations and breaking down the joint family, which traditionally took care of the sick, the old, the handicapped, the widows, and the orphans. Monetization of the economy encouraged mobility in society at all levels. Money became a central value; people began to be individualistic. Nuclear families came into existences, and the sick, the old, the handicapped were viewed as economic burdens. The caste system shifted its emphasis from purity-pollution; it began to acquire a competitive class character. The church responded to this situation by charity measures. In the wake of independence, therefore, the church was identified with charitable institutions.

The main ideology underlying these efforts to respond to the problem of poverty and human suffering consists in these tenets: society is made up of the rich and the poor; poverty cannot be eradicated but can be lessened; the rich must share with the poor and help them. The seven corporal works of mercy and scriptural texts such as "charity covers a multitude of sins" (1 Pt 4:8) made almsgiving and charitable donations very desirable and meritorious.

With this understanding of poverty, the rich again have a very positive self-image; they are benefactors, good and generous. Money becomes a deciding factor in starting, maintaining, and developing charitable undertakings.

THE INSTITUTIONAL AND INPUT MODEL

Due to the interplay of several national and international forces after independence, a shift took place both in the consciousness concerning poverty and the strategies to overcome it. There was the pressing need to rebuild the nation socially, economically, politically, and culturally. Nehru gave a clarion call to citizens to involve themselves in the reconstruction of the nation. This included building up a good infrastructure of educational and health institutions as well as the promotion of industrial development. The Hindu revival attempted to assert the relevance of Hinduism for Indians and to marginalize Christianity. The flow of missionaries to India was stopped, and Christians were branded as unpatriotic for professing a foreign-based religion and were looked down upon as belonging to the low castes. Hence there was a need for the Indian church to assert that it was in no way anti-national or unpatriotic. The establishment of international aid agencies, mostly supported by the church, during the development decade of the 1950s bolstered the idea of development as growth from inferior to superior status.

The church responded to these forces by starting educational and health institutions in large number and by establishing social service societies.

The main ideology underlying these ventures is that poverty and human misery can and should be changed and even eradicated. The causes of poverty are the underdevelopment and under-utilization of natural and human resources. The only way to remove poverty is to maximize both human and national resources. Acquisition and development of human skills through education and training, both technical and professional, and increasing productivity through technological devices and productive investments appeared essential. In this context, promotion of education, health, employment of technological devices, and acquisition of credit for productive purposes were considered ideal means to remove and eradicate poverty and human misery.

This way of interpreting poverty gives a very positive self-image to the educated, the professionally and technically skilled, and to those who offer financial help toward the realization of development projects. Here the important factor is again money, which plays the deciding role in starting and continuing the various projects. Dedication plays a role here too, but it is not necessarily a sine qua non.

ORGANIZATION AND PARTICIPATION OF PEOPLE

The so-called Angry Seventies brought a new consciousness in the understanding of poverty, as well as fresh ways and means of meeting this problem. There was an enthusiasm to put into practice the teachings of Vatican II, especially its acceptance of pluralism in theological approaches and its concept of the church as people of God. Further the realization began to emerge that the input model of projects benefitted only the middle class and the rich. In addition, the growing influence of Marxian analysis and its explanation of poverty, as well as the influence, especially from 1969 to 1971, of the Naxalite movement, an extreme leftist branch of the communist party movement that advocates violence as the only means of destabilizing the rich class, all began to shake up the rich. There was also an increasing consciousness about neocolonialism as well as about the oppressive measures adopted by the national elites toward the poor. There was then the emergence and spread of liberation theology from Latin American countries, and the influence of the CELAM conferences at Medellín in Colombia in August 1968 and at Puebla in Mexico in January 1979 (Ferm 1986, 7ff.). Further, the declaration of an emergency period in India, lasting nineteen months starting from June 25, 1975 and ending in change of political power, gave signs of hope for people's movements. The government policy encouraging adult education opened up new possibilities to organize people in villages.

The dialectical relationship among these various forces created a shift in the concept of poverty and in the ways of surmounting it. The response consisted in organizing people at the grassroots level, especially the illiterate and oppressed, in order to give them a critical awareness of their situation and the forces responsible for it. This critical awareness led many groups to take measures to liberate themselves from the overt and covert mechanisms the rich were employing to keep them poor and subjugated. In order to help people gain this awareness and to inspire self-confidence as they struggled against injustice, several training programs were conducted in which cultural media and group discussions were used. This type of work with oppressed groups is on the increase, and not among Christians alone. Non-Christians also form groups to organize the people. All come under the general umbrella of social action groups or non-party political formations or grassroots groups. In spite of their different ideological leanings, the various groups work jointly.

The ideological underpinning of the above-mentioned praxis is that poverty is a manmade phenomenon maintained by unjust socioeconomic, political, religious, and cultural mechanisms operated by the rich groups and classes. These manmade structures can be changed only if people become conscious of them, organize themselves, and are empowered to act together toward social transformation.

In this way of thinking, the rich get a very negative self-image. They are in no way benefactors or saviors of the poor. It is the poor who save not only themselves, but the rich as well. People who work along these lines require deep commitment to the poor and oppressed. If this commitment is not present, nothing can help. Money plays a very secondary role. This is amply illustrated by the fact that government, which allots plenty of money for adult education aimed at awareness, literacy, and functionality, has not succeeded much in these programs, whereas several voluntary organizations with meager financial resources have succeeded to a great extent. The deciding factor is the commitment of those engaged in this work.

THE NEED AND URGENCY OF LIBERATION THEOLOGY

The next question we must ask is what repercussions have all these approaches to the problems of poverty and oppression produced on the practice and understanding of the faith of the people, as well as on the theologians. In other words, have these changes and evolutions led to a new theological climate in India?

Clearly, working for the betterment of the poor has undergone a qualitative change from giving benefits to the poor—the crumbs that fall from the table of the rich—to acknowledging the rights of the poor. The poor refuse today to accept blindly the present unjust situation as God's will or as an occasion to gain merits for the afterlife. On the other hand, the poor are very sensitive to life and hence also to the sense of the sacred, the Divine. But as their critical consciousness grows, a feeling of restlessness and sometimes cynicism about pious devotions, rituals, and so on, through which the sense of the sacred was fostered, begins to creep in.

Vatican II faced this situation with a certain reformist attitude of popularizing the word of God. This reformist tendency found resonance among the people, especially among the oppressed who were sensitive to what was happening to them. They started reading the word of God, which they found to be on their side. They began to ask the meaning of being a Christian in a situation of oppression and violence. This created new stirrings in the church and slowly the message of liberation began to spread.

Further, those who were working with the poor and the oppressed gradually became convinced that the main basis for their work is commitment, not the power of money. They felt the need for an inner energy to sustain and increase their commitment. Experience showed them how faith and God-experience could serve as the source, as the mobilizing force for their commitment and work. In this way a liberation theology began to emerge.

A few theologians who have been in solidarity with the poor and oppressed began systematically to articulate liberation theology. They found that in addition to other sources such as scripture and the magisterium, the poor and their experiences serve as a *locus theologiae*.

Theology of liberation is a process of life-synthesis that goes on. Such a process calls for transition from theology as an intellectual synthesis made in the libraries to life as the focus of all theologizing (Puthanangady 1986, 307). If the church becomes the church of the poor, if this community is critically conscious of the mechanisms of injustice and oppression and undertakes liberative actions, and if this life-dynamics is celebrated in word (Schottroff and Stegemann 1984) and sacrament, then a liberation theology can flourish in India.

CONCLUSION

Though social injustice, exploitation, and oppression have been present down through history, they transform themselves from crude manifestations into more subtle ones. That is why a prophetic stand and action (Gottwald 1983, 101ff.) on the part of Christians is called for more than ever before. This study has indicated both the reality of the present forms of exploitation and oppression as well as the challenges that come to us from God through the historical struggles of the people.

REFERENCES

Das, Arvind N., and V. Nailakant, eds. 1979. *Agrarian Relations in India*, Manohar Publications, New Delhi.

Drucker, H. M. 1977. *The Political Uses of Ideology*, The Macmillan Press Ltd., London (reprint).

Ferm, Deane William. 1986. *Third World Liberation Theologies, An Introductory Survey*, Orbis Books, Maryknoll, New York.

Frykenberg, Robert Eric, ed. 1977. *Land Tenure and Peasant in South Asia*, Orient Longman, New Delhi.

Gottwald, Norman K. 1983. *The Bible and Liberation, Political and Social Hermeneutics*, Orbis Books, Maryknoll, New York.

Hiro, Dilip. 1979. *Inside India Today*, Monthly Review Press, London.

Mandelbaum, David G. 1970. *Society in India, Change and Continuity*, vol. 2, University of California Press, Berkeley.

Nisbet, Robert, and Robert G. Perrin. 1977. *The Social Bond*, Alfred A. Knopf, New York.

Puthanangady, Paul, ed. 1986. *Towards an Indian Theology of Liberation*, Indian Theological Association, Bangalore.

Refebure, Henri. 1978. *The Survival of Capitalism*, Allison and Busby, London (reprint).

Schottroff, Willy, and Wolfgang Stegemann, eds. 1984. *God of the Lowly, Socio-Historical Interpretations of the Bible*, Orbis Books, Maryknoll, New York. (Originally published as *Der Gott der Kleinen Leute: Sozialgeschichtliche Bibelauslegungen*, vol. 1, *Altes Testament*, and vol. 2, *Neues Testament*, Chr. Kaiser Verlag, Munich and Borckhardthaus-Laetare Verlag, Gelnhausen/Berlin/Stein, 1979.)

Sen, Sukomal. 1979. *Working Class of India*, K.P. Bageli and Company, Calcutta (reprint).

Sethi, Harsh, and Smitu Kothari, eds. 1983. *The Non-Party Political Process: Uncertain Alternatives*, UNRISD/Lokayan, Delhi.

Shah, S. A., ed. 1983. *India: Degradation and Development*, part 2, Venkatarangaiya Foundation, Secunderabad.

3

Bhakti and Liberation Theology for India

WALTER FERNANDES

Can *bhakti* become an inspiration for liberation theology in India? This question cannot have an immediate answer because the very meaning of *bhakti* keeps changing according to its context. There is, first of all, the Brahminic meaning of *bhakti* understood as devotion to atman and interpreted more or less in a contemplative sense, with little or no link with the surrounding social reality. The second is the *Krishnaleela* of the *Bhagavadgita*, which has been used as the basis for political action. It combines an emotional devotion to a personal God with a call for action. There is, thirdly, *bhakti* as equality before a personal God, which has been used as a tool for social transformation. One can also find other combinations of these concepts, some of them concentrating on action, a few on equality, and others on contemplation.

Not all of these interpretations can be used as the basis for a liberation theology in India. Greater discernment of the situation and analysis of the society in which these concepts evolved is esssential before one attempts any liberation theology based on *bhakti*. What is needed is not merely a study of the texts and sources, but their socio-historical context. As Friedheim Hardy would put it, the texts and sources themselves have to be situated in their milieu and analyzed according to the social and political context of the historical moment in which they evolved (Hardy 1983, 11).

In this chapter, therefore, we will focus not on the *bhakti* texts but on the sociopolitical context in which they originated. In doing this we shall every now and then refer to the doctrine. For this we shall depend exclusively on secondary sources, taking the doctrinal and theological details for granted rather than going into them explicitly.

THE MAIN TEXTS

The main sources of *bhakti* are the *Bhagavadgita*, a part of the *Mahabharata*, and the *Bhagavata-Purana*. The *Bhagavadgita* (Song of the Lord), often referred to simply as *Gita*, belongs to the post-vedic period, that is, 600 B.C. to A.D. 300 and is connected with the main battle of Kurukshetra. When the Pandava leader Arjuna hesitates at the thought of a fratricidal war with his cousins, the Kauravas, Lord Krishna, who has become his charioteer, urges him to fight on. The theme later applied to political action is that *bhakti*, devotion to a personal god, should be seen in deed. A second theme, also used later, is social integrity and equality based on work (de Bary 1966, 274-76).

The *Bhagavata-Purana* is the best known of the eighteen major and eighteen minor *Puranas*. All of them seem to have taken shape from the third to the fifth centuries, known as the golden age of Indian literature. They were probably completed during the four centuries that followed. The doctrine of equality based on devotion to a personal God found in the *Bhagavata-Purana* would prepare the way for the medieval *bhakti* movement (Basham 1954, 140-43).

Both the *Bhagavadgita* and the *Bhagavata-Purana* are non-Brahminic scriptures. The *Gita* probably belongs to the Kshatriyas and is a part of the power struggle between them and the Brahmins. Like the French bourgeoisie, which led the political revolution in the name of equality but only transferred power from the aristocracy to itself, so also the Kshatriyas used the language of equality. They struggled to acquire power for themselves. However, the concept of equality enshrined in the *Gita* would later be used by the other classes.

The *Bhagavadgita* and the *Bhagavata-Purana* belong to the first period of *bhakti*. This was followed by Brahminic reaction as well as efforts of the king to monopolize power. Ritual and caste rigidity as well as efforts at the king's divinization characterized this period. There was also reaction to this rigidity on the religious plane and efforts at the social level to reform the caste system. The third stage was the Muslim era, when *bhakti* received a new interpretation. The social dimension it acquired should be situated in the context of reduction in the power of the Brahmin and the Kshatriya. Finally, the fourth and most recent stage of the reinterpretation of the *Bhagavadgita* came during the freedom movement at the end of the nineteenth and beginning of the twentieth centuries. This reinterpretation began with Aurobindo, was taken up by Tilak, and was continued by Gandhi.

THE FIRST STAGE OF *BHAKTI*: BRAHMIN-KSHATRIYA COMPETITION

Buddhism, Jainism, and most of the *Bhagavadgita* have to be situated in the context of the Aryan conquest in the middle of the second millennium and the threat it posed to the egalitarian ideology of the tribals and the political power of the rulers (Ghurye 1957, 74-75). At the popular level, society in northern India, where the Aryans came first, was tribal and egalitarian. At the political level, power had been monopolized by petty kings who ruled over the land.

KSHATRIYAS AND EQUALITY

Into this egalitarian society the Aryans introduced caste-based inequality. Where the chieftains held sway, the conquerors attempted to impose their own brand of political power. The result was major social change. The four *Vedas*, probably written between 1500 and 600 B.C., show the transition from a pastoral to an agrarian society and from an egalitarian to a priest-centered caste society (Dumont 1970, 88-89). Efforts were also made by the conqueror to coopt the popular religiosity of the conquered peoples by including many tribal gods into the Hindu pantheon and by integrating them into the Brahmin-ruled apparatus. Obviously, this process took a long time because the arrival of the Aryans was not a concentrated invasion but a gradual migration, reaching the Gangetic Plains in eastern India only around 800 B.C. (Basham 1954, 26-28, 53-55).

At the political level, the arrival of the Aryans threatened the rulers who had appropriated most of the power to themselves. The conquerors were later identified with the Brahmin and the local rulers with the Kshatriya. The local rulers resorted to the tribal egalitarian ideology to demand equality for themselves. Through this conflictual process and negotiation, Brahmin and Kshatriya came to a mutually convenient structure of sharing power within a religious structure that was not institutionally organized. As such, the priest did not have a hierarchical structure independent of the king. He depended on the ruler for his material sustenance. In a politically fluid state, the king, on his part, needed legitimation from the Brahmin to be recognized as the ruler (Spellman 1964, 76-77). This need became greater as political instability increased. Beginning from the Nandas, all the rulers have been of Shudra origin (Panikkar 1956, 4). It was, therefore, essential for them to be accepted as Kshatriyas, the ruling caste. They did this, after assuming power, by getting the Brahmin to invent a new genealogy linking them with the (Kshatriya) Rajputs of Rajasthan, thus turning Shudra into Kshatriya.

Thus power was shared by keeping the priest materially dependent on the king, and the king ideologically dependent on the priest. In this joint enterprise, the king was the very foundation upon which all religious activity rested (Spellman 1964, 10-12). He regulated sacrificial actions just as he regulated other functions of the state. The whole state took part in the sacrifice with a definite function assigned to each section. He protected the Brahmin and divided his time between different administrative and religious duties, thus turning the state into a religious action.

This mutual dependence of Brahmin and Kshatriya was meant to maintain an order that was beneficial to both of them. But conflict was bound to arise between the two, and this took many forms. Every now and then the scriptures reflect this conflict. Some of the writings suggest that the king's power came from the priest, while others claim that the Brahmin's power came from the king (Ghurye 1957, 49-50).

The *Bhagavadgita* and the *Bhagavata-Purana* must be situated within this context of power conflict between the two dominant castes. They need to be viewed, on the one hand, within the context of constant wars of conquest and the call to action, and, on the other hand, in light of the effort of the priest to divert attention from the struggle for equality through a contemplative type of spirituality.

The *Bhagavadgita*, therefore, has at least two main streams of thought. First, it tries to find a balance between *kama yoga* (contemplation or love) and *karma yoga* (action). Second, it preaches equality based on work, not on birth (Panikkar 1956, 17-18). The ruler, who was demanding power from the priest, has recourse to an egalitarian ideology to achieve it. In other words, the Kshatriya declares himself equal before the Brahmin.

However, the underlying feeling is that of equality based on *work* not equality of *human beings* as such. Through this subtle distinction the *Bhagavadgita* plays the double game of giving religious sanction to the caste system while at the same time denying hierarchization. It claims that the creator apportioned duties. Everyone should, therefore, do *dharma* (religious duty). In the same breath the devotee is told that there is no such thing as pure and impure work. It is not the work but the way of doing it that matters. This distinction based on work safeguards the power of the ruler and justifies his role as political ruler of the people. Simultaneously, the cooperation of the egalitarian tribal society is obtained by declaring the equality of all (Ghurye 1957, 64-68). Thus, like the conquerors, the rulers (Kshatriyas) too coopt the people's ideology, but use the tribal sense of equality for their own benefit.

EQUALITY AND THE PEOPLE

Though the rulers used this egalitarian teaching to keep themselves in power, the thought of equality itself became the basis of the people's ideology and eventually turned into the *bhakti* movement, which challenged the caste system itself. One important reason this ideology became all-pervasive is that it was presented in the language of popular religiosity. The Krishna myth, which is the idiom of the *Bhagavadgita*, has absorbed many aspects of the people's culture and religion, such as devotion of the *gopis* (milkmaids) to Krishna, songs taken from the tribal culture of Mathura, and the people's link with forests, trees, flowers, and rivers (Hardy 1983, 29-30).

The God thus worshipped was not an intellectual and distant being, but someone close to the devotee. He was found in plants, flowers, and trees (Gonda 1970, 111-13). These aspects added to *bhakti* the emotional element required to bring it close to the low castes at a later date. Thus it was not merely the egalitarian doctrine of the *Bhagavadgita* or the *Bhagavata-Purana* that made it acceptable to the poor. The Kshatriyas preached the doctrine of equality in order to legitimize their own domination. But the popular ethos and the regional language, as against the Brahmin's Sanskrit, through which equality was presented would bring it close to the people.

Of course, no one form of popular religiosity existed all over the country. The elements of spirituality and popular expression differed from place to place. The initial Krishna cult, the *Gopi* emotion, and the references to trees and forests gave the *Bhagavadgita* a tribal background around Mathura, which is assumed to be the birthplace of Krishna. In Tamil Nadu the egalitarian ideology was taken over by the Alwars and Nayanmars and given an expression and meaning relevant to the local situation. Other forms were found elsewhere. But the emotional and popular aspects were retained in all of them (Hardy 1983, 34-35).

BUDDHISM AND JAINISM

Apart from the *Bhagavadgita,* the local rulers' challenge to Aryan domination and the caste system accompanying it took the form of Buddhism and Jainism in the fifth century B.C. Both went beyond equality based on work; they, Buddhism in particular, declared all human beings equal. Buddhists are told that to the pure all things are pure and that there is no such thing as superior or inferior caste (de Bary 1966, 194-95).

It is also true, as Ghurye asserts (Ghurye 1957, 72-74), that the Buddhist (and possibly Jain) claims to equality remained only pious words. Buddha did not choose anyone outside the two high castes for his core group of disciples. His followers further strengthened this trend and caste conflicts ensued. Thus Buddhists too used the egalitarian ideology to claim equality for the Kshatriyas before the Brahmins and not to promote those below them. But they too would be instrumental in spreading this ideology to the people because their scriptures were written in Pali, the people's language, not in the conqueror's language, Sanskrit. Jainism later spread this ideology in Gujarati and made a major contribution to its literature. These thoughts were eventually expressed by the *Bhagavata-Purana*, also in the popular idiom (Hardy 1983, 28).

THE SECOND STAGE OF *BHAKTI*: BRAHMINIC REACTION

Conservative reaction was bound to follow. It built over the centuries and reached its climax between the sixth and eighth centuries A.D. At first, reaction took the form of rigid adherence to the ritual, although this was to be questioned by some as being too priest-oriented. Others who heard the demands of equality introduced some reforms in the caste system. The timing and expression of these developments differed from place to place.

To begin with ritual rigidity, Hinduism slowly became a religion of several gods, each of them presiding over a department of human life. These gods were ever ready to grant the desire of the devotee who performed the sacrifice according to the rules. Rigid adherence to the ritual became the center of religion. *Yajna* was the main work of the person in the world, with other duties like *danas* (charity) and *vratas* (vows) becoming subsidiary. The other side of the coin was *tapasy,* the ascetic of austere life of the *rishi* or *muni* (monk). Unlike the common person in the world, the *muni* devoted himself fully to God and was a symbol of the victory of spirit over matter.

Hinduism was thus a priest-centered religion that divided society in two: ritual-based worship for the masses, and an ascetic life for a chosen elite. The masses had to depend on the priest for the ritual. The elite had to be honored because they had given up the world. This ensured the power of the priest over the common person (Sharma 1966, 10-12).

Such a religion was bound to cause reaction both from the ruling classes and from the common people. Initially protest came from the theologians and the kingly class. At the theological level, many claimed that such a ritual-based approach to religion did injustice to the *Vedas*. They protested that the essence of religion was not merely that devotees prostrate themselves before the gods, but that they do it in a spirit of righteousness and purity. "Is it only the material act of worship that matters? Do the heart and head of the devotee have no place in religion?" they asked. In other words, they claimed that the *Vedas* demanded that worship should not be merely a ritual but should have some effect on the life of the worshipper (Goswami-Sastri 1965, 3-13).

On the other extreme, protest against a ritual-based religion took the form of atheism—the *Nastika* doctrine. These theologians claimed that in the present religious sacrifice was meant only for the benefit of the priest and not of the worshipper or of the dead for whom it was offered. "Can the dead eat? Or is the sacrifice meant in fact to fill the stomach of the priest?" they asked. They also claimed that the priest ensured his own control over the common person by claiming monopoly over the sacrificial rites (Goswami-Sastri 1965, 3-13).

KINGS' SUPREMACY

Simultaneous to the Brahmins asserting supremacy, kings also began to affirm their rights. Two opposing traditions on the very meaning of the state originated from two geographical regions separated by the Ganges, although both have the concept of the fallen state. The Aryan tradition, which grew with their migration toward the Gangetic Plains, is more king-centered than the Kosala-Magadha approach. The latter theory, linked more to Buddhism than to Brahminism, is closer to the social contract, in which the king is a trustee of the people. The people appoint the ruler and military leader to judge the wrongdoers when stealth and dishonesty become part of life. The Aryan of Brahminic interpretation, on the contrary, is king-centered. The divine appointment of the king is more or less taken for granted (Spellman 1964, 10-12). In this approach,

> society in its original state is anarchy; without laws and a king to rule, the strong dominate and ruthlessly exploit the weak, just as big fish eat up their smaller companions. Without understanding this idea, there can be no understanding of kingship in ancient India. Although this concept of human nature existed in other countries, it was in India that it reached its highest development and became the central theme of political philosophy (Spellman 1964, 5).

By post-vedic times the king had become the source of good and evil in his kingdom. Welfare, good rains, sickness, calamities, and death among his people owed their origin to the king (Spellman 1964, 211). His role, therefore, was to preserve the *dharma* imposed on the people by the priest. The Aryan tradition even thought of the life of the people as a way of judging the king's *dharma*.

> If the people committed sin, it followed that they were not being properly cared for and restrained by the king. It also implied that the king was not setting a good example since the people followed the path of conduct shown by the king. Therefore, the king shared part of the sins of those people who were not restrained by him (Spellman 1964, 221).

The Kosala-Magadha tradition paid much less attention to *rajaniti* (the king's justice) as well as to the priest's *dharma*.

Given that both the king and the priest were demanding supremacy, occasional conflict between the two was inevitable. But it was between two dominant castes. The people rarely entered the picture (Basham 1954, 99-100). By and large there was collaboration between the two. At the time of reaction to Buddhism and in the age of imperial expansion, the concept of a universal emperor would grow.

People's Demands

Amid this priest-king conflict, popular demands could not be ignored. These demands came mainly from the South. Initially an effort was made to coopt these demands; later reforms were introduced.

Cooptation in theology took the form of *shraddha bhakti*, which came to be accepted as an attitude required in the devotee. It was an attitude of total devotion to God, but of an intellectual type with inadequate links with the world around. Monotheism was stressed against the polytheism that resulted in ritual rigidity. The devotee was made the center of worship, not the priest who exercised his power over gods presiding over different areas. This slowly grew into the atman concept popularized mainly by Sankara (A.D. 788-820). God remained a contemplation-oriented God; consequently, the spirituality of losing oneself in atman took the devotee away from the struggles that threatened the power of the king and the priest. In that sense, this individualistic spirituality was as alienating from the reality of the world as the earlier rigid, ritual-based religion of the Brahmin (Goswami-Sastri, 1965, 22-33).

This thought was taken up in the eleventh century by Ramanuja, who was influenced by the Tamil poets. Ramanuja was much more open to other castes than Sankara. He seems to have had some untouchables among his disciples, and he tried to find ways of integrating them into the caste system. Without questioning the caste system itself, he wanted to give to the Shudras a new type of sacred thread to bring them on par with the three "twice-born" castes. Briefly, at a time when reaction to popular aspiration had taken a rigid form through the priest-centered religion, when the king was attempting to assert his own authority through divinization, and when the theologian was evolving an otherworldly religion, Ramanuja and his followers attempted some reforms without changing the caste system itself (Ghurye 1957, 107-8). Though these steps may have been of a coopting nature, they prepared the ground for later interpretation of *bhakti* as equality.

THE THIRD STAGE OF *BHAKTI*: THE MUSLIM ERA

Internecine wars had weakened political India and by the end of the first millennium had created the infrastructure required for the Muslim conquest of the subcontinent. Simultaneously, the religious revival of the preceding centuries had made Hinduism culturally impregnable even when it was politically vulnerable. As a result, an assimilationist Hinduism failed to absorb Islam, and Islam, which had submerged other conquered lands, subjugated political India but failed to eliminate Hinduism.

However, the loss of political power also had an impact on the social field. The Hindu ruler lost absolute power and became a vassal of the Muslim emperor. Brahmin domination too was weakened. These changes made it easier for the subordinate classes to assert themselves, at least to a limited extent. Conversion movements to Islam and the spread of the *bhakti* ideology through the regional languages further supported the aspirations of the people.

DEFENSIVE MOOD

As far as Hindu society was concerned, the first feature of this era was the loss of power of its ruling classes. By the middle of the Muslim age in

India, their mood was defensive. The power of India's ruling classes had been partially broken. The Hindu king was not there anymore to defend the *dharma* and maintain the status quo of caste domination. The Brahmin had lost some of his supremacy since Sanskrit was no longer the only dominant language.

After the arrival of the Muslims, caste councils continued to function. Hindus retained their personal law as well as internal autonomy. They also continued the use of Sanskrit. However, Sanskrit lost its monopoly. At the imperial court, initially Arabic and later Turkish and Persian became the official language. Muslim law replaced the Hindu code and the Ulama the Brahmin. A section of the ruling classes adapted itself to the changed situation by reaching a compromise with the new imperial regime. Many former rulers were integrated into the Muslim military-administrative apparatus. Eventually a section of the Brahmins also joined the Muslim administration (Nizami 1961, 156-58). Their loss of power and later the alliance of a section of the ruling classes with the Muslim imperial government put the remaining Brahminic and other upper classes on the defensive.

The second factor that called forth the defensive mood of the ruling classes and supported social change in favor of the subordinate classes in the Muslim era was the conversion of a large number of people from the low castes to Islam. These conversions, which had begun during the early sultanates, gave a religious expression to the social aspirations of the low castes.

So much has been said about the forced conversion of Indians to Islam during these centuries that it is often forgotten that the majority of them were converted not by the politician but by the missionary. There certainly were conversions of convenience, mainly among the upper classes, for example, the merchants whose change of religion seemed linked to political patronage. But these were not the norm. Had conversions by forces or for political patronage been the norm, the number of Muslims should have been largest around the centers of Islamic power. But their numbers are relatively small around places like Ahmedabad, Ahmednagar, Bijapur, and Delhi. On the other hand, places like Bangladesh, where the majority of people are Muslims, were converted to Islam only in the sixteenth century (Ikram 1961, 189-90).

Hence, explanations other than political expendiency have to be found for this phenomenon. First of all, most conversions to Islam were from among the low castes, not from the merchant or other classes who could have reaped material benefits through change of religion. Second, only exceptionally did missionaries accompany the politicians. *Sufi*, who were members of Muslim religious orders, did the conversion work. They were not organized as missionary orders but were moved by individual zeal (Mazaheri 1970, 966). All these orders adopted many popular Hindu customs and religious practices in their lives and followed the *bhakti* devotional pattern in their propaganda. Like the *bhakti* teachers, they too went around singing *kirtans* (devotional hymns), many taken from the Hindu ethos, and appealing to the personal devotion and emotional life of the masses. In addition to the *bhakti* type of popular religiosity, another factor that attracted the subordinate classes to Islam was the equality that the *sufi* preached.

In other words, in areas where Brahminic reaction to *bhakti* and Buddhism was not as strong as elsewhere, and where the *sufi* communicated their message of equality through the popular medium, they found a response among the low castes.

REGIONAL LANGUAGES AND *BHAKTI* AMONG HINDUS

Conversion to Islam was not the only religious expression given to the aspirations of the oppressed to be equal. Within the Hindu fold itself, *bhakti* became the expression of the untouchables who were demanding not merely positional change within the caste system, but structural change. The message spread partly through popular religiosity and partly because of the regional languages, which became the third factor that made it possible for the subordinate classes to demand equality. Like Buddhism and Jainism, *bhakti* too valorized regional languages in religious renewal. If on the one hand, the movement became popular through the use of the regional medium, *bhakti* in its turn helped the growth of these languages. Bengali, Gujarati, Hindi, Kannada, Marathi, and Telugu were already popular languages with their own literature. Around the thirteenth century they had reached the stage of having major epics. In the composition of these epics, their poets broke away from the classical Sanskritic mold and developed a poetry based on a nonclassical meter (Harrison 1960, 30). During these centuries the *Mahabharata* and *Ramayana* were reinterpreted in the regional languages. These were not literal translations but reinterpretations with each culture developing its own myths based on the popular movements and devotions in the region.

Briefly, it was a non-Brahmin, and in many cases, even an anti-Brahminic movement. It had its beginnings in the South. The Chola dynasty, the symbol of Tamil greatness, had united the southern peninsula from the ninth to the thirteenth centuries and had revived it as a commercial and cultural center. In this atmosphere the religious reform movement started, with the Alvars and Nayanmars adapting the revival of the Hindu golden age to the needs of the masses. The poets found their base in the *Bhagavata-Purana* the "scripture-story" of the non-metaphysical type of popular Krishna.

In the Muslim age this movement spread to the rest of the southern and western regions. Brahminism had reached these regions only in the first millennium and had thus taken a rigid form. Reaction to Brahminism was therefore stronger precisely in these regions. As a result of the *bhakti* movement, all the three southern languages evolved their own version of the *Puranas.*

Thus *bhakti* combined low-caste upsurge, popular spirituality, and the emergence of regional languages. To call it an anti-Brahmin movement is to oversimplify. That element was certainly present, but it should probably be called a cross-caste movement. More than anything else, it was a major break from the traditional caste system, which had till then allowed only positional mobility, and that to the middle castes alone. The untouchables were excluded from any hope of upward mobility. *Bhakti* in the Muslim era became a movement for structural, not merely positional, change. It challenged the very idea of inequality and included the untouchables in its purview, though ultimately it would move only toward positional change (Srinivas 1972, 30).

Moreover, its proponents were not merely from the low castes. It was thus a dialectic of opposite groups. While pushing for equality, it included both the interests. On the part of the Brahmins it was probably an effort to moderate and, if possible, to coopt this emancipation by making Hinduism broad-based and giving the low castes a place in it. As early as the eleventh century, Ramanuja had set aside a day in a year for the Shudras to enter the temple, till then closed to them, and had tried to provide them with an alternative to the Brahmin's sacred thread (Ghurye 1957, 108-9). This trend continued and the untouchables hoped for many reforms.

> Through *bhakti* the Hindu faith of each region found some of its most honored expressions in the regional language. Recorded expressions of the *bhakti* spirit during the centuries of Islamic attacks on Hinduism became a strong link for each region with its past. The regional language, through its use as a vehicle of religious thought and love, became something far more meaningful to each region than mere patois or folk language. When western political and social ideals stirred nineteenth-century India, the highly developed Indian regional languages provided an obvious outlet for the rising generation of Indian leaders (Harrison 1960, 53).

THE FOURTH STAGE OF *BHAKTI*: THE BRITISH ERA AND THE FREEDOM MOVEMENT

The impact of the *bhakti* movement was still being felt in the nineteenth century, but it diminished with the consolidation of British power. Colonialism essentially controlled the indigenous populations through the collaboration of a few upper-class elements. This involved the strengthening of the existing dominant sections from the Brahminic, administrative, landholding, and other classes that derived the greatest benefits from British education and jobs in the administration.

In the nineteenth century the impact of *bhakti* and of the caste struggle was such that the untouchables had some hope of liberation within the Hindu fold. However, the primary objective of colonialism was not social reform or strengthening the local leadership in itself. It was a commercial enterprise which required the control of the local population. To achieve this, the local dominant structures, most of them feudal in nature, had to be supported, and if necessary, distorted, but not destroyed (Qudeer 1985, 216).

Apart from the traditional ruling classes, the colonial age witnessed the emergence also of Indian capitalism. A few groups like the Parsis, Marwaris, and Vanias, who controlled Indian trade before the arrival of the British, had kept a toehold in it even in the colonial age. These groups became the capitalists in the western region. In the rest of India, moneylenders, *zamindars* (landlords), and other feudal elements took control of commerce, initially as agents of the British and later as the new capitalists during the freedom movement (Sarkar 1983). Briefly, commercialization was linked with modernization. But colonial policies interacted with the local infrastructure. While capitalism grew in the colonizing country, it strengthened the feudal forces in the colony. That in itself is not surprising because change is brought about through an interaction between external inputs and internal forces (Martin 1978). The internal forces in India at that time were predominantly feudal, although they were under attack from the *bhakti* movement. However, by getting the collaboration of the ruling classes, colonialism strengthened these forces and further weakened the subordinate classes that were struggling for equality.

The legal system, particularly land laws, also had to be changed to suit colonial needs. As a result, the landholding pattern was changed and the *jajmani* system of division of labor was weakened in areas where the impact of colonialism was felt the most. The net result of these interventions was that the impact of the *bhakti* movement was lost. The untouchables were thus deprived of the last hope of freedom from caste within the Hindu fold. If they wanted liberation, they would have to search for it elsewhere.

Thus these changes brought about a deterioration in the status of the untouchables, and with other events led to the conversion of a large number of untouchables to Christianity, Islam, Sikhism, and other religions that preached equality (Fernandes 1981, 23-24). These conversions were a threat to the Hindu ruling classes, particularly because of the constant missionary attacks on the caste system as the very embodiment of the injustice perpetrated by Hinduism. Besides, in order to legitimize colonialism, the foreign rulers devalued Indian (considered Hindu) culture and presented it as barbarian. All these aspects put the Hindu upper classes on the defensive.

Religious Revival

The religious revival during the freedom movement has to be understood in this context. The elite had gained access to British education and the administrative posts that took control of the freedom movement. The commercial classes founded it. The elite had to react to the colonial devaluation of Indian culture; religious revival was their response. The missionary attacks on Hinduism had to be counteracted and conversions prevented. The upper-class response was social reforms. This was achieved through a combination of caste reforms, religious revival, and the promise of a better life in independent India.

Initially some attempted purely secular change in the country. Though they succeeded in enacting radical legislation, most of the reformist laws could not be implemented since they lacked social legitimacy. Another group attempted religious revival. While it functioned as the rallying point to bring the Hindu masses together, revival alone could not provide the basis required for social reform or economic development. In fact, it functioned as a divisive force and was often exploited by the commercial and related classes to take control of the freedom movement (Shankardass 1982).

Others, however, realized that a purely secular approach to social reform was not acceptable in a country like India; a religious base was essential. That is what reformers like Tilak, Aurobindo, and Gandhi did. They began with the *Bhagavadgita* as the basic text. Tilak and others who wanted a political struggle alone to free India from the British used the text to proclaim their call to action. While accepting this call, Gandhi used the same text to propagate his call to *satyagraha* (nonviolent, cooperative fight for truth) against the foreigner, who followed the double strategy of divide-and-rule and violent action. He used *bhakti* to proclaim that the *Vedas* made no distinction among different types of work. All work is equal as long as it is done out of devotion to one God. Whatever the work done, all the castes are equal (Gandhi 1949).

Such a call to a return to the vedic times of equality and justice had already been given by Dayananda Saraswati and other religious reformers with a social base. Gandhi combined the social and religious into one. He presented the future society of *bhakti* of justice and equality as *Rama Rajya,* the return of the rule of the mythic king Rama, in whose kingdom truth and justice prevailed. Through this return to the past, the leaders were in fact proclaiming a future society that Free India had to commit itself to build and were giving it a religious basis (Karunakaran 1970, 16-17).

IMPLICATIONS FOR AN INDIAN LIBERATION THEOLOGY

The above bird's-eye view of *bhakti* has shown the growth of this concept in Indian history. A few aspects stand out in this analysis. The first is the close link between religious thought and social reality, and the second is the choice of the class in the development of a thought in a given age. The upper classes, like the rulers who want to be equal to those above them, know that the egalitarian ideology of the tribal society has to be accepted. The ruling classes feel threatened by such an ideology and attempt to coopt it. But given power relations favorable to the subordinate classes, as during the Muslim rule, these classes are able to use religion to demand equality. Third, the freedom struggle showed that religious revival alone is inadequate; it can in fact be a divisive force. Hence in a plurireligious society, the option has to be interreligious. The role of popular religiosity too stands out in this bird's-eye view. We shall analyze these aspects in the concluding section.

RELIGION AND SOCIETY

The first aspect that stands out in the study of *bhakti* in Indian history is the close link between religious thought and social reality. Theology and philosophy are based on the socioeconomic situation and domination-dependency relations. They legitimize or question the existing social order. Likewise, in a country like India, social change requires a religious basis. The history of the *bhakti* movement, as well as that of the tribal, freedom, and other sociopolitical struggles, shows how religion is capable of providing such a base. That is also the lesson of liberation theology in Latin America and of many other reformation and revolutionary movements in world history.

More often than not, theology legitimizes the domination of the ruling classes. But at every moment in history, a minority that struggles for the rights of the subordinate classes has been able to find protest elements in religion. Theology calls them the prophetic part of proclamation. These elements bear witness to a different type of a world. In a situation of power and powerlessness, these are the elements that support this minority in its option for the powerless, when the majority, including mainstream theology, are with the ruling classes. The history of *bhakti* as well as that of other movements elsewhere has shown that the prophetic elements are always a minority. The struggles and the religious base this minority give to it may be forgotten by history, which is controlled by the ruling classes. But they give an impetus to change in favor of equality and service in an unequal and unjust society. This message may, at times, be coopted by the ruling classes, but not without social negotiation and reforms in favor of the oppressed (Joshi 1989, 162-78).

A CHRISTIAN PERSPECTIVE AND OPTION FOR THE POOR

An immediate implication of this understanding of history in general and of *bhakti* in particular is that the use made of religion depends on the option one has chosen. There has been the contemplation-related otherworldly atman interpretation of *bhakti*. The *Bhagavadgita* has been used to proclaim the political action-related *Krishnaleela*, or at a later stage the struggle for the country's freedom. At other times, when power relations were favorable, the subordinate classes have used the concept of *Bhakti* to demand the equality of every human being.

What this means is that a genuine people-related theology begins with an option in favor of those who are otherwise excluded by the powerful. The classes thus excluded have to be identified, as well as the prophetic elements in religion that can support their struggle. For a Christian, these elements are available in the life of Jesus, who died that others may have life, who came to serve and not to be served, who became a slave that others may be free.

In other words, a personal option for the marginalized, through the message of Christ's freedom, is the first step for a Christian. Others have to take similar steps from their own religious perspective. For a Christian the starting point of this people-related theology has to be the historical Jesus of Nazareth, who lived, struggled, and died among his people. In other words, this theology begins with the human Jesus and goes on to reflect on his divinity, and not the other way about (Sobrino 1978, 3-4). The assumption of this approach is that "God is at work, through His own free choice, in the struggle for justice and the expectations of hope" (Sobrino 1978, 5).

The second aspect of this option is that such a historical Christ has to be found in the everyday life of the poor. Hegel, the German philosopher, once said that the reading of the daily newspaper was the prayer of modern man. His observation was a profoundly theological one. If a person opens the newspaper and comprehends God's revelation in the concrete course of salvation history, then he or she really is praying for it is in concrete history that God reveals God's self. But the truly important news may not be in the headlines; it may be buried away on the fourth or sixth page of the newspaper. Faith has to discern where the important news, the concrete revelation truly is (Dussel 1976, 139).

AN INTERRELIGIOUS OPTION FOR THE POOR

The third feature of an Indian liberation theology is its interreligious nature. There is always the temptation to transplant into India the experiences of another continent and to develop a Christian liberation theology for India. The history of the freedom movement as well as post-independence developments in the country have shown that when focus is on only one tradition, then religion can become a divisive force. In fact, the ruling classes may deliberately use this emotional force to divide the marginalized groups that are demanding their rights (Fernandes 1988, 7-12). There is always the danger of following the same divisive path in the name of Christ and speaking in terms of a Christian liberation theology for India. There is always the danger of transplanting the experience of another continent.

What Paulo Freire says in the context of non-formal education is relevant also to liberation theology:

> We also learned not to attempt to impose on the Chilean context what we had done in different circumstances in Brazil. Experiments cannot be transplanted; they must be reinvented. One of our most pressing concerns when we were preparing as a team for our first visit to Guinea-Bissau, was to guard against the temptation to overestimate the significance of some aspects of an earlier experience, giving it universal significance (Freire 1978, 9-10).

A liberation theology in India cannot be Christian. It must be interreligious. Hindus, Sikhs, Muslims, and Christians have to search together, each person finding inspiration in his or her own religious tradition and respecting one another's expression. Together they have to search for a genuine *bhakti* in the Indian reality, knowing that every religion has a protest and a prophetic element, though it may not always be commonly expressed. The same scriptures, for example, have been used as support by the subordinate classes in their struggle to be equal as well as by the ruling classes to assert their domination. The dividing line is the class option. This is the challenge in India. It must be an interreligious option. To evolve a liberation theology, people of different religious traditions have to search for the prophetic elements in the context of their common option to support those who are struggling to free themselves from oppression.

The Role of Popular Religiosity

Another aspect that stands out in the history of the *bhakti* movement is the role of popular religiosity. *Bhakti* was propagated, particularly in the Muslim era, through popular religiosity and the local medium. It was an expression of the common people's aspirations through their language, culture, and religiosity. The theologian's option for the poor was thus expressed through the people's culture and religiosity.

It is from this point of view that one should perhaps analyze what is called indigenization, an effort to move away from the foreign image of the church and implant it in the indigenous soil. However, the "Indian" culture that is attempted by this inculturation is predominantly of the Brahminic and Sanskritic variety, the type presented as Indian culture by the revivalists during the freedom movement. Those who belonged to this culture are real Indians. The rest are marginal. When such revivalists say that the church should be indigenized, they expect Christians to identify themselves with this sanskritized Brahminic culture.

That, in reality, is the type of indigenization most Christians working for inculturation have come to accept. Most elements from "Indian" culture that are given a Christian form belong almost exclusively to the Brahminic ritual and philosophy and other forms of dominant cultural expression.

The Sanskritic nature of indigenization is the main reason tribal Christians do not accept inculturation. They have a rich culture of their own, considerably different from the Hindu culture. They are attempting their own inculturation both in their social and liturgical life. It is based not on the Brahminic but the tribal socio-cultural expression. In many areas cultural revival among the tribals has become a rallying point that builds a tribal community and supports it in its struggles against its oppressors. In fact, many of the leaders have learned not to let their religion divide them. Those who formerly called themselves Christian tribals or Sarna tribals today refer to themselves as tribal Christians. They give priority to their tribal belonging. Their culture, therefore, becomes the rallying point irrespective of their religion, which gives them additional inspiration but does not divide them. The lessons of this process of change have to be learned by those involved with the oppressed. A genuine liberation theology has to opt for popular culture, popular religiosity, and a popular idiom. Scriptures like the *Puranas* are certainly important, but one cannot stop at the scriptures. One must go to folklore, popular expressions, imagery, and so on. One has to identify the protest elements in the festivals and other expressions of each culture and use them as the starting point. That is where the Christ of reality lives for a Christian today. Other religions have to find their own starting point. It is in this reality that the people are united in God in their aspiration for liberation and can continue to work together, even while belonging to different religions in India.

CONCLUSION

We have analyzed in this chapter social and political processes that made it possible for the subordinate classes to use religion, particularly *bhakti*, in support of their struggle for equality. We have studied the role played by various classes and the option that has to be made if *bhakti* is to become an expression of the struggle of the oppressed. The role of popular religiosity and culture was analyzed in this context. We saw how they have functioned as the expression of people's struggles, and even today become a rallying point among the tribals.

It is in this context that we analyzed other processes such as the freedom movement and inculturation. It is clear that the meaning of action has to be rediscovered, not merely from texts such as the *Bhagavadgita* and the *Bagavata-Purana*. It has to be reinvented in the processes that have made *bhakti* relevant to the oppressed (Amaladoss 1985, 34-35). In this one can borrow much even from the dominant religion. But the starting point has to be an option for the subordinate classes, identification with their aspirations for equality, and involvement in their struggles.

REFERENCES

Amaladoss, Michael. 1985. *Faith, Culture and Inter-religious Dialogue*, Indian Social Institute, New Delhi.
Bary, W. T. de. 1966. *The Sources of Indian Tradition*, vol. 1 and 2, Free Press, New York.
Basham, A. L. 1954. *The Wonder That Was India*, Fontana Collins, London.
Dumont, Louis. 1970. *Homo Hierarchicus: The Caste System and Its Implication*, Vikas Publications, New Delhi.
Dussel, Enrique. 1976. *History and the Theology of Liberation*, Orbis Books, Maryknoll, New York.
Fernandes, Walter. 1980. *The Indian Catholic Community: Its Peoples and Institutions in Interaction with the Indian Situation Today*, PMV Asia Australia Dossier 12-13, Brussels.
———. 1981. *Caste and Conversion Movements in India: Religion and Human Rights*, Indian Social Institute, New Delhi.
———. 1988. *The Role of Christians in National Integration*, Indian Social Institute, New Delhi.
Freire, Paulo. 1978. *Pedagogy in Process: The Letters to Guinea-Bissau*, Seabury Press, New York.
Gandhi, M. K. 1949. *Cent Per Cent Swadeshi*, Navjivan Publications, Ahmedabad.
Ghurye, G. S. 1957. *Caste and Class in India*, Popular Book Depot, Bombay.
Gonda, J. 1970. *Visnuism and Sivaism: A Comparison*, The Athlone Press, University of London, London.
Goswami-Sastri, Mahamahopadhyaya Pandit Bhagabat Kumar. 1965. *The Bhakti Cult in Ancient India*, Chowkhamba Sanskrit Series Office, Varansi.
Hardy, Friedheim. 1983. *Viraha-Bhakti: The Early History of Krsna Devotion in South India*, Oxford University Press, Delhi.
Harrison, Selig S. 1960. *India: The Most Dangerous Decade*, Princeton University Press, New Jersey.
Ikram, S. M. 1961. *A History of Muslim Civilization of India and Pakistan*, People's Press, Lahore.
Joshi, P. C. 1989. "Religion, Class Conflicts and Emancipation Movements: Some Reflections," *Social Action* 39.
Karunakaran, K. P. 1970. *Religion and Political Awakening in India*, Meenakshi Prakashan, Meerut.
Martin, Roderick. 1978. *The Sociology of Power*, Ambika Publications, New Delhi.
Mazaheri, Ali. 1970. *Le Monde Musulman: Histoire de L'Humanite-19ᵉ siècle*, vol. 5, Unesco, Paris.
Nizami, K. A. 1961. *Religion and Politics in India in the 13th Century*, Asia Publishing House, Bombay.
Panikkar, K. M. 1956. *Hindu Society at Cross Roads*, Asia Publishing House, Bombay.
Qudeer, Imrana. 1985. "Health Services System in India: An Expression of Socio-Economic Inequalities," *Social Action* 35.
Sarkar, Sumit. 1983. *Modern India 1885-1974*, Macmillan, New Delhi.
Shankardass, Rani Dhavan. 1982. *The First Congress Raj*, Macmillan India, New Delhi.

Sharma, S. R. 1966. *The Crescent in India: A Study of Medieval History*, Asia Publishing House, Bombay.
Sobrino, Jon. 1978. *Christology at Crossroads: A Latin American Approach*, SCM, London.
Spellman, I. W. 1964. *Political Theory of Ancient India*, Oxford University Press, Oxford.
Srinivas, M. N. 1972. *Religion and Society Among the Coorgs of South India*, Asia Publishing House, Bombay.

4

Dominant Trends in Hindu Thought

IGNATIUS PUTHIADAM

To write with accuracy and completeness on modern and contemporary Indian thought, and yet to omit sweeping generalizations, is an almost impossible task. Today India's population is over eight hundred million. Her cultural and religious heritage is vast and varied. Her present and immediate past are built on two or three millennia of history. As we calmly reflect on modern Indian thought, we slowly realize that there is, first of all, a modern Hindu thought or, to be more accurate, that there are many strands in modern and contemporary Hindu thinking. There are also Islamic, Sikh, and Christian thoughts in India (Titus 1979; Boyd 1969). Marxism too has assumed a new form in India (Nevett 1954). Each of these is different from the others in origin, in purpose and development, and in the conceptual tools used. Thus the sheer vastness and variety of the present thinking in India forces us to limit the scope of this contribution very considerably. Since India is eighty percent Hindu, and since the dominant cultural and religious influences are arising from the Hindus, and above all since the Hindu world-views are what individualize and characterize India in the world at large, we shall deal here only with the dominant trends in modern and contemporary Hindu thought.

From the outset, however, let us be constantly reminded of two important truths. *Hinduism* is a verbal symbol that signifies a conglomerate of religious sects and subsects, and schools of philosophy and theology that in many respects are doctrinally and ritually opposed to each other. Yet there are a certain number of common tenets and practices that give an inner unity to Hinduism. For example, belief in *karmasamsara*, final liberation, yogic practices, and so on, are accepted by all the groups, though each school and sect has its own way of interpreting these common tenets (Dasgupta 1932, 71ff.).

BACKGROUND

India was known to the West even prior to the Roman period. But the discovery of the sea route to India by Vasco da Gama in 1498 brought the massive entrance of the West into the country and into the hearts and minds of the Hindus. With the coming of British political power in 1757, new cultural, social, political, and religious factors, unknown and unsuspected till then, forcefully found their way into the placid, resigned lives of millions of Indians.

Before the consolidation of British supremacy over the Indian subcontinent, the Hindus had submitted to centuries of Moslem rule and law, especially in the North. Islam—strictly monotheistic, fanatically missionary, lacking caste distinctions or priestly class, permitting its followers to eat beef—was at first violently opposed to the so-called idolatrous, polytheistic, caste-ridden, ritualistic Hindus, who venerated cows and practiced nonviolence. In the beginning, as the Moslems streamed into India, they destroyed temples, killed and maimed the Hindus, forced them to become Moslems, burned their sacred books and articles. Islamic political and religious dominance meant slavery to the Hindus. They built walls around themselves by making the caste system more rigid and by insistence on conformism.

But slowly the relationship between the conquerors and the vanquished changed. Political, religious, and cultural reasons were behind the change. From intolerance and persecution to tolerance and coexistence, to a sincere effort to understand and appreciate each other, to positive assimilation and cooperation was the path of change (Majumdar 1970, 384, 571).

Islamic monotheism, sense of morality, social equality, and *sufi* mysticism profoundly influenced some of the Hindu thinkers. Religious men like Kabir and Nanak tried to transcend the limits of Hinduism, and Nanak tried to transcend the limits of Hinduism and Islam and initiated movements embracing both. Kabir, who lived in the North toward the close of the fourteenth century, rejected the rituals and practices of both Hinduism and Islam, insisting on internal attitudes and dispositions. Nanak, the founder of Sikkism, lived in the fifteenth century. His mission was to put an end to religious conflicts. In the sixteenth century the emperor Akbar attempted to establish a universal religion (*Din-i-Ilahi*). He invited two Jesuits to his court to help him in his work. Islamic-Persian and Indian elements fused in a creative way and produced masterpieces in painting and architecture and music. A new language, Urdu, was created and vernacular literatures grew. There was a general awakening in the country. *Bhakti* gathered momentum, and devotees poured out their hearts in exquisite mystical poetry.

Yet with the decline of the Moghul power, decadence once again enveloped the land. The subcontinent split into innumerable warring kingdoms with no economic, political, or social stability. Periodic famine and pestilence decimated the population. The creative potential of the Hindus and the Moslems dried up. The Hindu society was split into over three thousand sub-castes (Dubois 1899). Immoral and debilitating socio-religious practices like *sati* (the widow burning herself on the funeral pyre of her husband), temple prostitution, child marriage, prohibition of widows' remarriage, veiling of women, neglect of education, the absence of the personal and the spiritual from religious life, and the insistence on externals and superstitious practices were rampant in the country. The result was the death of thought, resignation, and total loss of freedom. India had lost the memory of its past and hence its self-identity.

Into this atmosphere the West came — dynamic, self-reliant, convinced of its material and spiritual superiority, intent on profit-making. Though the overriding interest of the West was commercial, both Catholics and Protestants wanted to propagate their respective faiths in the land. Together with the merchants and the missionaries and especially with the definitive domination of the subcontinent by the British, western education, British-type schools and universities, liberal ideas and ideologies, and the Christian ethos reached India. Ideas centered on the human person — the dignity, freedom, and equality of all — western technology, natural sciences, and the scientific spirit, a sense of the value of the world and of the need to transform it by human ingenuity, a feeling for history and its significance, all these forced their way into India (Majumdar 1970, 842ff.). Surely the British, who introduced the English system of education and their language, and the missionaries, who started a network of educational institutions of various grades in the land, had their private interests and objectives: the perpetuation of British domination by means of the semi-westernized Indians, and the propagation of Christianity and Christian ideals through the indirect method of education.

Again, the Westerners were instrumental in discovering India's past. They were the pioneers in the historico-critical study of Indology in its various aspects (Gonda 1978, 1-6). India's past with its rich philosophy and theology, literature and art, and political and social systems opened the eyes of the West to the inherent worth of India's culture and forced Westerners to look on Indians with respect and consideration.

Again it was the West, chiefly England, that politically and economically unified the subcontinent and gave to its people at least a semblance of order, justice, and peace. Even the cultivation of the vernacular languages of the land in a truly scientific manner is to a great extent the work of the West.

Europeans, primarily the Christian missionaries, brought to the Indians a new social consciousness and responsibility. Any foreigner who walks through the streets of India is struck by the immense social evil. The Christians in words and deeds pointed out these evils and blamed chiefly the Hindus for their utter neglect of their fellow human beings. In a caste-ridden society that believes in the inexorability of karma, how could there be true concern for others? Thus the West challenged India in every sphere of human life: political, social, cultural, and religious. Can India stand on her own legs and find solutions to her problems? Can Hinduism be the foundation of a new India? Can the stagnant society of India be resurrected by a reinterpretation of her age-old world-views and beliefs? Almost all the Europeans and many English-educated Indians were convinced that India had to discard her traditional values and beliefs and embrace Western ways and ideas in order to become really modern.

Some of the Hindus, steeped in their traditions and sensing the danger to their religion and way of life, reacted sharply to western influences. Their answer to the all-embracing European challenge was revivalism. They opposed Christianity chiefly because, in their view, the Christian missionaries were the agents of a foreign religion and culture.

Between these two extreme positions are the Hindu *reform movements*. Their advocates were ready, even eager to learn from the West. Many of them studied in western-style schools or in missionary institutions. Some even went to England for higher studies. They embraced the scientific spirit and liberalism of the Europeans. English became the medium of their communication. Yet they did not throw away the past of their country. Using the very methods learned from their conquerors, they reached back to their ancient heritage and tried to reinterpret and reform Hindu beliefs and practices. Acutely conscious of the social evils surrounding them and infecting their society, they launched a program of reform. The weakness and ills of their people and the dynamism and strength of the Europeans forced them to reflect and to find creative solutions to their problems. Thus Hinduism entered on a period of renaissance and far-reaching reforms. This renaissance was above all a renaissance in thought, and our purpose is to analyze the main trends of this renascent Hindu thought, which is still a living and ongoing movement.

MODERN TRENDS

Hinduism in its meeting with the West had to face three important problems: the sociopolitical problem; the religious problem; and the problem of mental attitudes and methods. The Hindus had the insight to see that at the source of all these major issues lay religious world-views that really formed and shaped all aspects of human life. Though externally most of the early movements and reflections had a social bias, the core of every Hindu attempt at revival and reform was religious.

Religious pluralism has been part of India's life and history for millennia. Hinduism with all its subsects, Buddhism, and Jainism existed side by side in India for centuries. With the arrival of Islam the problem became more acute. Religious individuals tried to go beyond the particularities of Hindu sects and of Islam to establish religious groups open to all. These religious groups were theologically and philosophically based on the idea of the existence of one God, who is the God and Father of both Hindus and Muslims. So when Christianity reached India, theologically or philosophically a new problem did not arise. But Christian propaganda methods and means were more powerful and more subtle than those of Islam. The early thinkers of the modern period therefore wanted to find a religious worldview that would at once advance the social welfare of India and check the progress of Christianity.

Raja Rammohan Roy (1772-1833), through a deep study of Hinduism, Islam, and Christianity, reached the conviction that monotheism was the basis of all religions. Monotheism is the source from which Islam and Christianity draw their unity, strength, and social equality. Hinduism in its earlier phases, according to Roy, believed in one supreme being alone. But later, idolatry and polytheism entered Hinduism, broke it up internally, and brought in moral and social degradation. Rammohan Roy and the society he founded (*Brahmo Samaj*) accepted this belief as their fundamental tenet: One Supreme God or Father is the source of all peoples and nations. Hence social equality and the freedom of all flow from faith in one God. These thinkers rejected trinitarianism, incarnation, or the possibility of God's appearance in any creaturely form as opposed to reason, unworthy of God, and pure imaginations of the human mind (Nalini 1934, 131). In fact even a fundamentalist and revivalist like Swami Dayananda Sarasvati (1824-83) believed that monotheism was the fundamental teaching of the *Rg Veda Samhita*. From a historico-critical point of view, neither the contention of Rammohan Roy that the *Upanishads* teach monotheism nor the conviction of Dayananda Sarasvati that the Vedic *Samhitas* are monotheistic in character can be sustained. Yet educated Hindus of their time accepted this basic tenet of the two great reform movements because it put Hinduism on a par with the other two religions.

These thinkers realized that for a healthy, moral, social, and religious life, monotheism was essential. In fact, Gandhi comes within this tradition. Though he did not write explicitly on monotheism, his basic belief was monotheistic (Datta 1961, 27).

What we see in this attempt is the old assimilative and synthetic spirit of Hinduism. Down through the centuries it has tried to assimilate whatever was good and beautiful in other cultures and faiths and transform from inside foreign ideas to bring them into accord with its world-view and pattern of thinking. Modern Hindu thinkers like Rammohan Roy desired to be harbingers of a universal humanism, to be prophets of a coming humanity in which East and West would meet and merge, though without losing their distinctive elements. The philosophical and religious striving of the *Brahmo Samaj* and the *Arya Samaj* was to establish monotheism as the fundamental religio-philosophical insight of Hinduism because that alone could be the basis of a universal humanism embracing Hindus, Christians, and Muslims.

Other thinkers like Vivekananda and Radhakrishnan opposed this trend of putting monotheism as the basis of religion, morality, and social reform. Insistence on a monotheistic, natural philosophy was considered too dangerous a concession to Islamic and Christian ideas and a betrayal of the traditional Hindu insistence on *anubhava* (experience). The basic goal of Hindu life is the experience of the Absolute. The *advaitic* (spirit-monistic) tradition, however, insists that a conscious being's ultimate goal is the immediate experience of the identity of one's self with the Supreme Self. From a really real point of view there is only One Reality. One without a second. The world of multiplicity, change, and history is not real from the Supreme point of view. Just as a rope snake is not real from the point of view of the reality of the rope, so also the world is not real from the reality of the Supreme Being, Brahman. A lower level of reality gives way to the higher. This does not mean that the world is unreal, or that it is an utter non-being. It only means that from the absolute point of view the changing multiplicity cannot be considered real. Yet the Reality underlying the many and on which they are superimposed, is the Absolute.

But what is important for us here is the philosophy of religion built upon these premises. Since there is only one Reality and that Reality is Being, Consciousness, and Bliss, the goal of every being is to realize and to become this Truth-Reality. In this world the experience of multiplicity, personal distinction, and so on, pertain to the sphere of illusion. If we can speak of religion at all in such a world-view, then the goal of religion is the experience of identity. Oneness of Reality is the truth. The immediate, intuitive experience of this Reality is the ultimate goal and bliss. But there are religions that teach a distinction between the soul and the Absolute. How can such tenets be reconciled with this absolutistic view? Religions, like Christianity, that at least in some forms teach the distinction between the Absolute and individual are not totally untrue. But they belong to a lower plane of truth. The absolute truth is *advaita*, which only a few spiritual adepts can reach. So religions that teach that the individual self is distinct from the Absolute, or those that hold the individual self to be nothing but a mode of the Supreme, embody only partial truths. These religions are needed because the inner aptitudes and fitness of those who follow such religions can grasp only such partial truths. But they, by a natural process of repeated births and spiritual growth, will one day reach the Supreme Truth.

MORAL THOUGHT

Classical Hinduism did not develop an explicit and elaborate ethical thought. Though laws and regulations were numerous, Hinduism did not reflect deeply on the roots of human activity, freedom, the progress of a person through action, and the ultimate norm of human actions. Along with this poverty of ethical thought, there was surely a lack of concern for other. Schweitzer calls the classical Indian world-view world- and life-negating. According to Schweitzer this is so because for Hindus the world is a stage play in which people must participate but not fully immerse themselves. Humanity's true home is eternity (Schweitzer 1980, 7ff.).

Modern and contemporary Hindus certainly controvert Schweitzer's views. Some of them think that the essential truths of democracy, dignity of the individual, equality of persons, and concern for others are all found in Hinduism. But the classical texts must be interpreted in the right way (see Radhakrishnan; Sastri and Yamunacharya 1955).

Modern and contemporary Hindu thought shows considerable divergence from the classical thought in the areas of morality and social obligation as it searches for a religio-philosophical foundation for its ethical and social endeavors. Even the terms Hindus use in their speeches and writings in English show the radical changes that are taking place in their thought. *Person, freedom, choice, decision, intellect, soul, dignity of the person, equality of all* are terms which embody ideas that have no exact equivalents in Hindu thought. That is not to say that Hinduism had no notion of person, freedom, and so on. But through contact with the West and by the use of a language and concepts which originate from a different thought-pattern, a profound change is taking place within Hinduism.

In thinkers like Rammohan Roy and Gandhi morality was the biggest concern. They wanted a moral regeneration of the people. Rammohan Roy was more interested in reforming the Hindu society than in elaborating a philosophical system. For this he wanted his people to give up polytheism and idolatry and embrace true spiritual theism which would bring them out of their moral degradation. Roy was convinced that strict monotheism alone could provide the firm foundation of morality. Moreover, he found the doctrines of Christ more conducive to moral principles and better adapted for the use of rational beings than any others that had come to his knowledge.

> By separating from other matters contained in the New Testament the moral precepts found in that book, these will be more likely to produce the desirable end of improving the hearts and minds of men of different persuasions and degrees of understanding (Roy 1820, vi).

To Gandhi, Truth is God and people are called to experiment with truth and to follow the glimpses of truth they receive. "To me God is Truth and Love; God is ethics and morality; God is fearlessness," says Gandhi. He was influenced by the West profoundly, yet he always considered himself to be an orthodox Hindu. To his mind the eternal religion, the law of righteousness, rests on *satya* (truth); *ahimsa* (positive and universal nonviolence); renunciation; passionlessness, equal love for all God's creatures; and *brahmacarya* (total self-control). Gandhi writes:

> Morals, ethics, and religion are convertible terms. A moral life, without reference to religion, is like a house built upon sand. A religion divorced from morality is like sounding brass good only for making noise and breaking heads. Morality includes truth, *ahimsa* and continence. Every virtue that mankind has practised is referable to and derived from these three fundamental virtues. Non-violence and continence are again derivable from Truth, which for me is God (Sen 1960, 155).

To Gandhi, and to many of the far-sighted Hindu reformers, liberation meant not the individual's emancipation from the painful cycle of birth and death, but a whole nation's emancipation from the bondage of desire, anger, avarice, sloth, and violence. Like Rammohan Roy, Gandhi absorbed the ethical teachings of Jesus (chiefly the Sermon on the Mount), the absolute and transcendent monotheism of Islam, and the placid calmness, renunciation, and *sannyasa* ideal of Hinduism. In his person he reinterpreted his religion. In his life and actions he showed tremendous concern for others. In the great ideals proposed in the *Gita*—selfless action, equanimity, complete surrender to God, utter fearlessness—he learned the way to love and care for the least important of his brothers and sisters.

In fact, after Rammohan Roy and Gandhi, Hinduism is not the same as it was before the time of Roy. By a process of reinterpretation, assimilation, discovery of the past, and acceptance of new ideas, Hindu ethical and social thought has changed beyond recognition.

The Hindu thinkers who followed the monistic trends in Hinduism were surely very concerned with uplifting India, especially salvaging Hindu society from its moral and social degradation. They found in the supreme *advaitic* truth *tat tvam asi* ("thou art that") the ultimate foundation a person's effort to love and serve others. Love your neighbor as yourself is a Christian principle. For these Hindu thinkers love of neighbor is founded on the fact that the reality of the neighbor and one's own reality are identical.

> We have always heard it preached, "love one another." What for? That doctrine was preached, but the explanation is here. Why should I love every one? Because they and I are one.... There is this oneness, this solidarity of the whole universe (Vivekananda 1962, 414-15).

Radhakrishnan and all the modern Hindu thinkers admit the need for morality in the human quest for the vision of the Supreme. Even Neo-Advaitins accept with Radhakrishnan that "the metaphysical truth of the oneness of *Brahman* does not in any way prejudice the validity of the ethical distinction on the empirical plane" (Radhakrishnan 1940, 621). Thus though ethics is indispensable and very significant in humanity's ascent toward the spiritual vision, yet they believe that it is ultimately transcended. To them, the religious plane, which is the true spiritual plane, is not reducible to the ethical. Ethics is the realm of the good; religion is the realm of the Universal Consciousness, God, the Good, the True, and the Beautiful. Here we can see the great difference between Raja Rammohan Roy and Gandhi, on the one hand, and the Neo-Advaitins on the other. To the former religion meant morality. To the latter religion is spirit-consciousness, though they do not countenance the idea that such a soul is or can be immortal. Thinkers like Vivekananda and Radhakrishnan preach with great eloquence the need of a spiritual and moral renewal of the world.

THE REINTERPRETATION OF OLD CONCEPTS

Since morality and social concern imply freedom, dignity of the individual, and so on, it became necessary for many of these thinkers to understand anew traditional Hindu concepts like karma, transmigration, caste, and others. To them karma means the freedom and determinism that rule human life; caste is nothing but occupational differences; and transmigration, the law of retribution. They are at the same time at pains to show that these are truths quite consonant with modern science.

Another point of great interest is the change that modern and contemporary Hinduism has undergone in its views on the reality and value of the world and history. Ancient and classical Hinduism did not place great value on the reality of the world. In fact, the dominant *advaitic* illusionism did not merely affect the *advaitic* school but also, to some extent, infected other schools.

It is a well-known fact that India in her earlier eras did not produce accurate, substantiated, and factual history. India was the land of myths and legends. For the Hindus of earlier periods what mattered was the spirit, untouched by matter and time. The spirit remained unsullied and untouched by the historical process like the lotus leaf untouched by water though immersed in it. At the same time the Hindus lived and thought too much in accordance with the rhythm and necessity of nature. Unless we can separate ourselves from nature, experience our freedom as transcending the necessity of nature, transforming it, and bringing newness into the predictability of nature's rhythm, we cannot conceive history.

Contact with western thought and Christianity in general, the existential experience of the struggle for independence, and social progress in particular have brought in a deep sense of the reality of the world and its value, a feeling for the concrete multiple realities and the meaningfulness of history. The *advaitic* theory of the illusoriness of the world and the general Hindu concept that humanity's final duty is to escape from this world were found to be insufficient bases for India's struggle for freedom. The uniqueness of the individual, his or her change in permanence, and his or her relatedness to others and to the world could not be left aside. Science and technology brought home to the Hindu thinker the value of multiple material realities. The classical Hindu views, which placed humans on a continuous line with nature and thought of them more as a process than as agents and directors of that process had to change. Today's Hindu thinkers speak of human freedom and responsibility as the center of the individual's personality, transcending groups and castes. Each person has a dignity and a worth irrespective of caste, color, or sex.

Modern thinkers taking up the old Hindu evolutionary theories have tried to interpret history as the evolution of the Spirit. Each individual, society, and the whole world is nothing but the evolutive manifestations of the Spirit, and history is the return of the manifest into the ultimate integration and unity of the Spirit. Aurobindo, Tagore, Radhakrishnan, and other neo-vedantic thinkers subscribed to some form or other of evolutionary philosophy.

Though history is a new dimension added to traditional Hindu thought, most of the modern Hindu thinkers are reluctant to take history seriously into the area of religion. According to most of them a religion cannot be founded on historical facts and around a historical person. Universal principles are the source and rallying point of a religion that wants to embrace the whole of humanity.

Even Gandhi, so concerned with the concrete and the multiple, used to say: "I have never been interested in a historical Jesus. I should not care if it was proved by someone that the man called Jesus never lived and that what was narrated in the Gospels was the figment of the writer's imagination. For the Sermon on the Mount would still be valid" (Gandhi 1963, 65-66). Surely none of the great modern thinkers questions the historicity of Jesus. But all believe that, in the field of religion, history as understood in the West should not be too much insisted upon. The relation between principle and person, the uniqueness of history, and the all-pervasiveness of principle are philosophical problems with which Indians, especially Christians, are grappling today.

UNION WITH THE UNIVERSAL SPIRIT

Of the many world-views India has produced in her long history, the West may be acquainted with the monistic illusory ideas of *advaita* and the more theistic-realistic world-view of the great *Bhaktas* (devotional teachers). But there is another world-view, which in a mystic vision sees the interconnection of all things, indissoluble union with distinction of the finite and the infinite the golden thread running through both; this view affirms a reciprocity and duality between the world and God. Hence reality is shot through with joy and love. Humanity forms at once a manifestation of the infinite and an individual unit capable of loving and enjoying in the very bosom of the universal spirit. Tagore is the great representative of this thought of distinction in unity and reciprocity in duality. He writes: "Truth is to realize one's unity with the entire universe, to merge the individual soul into the universal soul. Sin is not mere action, but it is an attitude to life which takes for granted that our goal is finite, that our self is the ultimate truth and that we are not all essentially one but exist each for his own separate individual existence" (Zaehner 1962, 253).

NEW METHODS AND ATTITUDES

What new methods and attitudes were produced in modern and contemporary Hindu thought by India's contact with the West? The answer is very complex. Yet we can give a rather general answer to this question. From the time of Rammohan Roy, because of the very religious, social, and political situation in the country, the *comparative method* became all-pervading at various levels of thought.

Religio-philosophical ideas were studied from the point of view of Islam, Christianity, and Hinduism. Buddhism, Jainism, and Zoroastrianism were also taken into account. Later on this already vast field was widened to include the religions of China. Even today the comparative method is pursued with great earnestness, though very often quite a few of the thinkers show only a very superficial knowledge of other religions.

From the West, India has learned the *historical method*. The Europeans' studies on Indology have taught the Hindus the importance of a historical approach in the study of ideas. Very often this historical approach lacks a critical sense. This is mostly because many Hindus have still not freed themselves from a defensive mentality. Christian missionary criticism of Hindu tenets has been so violent and unreasonable in the past that even now many thinkers are interested in showing the West that their religion is equal or superior to Christianity. This defensive mentality may be seen in facile comparisons and uncritical equations at every level of thought.

The *rationalistic-scientific* method and its resultant mentality can be seen in almost every modern Hindu thinker. Rammohan Roy's philosophy of religion is very much the result of the influence of the eighteenth-century rationalistic deism of England. The whole of *Brahmo Samaj* resolved that reason and nature should be considered the source of all truth. Among Hindu thinkers there is a general tendency to look down upon theology, which according to them is nothing but unreasoning dogmatism, and to present Hinduism and Hindu thought as philosophy. Rationalistic-scientific methods and attitudes may be seen also in the rejection of the Hindu myths and legends and in the earnest efforts made by educated Hindus to reinterpret traditional concepts in accordance with the demands of science and reason.

Others, more faithful to Hindu tradition, plead for the capacity in the conscious being to intuit immediately the infinite and to enter into communion with the universal spirit. From a Western point of view, their attitude may seem contradictory. On the one hand, they insist on the need of testing and experimenting with every truth, including religious ones, and they extol the power and range of reason. On the other hand, they accept the Spirit as intuitive and unitive beyond the reach of all the functions of reason, that is, analysis and synthesis.

The final purpose of the comparative, historical, and rational-scientific methods is the mobilization of the wisdom of the world, the evolution of ideals, habits, and sentiments that would enable India to build up a world community and live in a cooperative commonwealth.

Indians always wanted thought to be integral and synthetic, all-embracing yet keeping the traditional values. This is particularly true of modern Hindu thought. In its search for a theoretical basis for the building-up of a modern India, it has tried to reach out to all the thought-systems surrounding and influencing it. But in the process of the discovery of the past, reinterpretation, assimilation, and synthesis, modern Hinduism has been to a great extent busy with immediate practical questions. Modern Hindu thought in the areas of philosophy of religion, morality, social concern, reality and history of the world, and methods and attitudes has constructed world-views, accepting insights from various sources and reinterpreting old ideas. Whether the world-view so obtained is logical, and philosophically and historically valid from a critical angle, is not a problem with which many Indian thinkers are concerned. If the solution is immediately satisfying, then it shows the truth of the solution and of Hinduism. In the years to come, when the defensive mentality of the Hindus fades away, Indians will be forced once again to rethink present-day trends in the light of India's past and search for solutions that touch the roots of reality. But for the present we can only say that Indian thought is in a transitional state, embodying great possibilities for the future. Given the historical and geographical situation of India, and the socio-cultural situation prevailing in it, we have sufficient grounds to hope that a new synthetic world and a more universal view are in the making.

REFERENCES

Boyd, R. 1969. *An Introduction to Indian Christian Theology*, CLS, Madras.
Dasgupta, S. N. 1932. *A History of Indian Philosophy*, vol. 1, Cambridge University Press, London.
Datta, D. M. 1961. *The Philosophy of Mahatma Gandhi*, Wisconsin University Press, Madison.
Dubois, L'Abbe. 1899. *Hindu Manners and Customs*, Clarendon Press, Oxford. This work provides a graphic picture of the Indian socio-religous situation.
Gandhi, M. K. 1963. *The Message of Jesus Christ*, Bharatiya Vidya Bhavan, Bombay.
Gonda, J. 1978. *Die Religionen Indiens*, vol. 1, Kohlhammer, Stuttgart.

Majumdar, R. C. 1970. *An Advanced History of India*, Macmillan, London.
Nalini, Ganguly C. 1934. *Raja Ram Mohan Roy*, YMCA Publishing House, Calcutta.
Nevett, A. 1954. *India Going Red?*, I.S.O., Poona.
Radhakrishnan, S. 1940. *Indian Philosophy*, vol. 2, Allen and Unwin, London.
———. *Eastern Religions and Western Thought*.
Roy, Raja Rammohan. 1820. *Precepts of Jesus: The Guide to Peace and Happiness*, Baptist Mission Press, Calcutta.
Sastri, K. A. Nilakanta, and M. Yamunacharya. 1955. "Religious Resources of Hinduism." In *Cultural Foundations of Indian Democracy*, YMCA Publishing House, Calcutta.
Schweitzer, A. 1980. *Indian Thought and Its Development*, Wilco Publishing House, Bombay.
Sen, N. B. 1960. *Wit and Wisdom of Gandhi*, NBCI, New Delhi.
Titus, T. M. 1979. *Indian Islam*, 2d ed., Orient reprint, New Delhi.
Vivekananda, Swami. 1962. *The Complete Works of Swami Vivekananda*, vol. 2, Advaita Ashrama, Calcutta.
Zaehner, R. C. 1962. *Hinduism*, Oxford University Press, London.

5

Theology of Liberation and Gandhian Praxis

A Social Spirituality for India

T. K. JOHN

"God always reveals Himself to us in some concrete shape," Gandhiji wrote in 1926 to the members of his ashram (Gandhi 1969b, 439). Again, while commenting on the central message of the *Gita*, the book that had been Gandhi's chief source of inspiration for years, he observed that "a *dharma* which does not serve practical needs is no *dharma*" (Gandhi 1969b, 152). Gandhi's perception and interpretation of God's intervention in history and his understanding of *dharma* are encapsulated for us in these two statements. He summarized all he did and said in his autobiography, which he named *My Experiments with Truth*. His aim was to find a way in which all people can live together as full human beings, in mutual acceptance and respect, orienting economic, political, social, cultural, and other activities to the benefit of as many members of society as possible. *Dharma* or religion should be the main source for such harmonious living, from which it would be possible to derive insights that could constitute the foundation of a new humanism, a new philosophy, and a way of life capable of inspiring all toward their ultimate destiny. Gandhi's life is an excellent illustration of the theory-praxis relationship, of an ideal and its realization, a vision and its actualization. In the following pages we will trace the genesis and meaning of the Gandhian praxis.

The distinguishing feature of the emerging theology of liberation is perhaps its insistence upon praxis. Truth is born of and tested in praxis. One is struck by the great similarity that exists between this theology and the

Gandhian interpretation of *dharma*, the remarkable fusion of theory and praxis.

The great teachers of the world, the founders of religions, and men and women of insight and wisdom, have left behind a rich heritage of ideas. But the impact of these insights on the daily struggles with the forces of decay and disintegration seems questionable. The problem facing us today is this: while the insights of science have found concrete application in technology, which has revolutionized the lives of people (to the point of creating the danger of the total annihilation of humanity), the insights of religion, intended to achieve a total transformation of human and social living, have failed to revolutionize societal relationships and praxis. It would appear that, having met with failure in this task, religion today is bypassed. Gandhi's chief achievement was his successful effort to bring about through religion such a transformation of the social order. The newly emerging theology of liberation holds much promise for a similar successful experiment in Christian living.

GENESIS OF THE GANDHIAN PRAXIS

Gandhiji was provoked by the experiences of exploitation and enslavement, of poverty and helplessness common at that time to the people of India and South Africa. These experiences set him on a prophetic path. Like the poisonous pink-yellow smoke that much later hovered over Hiroshima and Nagasaki, a strange smoke hovered over the entire Indian subcontinent during the childhood days of Mohandas Karamchand Gandhi. It was the presence of the mercantile power that had landed stealthily on the Coromandel coast. This mercantile power subsequently grew into the large military, political, administrative, and economic force under which the country lay writhing. That cloud had obscured the vision of the people for years, choked the life-breath of their culture, and drained their economic resources, leaving deep wounds which are yet to heal. In England, and later in India, Gandhi was appalled by the maneuvers and manipulations of the Christian preachers and missionaries who tried to get him into their net. In South Africa he experienced directly the superiority complex of the whites and their contempt for the dark-skinned and the blacks. The treatment meted out to Gandhi and his fellow citizens by the ancestors of the racist movement in Britain and of the apartheid regime in South Africa challenged Gandhi to the core. But the worst came when he found that the religion of these colonial masters had neither the vision nor the moral courage to denounce these ungodly practices.

Providence brought the young lawyer into contact with the works of three prophets of countercultural protest: John Ruskin, Leo Tolstoy, and Henry Thoreau. The Sermon on the Mount also had a deep formative impact on him. His early education through the stories of Harischandra and others had already given him a love for the *Gita*. The inspiration from all these sources became a force, a stream capable of initiating actions that would come into effective confrontation with the unjust system. It occurred to Gandhi that the economic, social, and political depravities of the colonial system were symptoms of a deeper malady that had its roots in the ethico-moral and even religious views and practices of the rulers. It was his conviction that morality is the basis of all human deliberations and decisions, and that truth is the substance of all morality, the sovereign principle that governs and guides all other principles and values. This journey through the realm of ethics, morality, and religion to the discovery of his own philosophy of action and involvement can be traced through five aspects.

SEEING GOD FACE TO FACE IS THE ULTIMATE HUMAN DESTINY

Gandhiji was not and never claimed to be a philosopher. His writings, his discourses, and his numerous letters were born of reflections upon his actions and involvement. His own leadership and participation in the struggles of his fellow citizens were aimed toward removal of the evils in the society and striving for the emergence of a new society. He called it by a familiar name, *Rama Rajya*, the society or nation governed by Lord Rama. To bring this about it was necessary to probe the depth of the human person, to discover his or her roots and destiny, and integrate these with the demands of daily living. It was in this process that Gandhiji discovered for himself the ultimate aim in all human endeavors and its bearing on temporal commitments. He categorically states:

> What I want to achieve—what I have been striving and pining to achieve these thirty years—is self-realization, to see God face to face, to attain *moksha*. I live and move and have my being in pursuit of this goal (Gandhi 1933, 87-89).

In line with the thinking and aspirations of humanity, especially of the founders of religion and seekers after God, Gandhi states here in simple terms that all his life and activities are guided by this transcendent goal. He never labors to prove either that God exists or that men and women are ordained to God.

TRUTH IS GOD: A POINT OF DEPARTURE

Gandhi always claimed that he was only a seeker after truth. "I am but a seeker after truth. I claim to be a votary of truth from my childhood. It was the most natural thing to me" (Prabhu 1955, 314). His unwillingness to commit fraud in the dictation class, his confession to his father of stealing gold from his brother's armlet, his reaction when he saw a drama depicting the story of Harischandra are some of his early experiences of truth. Doing the truth became an early habit with Gandhi. Although the well-known saying, God is Love, attracted him, truth had a still deeper appeal for him, so much so that later he would say that to find the truth in all its fullness is to realize by oneself what is one's destiny (Prabhu 1955, 3).

> My prayerful search gave me the revealing maxim, Truth is God, instead of the usual one, God is Truth. That maxim enables me to see God face to face as it were. I feel Him pervade every fibre of my being (Prabhu 1955, 4).

He concluded that devotion to Truth is the only justification for our existence and that all our activities should be centered on Truth, governed by Truth, and enable us to move toward the attainment of Truth in its fullness.

Truth: Absolute and Relative

Inaccessible, invisible, intangible, ungraspable, and transcendent — these are some of the epithets with which the learned have described God. This is especially true in the *Upanishads*. Gandhi, who claimed that he was a "practical dreamer" (*Harijan*, November 17, 1933), one who is desirous of converting his dreams into realities, did not want to speculate on the nature of God or expound the mysteries of God or try to prove God's existence. He was deeply aware of the presence of the Divine in and around him and came to the conclusion that Truth as God is a concretely realizable goal, however limited. This goal becomes real by means of a faithful adherence to what he called the relative truth:

> But as long as I have not realized this Absolute Truth, so long must I hold by the relative truth, as I have conceived it. That relative truth must, meanwhile, be my beacon, my shield and buckler (Gandhi 1933, 8).

This perception of the relative truth as linked ontologically with the Absolute is based upon the *Upanishadic* insight about the relation between the empirical realities and the Supreme. The empirical realities are termed truths, or fragments of truths, emanating from the Absolute Truth. Here Gandhi discovers his way to the Supreme: relative truth, consistently pursued, will inevitably lead one to closer and closer approximations of the Absolute Truth or God. One of the merits of this distinction between absolute and relative truth lies in the acceptance of the need and possibility of a self-corrective process of experimentation with one's own vision of life and one's goals. The very term *experiment* implies a disclaimer of any finality or absoluteness in what one finds as truth and a certain open-endedness as far as the outcome is concerned. Therefore this distinction does away with any claim to fullness of truth which often leads to intolerance of other perceptions and prevents progress in investigation. For Gandhi, it implied a willingness to admit one's failures, the humility to be a seeker and not a possessor of truth, and a desire for harmony between thought, word, and action.

REALIZATION OF TRUTH: THROUGH SERVICE OF HUMANKIND

Gandhiji's new way may be best understood in the context of India's long history of men and women searching for God. Some have undertaken this journey by going to holy places, shrines, and sacred rivers. Others have spent their time in rituals and sacrifices. Some have sought God in yogic practices and in meditations. Still others frequented caves and mountains in search of the Absolute. In any case, rigorous austerities, the renunciation of personal and family possessions and relations, and insistence upon meditation and other techniques characterize most ventures in this line.

In the religio-cultural history of India, Gandhi's insight is significant as a corrective to a great tradition. Drawing inspiration from the theology of the *Gita*, and led by his instinct, Gandhi came to the conclusion that his path was different: "For me the road to salvation lies through the incessant toil in the service of my country and of humanity" (Prabhu 1955, 5). In place of renunciation and rituals, offerings and pilgrimages, worship in temples and other observances—the activities normally held as religious— Gandhi offered a new approach to the same goal, namely, service of humankind. In this way Gandhi restores to each individual his or her role as a dynamic agent of the historical process in which each person's contribution becomes significant. It is the free response to the revelation of God in history that renders a person religious or ethical. It is in history and in its struggle that we discover ourselves. Concretely this is a call to accept others in their totality, to love them as they are, to care for them in all their needs, to share all their sufferings, limitations, and agonies as well as their joys and aspirations. This then is the normal way to the realization of Truth. In other words, the service of others is a participation in truth, moving toward the fullness of truth. As Gandhi says:

> The immediate service of all human beings becomes a necessary part of the endeavour simply because the only way to find God is to see Him in His creation and be one with him. This can only be done by the service of all (*Harijan*, August 29, 1939).

This conviction becomes almost an axiom for Gandhi: "I am endeavouring to see God through service of humanity" (Prabhu 1955, 5). The significance of this saying cannot escape anyone.

First, it implies that there exists a fundamental unity in all creation, especially among all human beings and between creation and God, so that to identify oneself with others and serve them is to be one with God. Gandhi says, "We all claim descent from the same God and hence all life in whatever form it appears must be essentially one" (Prabhu 1955, 5). The commitment each one makes for the removal of suffering and evil is only a first step toward an active and creative identification of oneself with everyone.

To talk about this basic identity and to allow bondage, poverty, illiteracy and discrimination in any form to go on unhindered is a transgression of this truth; it is dishonor to God. Gandhi says:

> We are all ... children of one and the same Creator, and as such the divine powers in us are infinite. To slight a single human being is to slight those divine powers and thus to harm not only that human being but to the whole universe (*Harijan*, February 11, 1939).

Second, Gandhi discovers in the depth of human service a meaning and value equal to and even surpassing that normally associated with rituals, sacrifices, and other so-called religious activities. The separation between religious and secular pursuits of people is thus corrected.

Third, this *sadhana* (way of life) enables one to be truthful to God through God's own creation. The service, especially of the poorest, the weakest, and the lowliest, is a great honor rendered to God because it is among them that God is found. Great faith and moral power are needed to discover God in such situations: Gandhi says:

> To relieve the distress of the unemployed, by providing them work, to tend to the sick, to wean people from their insanitary habits, to educate them in cleanliness and healthy living conditions, should be the concern of every seeker after truth (Gandhi 1969d, 43).

Fourth, by such an attitude of service, religion is rescued from its alienation, is given a new meaning and orientation, and is accorded an honored place in human endeavors. Every activity undertaken in pursuance of the noble goal of serving God's people becomes a sacred action.

Finally, a privileged place and role is assigned to liberative actions and projects. The people Gandhi wanted to serve, whether in India or in South Africa, were those whom internal discord, poverty, political subjugation, and economic exploitation had condemned to servitude. To serve them meant to raise them morally, economically, spiritually, and culturally. The first step must be to infuse in all a spirit of self-respect and self-reliance. For Gandhi, the pursuit of Truth was through those forms of political action that restore the dignity and impart courage and self-respect to people. Action for social justice and participation in the national struggle for political, economic, cultural, and religious freedom became a new kind of *sadhana*. The emergence of a new society is thus a means in history. For Gandhi, self-realization, which is the attainment of Truth as God, was through this service of his brothers and sisters in need.

The whole of my activity whether it may be called social, political, humanitarian or ethical is directed to that end. And as I know that God is found more often in the lowliest of his creatures than in the high and the mighty, I am struggling to reach the status of these. I cannot do so without their service. Hence my passion for the service of the suppressed classes (*Young India*, September 11, 1924, in Hussain 1959, 35).

RELIGION IN ACTION: TOWARD A NEW SOCIETY

Gandhi's efforts to put an end to British rule in India were only a prelude to the transformation of India according to his own convictions. For him, the principle and long-term task was the reconstruction of society. Eighty percent of the population of India were peasants. Most of these were landless agricultural laborers; others were bonded laborers living permanently in serfdom. Semi-feudal and exploitative systems of production, the fragmentation of holdings, tenancy, and an abysmal poverty had made the masses helpless and enslaved. Mass illiteracy, a fatalistic otherworldliness and traditionalism had made any revolt or mass uprising against the oppressive forces almost impossible.

This situation was further aggravated by the presence of the colonizers, who had, by means of the gradual introduction of western technology, trade, and commercial practices, destroyed India's traditional cottage industries and handicrafts. A culture of healthy relationships had existed at the village level prior to the disaster of colonization. Now the largest sector of the Indian population remained in a state of helplessness and inaction.

Indian society was subject to yet another evil. The caste system had stratified Indian society into numerous social units maintaining themselves in an unequal and mutually exclusive coexistence. The upper class maintained its domination and exploitation of the lower classes. The worst hit in this were the outcastes, who later became the untouchables. Neither the Buddhist revolt nor the presence of Semitic religions like Islam and Christianity was able to effect any change in this set up. Even reform movements like *bhakti* and the influence of western ideologies were not able to remove the evil of caste from this fossilized Indian society.

The nature of the task Gandhi undertook became gradually clear to him. In order to bring about a transformation of Indian society, the first thing to do was to create an awakening among the masses, to organize them, and to channel their newly awakened enthusiasm in such a way that they would collectively participate in that deeper freedom movement he had initiated, of which political freedom was only a prelude. No large-scale social upheaval is possible without this awakening of the masses. What the intelligentsia of the day, involved in the Indian Renaissance and freedom movement, was not concerned about, Gandhiji attempted. When he talked about service of the people as his way to the realization of Truth, what he had in mind was just such a transformation of the masses. The new society he envisaged for himself, and which he raised on the horizon of the Indian nation at the beginning of the new struggle, was one which had deep roots in the religio-cultural soil of India, namely, *Rama Rajya*, the kingdom of Rama.

The strategy invented and employed by Gandhi to bring about such an awakening among the masses, to organize them, and to lead them, was known as the constructive program. It included bread-labor and cottage industry, basic education, eradication of untouchability, working for communal harmony, and so forth.

The first and most important area Gandhi chose to study and to work in was economic. The masses were in abject poverty and dependence. Gandhi's invention of the spinning-wheel symbol, his insistence on bread-labor, his efforts to promote cottage industry, and similar ventures were to enable people to labor and produce for themselves what they needed and to get rid of their enslaving economic dependence. Gandhiji wanted the fullest utilization of human power, then largely untapped, in a situation in which rapid progress was not possible because of the scarcity of capital. It was his conviction that the means of livelihood for the majority of the population would come only from their own labor and limited resources, and these were found in agriculture and cottage industries. The boycott of foreign clothes, which Gandhi advocated at one time, was intended to make the peasants of India produce their own clothes by their own labor. Not only honor, dignity, and self-respect, but also a good measure of economic independence would result from such a policy.

The depth of integration of the economic and the religious sectors achieved by Gandhi through such programs is seen in some of his comments, for example,

> To a people famishing and idle, the only acceptable form in which God can dare appear is work and promise of food as wages. God created man to work for his food and said those who are without work are thieves (*Young India*, October 13, 1921, in Hussain 1959).

Inseparably linked with this economic program for mass awakening was Gandhi's plan for basic education. It was his contention that education should serve the practical needs of the people. A production-oriented and need-fulfilling education supported the liberative economic program launched by Gandhi. Each village should be autonomous as far as these two programs were concerned. He stood for the independence of each village, yet also for voluntary interdependence of all such villages and a better human fraternity in which service and not competition motivates people to work and produce. To eradicate prevailing mass illiteracy, poverty, and unemployment, Gandhiji envisioned dovetailing education into the economic activity of the villagers.

Diametrically opposed to the ideal of fraternity was the problem of untouchability, which Gandhi declared to be immoral. He urged the nation to work for its complete eradication. He said again and again that this curse of untouchability militated against all the basic values cherished by him, promoted by all religions, and desired by all authentic devotees. He launched several programs aimed at its eradication: education of the nation, fasts, and other forms of nonviolent actions. He also organized the untouchables and gave them a new name *harijan* (children of God).

By working for the emergence of a new society based more on ethical and moral rather than on purely economic foundations, Gandhi desired to serve the people of the country. He regarded this service of the people his *marga* (path) toward the realization of Truth.

> My God is myriad-formed, and while sometimes I see Him in the spinning wheel, at other times I see Him in communal amity, then again in the removal of untouchability; and that is how I establish communion with Him according as the Spirit moves me (*Harijan*, May 8, 1937).

THE ROOTS: PRAXIS IN EARLY HINDUISM

The Indian quest can be presented as a movement from meaninglessness and unreality to meaning and reality; from annihilation and disintegration to life and deathlessness; from confusion, obscurity, and darkness to clarity and light; from change, impermanence, and delusive phenomenal existence to existence in fullness. The ways of knowledge and enlightenment, of sacrifice and ritual, and the way of love and surrender were means that emerged in the course of India's long march through history. There is one feature common to all these ways: an insistence upon praxis, upon doing.

Among the many schools that sprang up in this context mention may be made here of the Sabdadvaita of the grammarians. According to them, the ultimate Reality is *Sabda-Brahman*; the universe, the world of empirical experience, is only a manifestation of the non-empirical *Sabda-Brahman*. What is significant is that a vital relationship exists between the material world and its root in the *Sabda* state. Cosmic existence is the *bhasya* (articulation), the expression of the *Sabda-Brahman*.

This vision is basic to the *Gita*. It affirms the essential link both between creation and karma (3:10), and between the manifest and the unmanifest. Thus action springs from Brahman (3:15), for God is ever engaged in action (3:22). If God were not always engaged in action, then the world would slip back into chaos (3:24). Indeed the very creation of the world was accompanied by a sacrificial action (3:10). Krishna will explain the meaning and goal of his unceasing activity: *lokasamgraha* (the welfare of all). The ancient practice of offering sacrifices is given a new meaning and interpretation: a *yajna* (sacrifice) is an action performed for the welfare of the world, for the betterment and well-being of the wider society. If God is ever involved in action, humans too are invited to do the same, and this becomes the privileged path to the Supreme.

Gandhi would wholeheartedly endorse and support this interpretation. In fact, he has said:

> Wherever we find anyone . . . who suffers when others suffer and who practices the supreme *yajna* of maintaining a sameness of attitudes towards all, there, we may be sure, Brahman is present (Gandhi 1969b, 161).

For Gandhi, *yajna* is any activity done for the benefit of as many members of the human society as possible. Instead of restricting the meaning and scope of *yajna* to the pouring of an oblation into the sacrificial fire, Gandhi saw it present in every form of physical labor that helps the wider society. For example, we know and worship God through physical labor because it leads to an increased production of food for the maintenance of society. Gandhi says, "If water was scarce and we had to fetch it from a distance of two miles, fetching water should be a *yajna*"(Gandhi 1969b, 164). But widening further the scope of *yajna*, Gandhi says that, taken in its widest sense, *yajna* includes every thought, word, and deed which is conducive to the welfare of the greatest number of people, and which can be performed by the largest number of people, and which can be performed by the largest number of men and women with the least trouble. Indeed, our body is given to us in order that we may serve all creation with it. We are all born with *yajna*, and so we are debtors to all creatures (Chandra 1946-47, 112-13).

Thus *karma* and *yajna*, two key terms in the ritual tradition of the Hindus, are given new meaning, endowing the service of humankind with a highly religious significance. It becomes a religious act.

There are several elements in the new meaning given by Gandhi to *yajna* and *karma*. First, the traditional separation between secular activity and religious activity is removed. The human person is seen as an integral reality, and his or her actions are integrated. This holistic perception of all human concerns is one of Gandhi's major contributions to the Indian religio-cultural heritage.

Second, the extreme individualism that characterized much of the ancient seeking after God is corrected and the whole human society taken into the ambit of religious activity. According to the earlier understanding, individuals sought their own merit by offering oblations to a particular god or their own individual liberation through ascetical and other practices. Gandhiji placed before religious seekers the needs of the wider society.

Third, the mutual relatedness of all persons and things in the universe, especially in society, is restored. The highly abstract *advaitic* concept is brought down to the level of social praxis. Conversely, without this economic praxis, by which and through which a person expresses his or her indebtedness to all, one cannot attain *moksha* (fulfillment).

Fourth, any place can become a place of worship and service. Gandhi never indulged in the practice of building temples, of visiting them, or of offering gifts in such sacred places. He never went on a pilgrimage. His shrine was, so to speak, the *harijan* colony or the *khadi* hall, and his pilgrimages were his travels through the Indian villages and towns in order to promote unity, amity, love, and service. He says:

> The best and most understandable place where He can be worshipped, is a living creature. The service of the distressed, the crippled and the helpless among the living beings constitutes worship of God (Gandhi 1969c, 296).

Finally, by giving a wider meaning to traditional terms, Gandhi challenged religion to play its true role in society. The removal of the evils in society is *dharma* (religious duty). The economic well-being of every member of society thus becomes a religious activity. Activities ordinarily confined to the realm of the secular are thus found to be endowed with a transcendent orientation. Half-starved, ill-clad, and illiterate human beings are no honor to the great God, whose worship is the professed concern of the professional religionists. Gandhi thus restored to religion dimensions it had lost in the course of history.

STRATEGY FOR A NEW SOCIETY: *SATYA* (TRUTH) IN PRAXIS

SATYAGRAHA

Having set his goal in life—realization of God as Truth by means of service of his brothers and sisters—Gandhi proceeded to the actualization of that goal. The starting point of his journey was the mass of enslaved and degraded human beings who surrounded him. The exploitation of the wealth of the colonized, their mental, cultural, and moral subjugation to the conquerors; the hatred and greed that destroyed the health of individuals and of society; the communal fights and the growing antipathy—these were some of the evils with which Gandhi was confronted. For him, all these evils were actually forms of untruth. To fight against them, to heal the society of its malaise, and to introduce revolutionary changes into it, Gandhi needed a new weapon. This he forged in the concept of *satyagraha*—truth in action.

The basic principle underlying *satyagraha* is that evil is overcome by good and untruth by truth, for the power of goodness and of truth is greater than that of evil and untruth. Love can overcome hatred. Effective love in the form of forgiveness can dissolve enmity and restore friendship. Promotion of mutual respect and understanding can ward off religious and other forms of intolerance. Tensions and conflicts can be resolved by negotiations and compromise, which are always based on the recognition of the pluralism of perceptions. These principles are gleaned from the teachings and practices of the great teachers and masters of humanity. All of Gandhi's campaigns against the moral evils current in his days in India as well as in South Africa are based on these golden principles. In other words, we have the unique case where the rich wisdom of humankind is gathered and converted into a technique of action.

Satyagraha has various renderings: insistence on truth, holding onto truth, reliance on truth, adherence to truth, release of soul-force or moral force, application of spiritual power. The term *satyagraha* was coined by Gandhi during the struggle against the oppressive forces in South Africa, as early as 1906, the first phase of the campaign to secure elementary human rights for the Indian immigrants. The word *sadagraha* (firmness in a good cause) had first been proposed to Gandhi. He welcomed the term with a modification.

> I therefore corrected it to "Satyagraha": Truth (*satya*) implies love, and firmness (*agraha*) engenders and therefore serves as a synonym for force. I thus began to call the Indian movement "*Satyagraha*" that is to say, the force which is born of Truth and Love or non-violence, and gave up the use of the phrase "passive resistance" (Gandhi 1969, 92).

The Sermon on the Mount, the *Bhagavadgita*, and the teachings of Tolstoy and Thoreau helped Gandhi to give a rich connotation to the new term.

First, *satyagraha* is the method of a movement intended to fight societal violence and injustice. It is an organized program of action, a campaign. In military campaigns, police actions, or organized violence, guns, tear-gas bombs, abusive words, false propaganda, manipulation, maneuvering and other forms of physical or psychological force are used. Surprise actions or moves, taking advantage of the weakness of the enemy, and denigrating the opponent are also resorted to. The chief aim of such all-out war exercises is gaining victory at any cost. In *satyagraha* the entire stress is on the replacement of these ungodly and dehumanizing weapons and strategies by truth, love, honest exchange, and noncooperation with unjust laws. The moral and spiritual force that flows from the dignity and worth of the human person is the real power in *satyagraha*. Thus, instead of attacking the enemy physically, the campaign initiated by Gandhi in *satyagraha* consisted of various steps to create moral pressure upon the opponent and make him withdraw all repressive and inhuman laws and practices. The actions are very concrete: surrender of titles and honorary offices, resignation from nominated posts to local bodies, withdrawal of children from the government educational institutions, boycott of courts by lawyers and litigants and establishment of parallel courts by the people for the settlement of disputes, boycott of foreign cloth and the manufacture of cloth and other essential commodities through the development of village and cottage industries. Actions such as these eventually gather momentum and then more decisive steps are undertaken, which may lead to civil disobedience. Obedience to unjust laws is regarded as immoral by Gandhi. An appeal is made to the conscience of the people, to the value of the human person, and a high regard is maintained even for the people against whom an action is organized. Rationality and morality are prime considerations.

Second, *satyagraha*, born of the conviction that truth will eventually overcome all evils, instills self-confidence in the hearts of the powerless. To refuse to do a thing that is against one's moral and ethical values is born out of the soul-force. It is the reliance upon the power of truth and of love (nonviolence) that gives the *satyagrahi* confidence. Fearlessness is essential for any warfare. Armed with truth and love, the *satyagrahi* conducts himself or herself in the humane way, but with a sense of fearlessness.

Third, *satyagraha* generates and promotes ethical values. It avoids every form of hatred, ill-will, or taking undue advantage of the weakness of the opponent. The objective of the campaign is the moral and ethical growth of all, including the opponent, and not mere short-term advantages. Thus *satyagraha* recreates and regenerates a disintegrating society or culture by making it move upward to a higher level of human existence.

Fourth, *satyagraha* aims at concrete actions for the immediate removal of the evils besetting a particular society: the avoidance of liquor, the boycott of foreign goods (because they perpetuate economic dependence and subservience), fasting, and the distribution of literature that explains and instills moral values and exposes every aspect of the unjust system of the opponent. Through these positive actions an effort is made to focus on truth and to lead people to an adherence to it, to effective faith in the power of truth. An awareness is thus created in the collective consciousness of the enormity of the evil operative in a particular society or structure and of the need to remove it and replace it with a new social order that will enrich and elevate human dignity in all, including the opponent.

Fifth, *satyagraha* reintroduced God into a godless political life. A state that ignores its sacred oath to live and operate on the basis of justice and the equality of all before the law rejects truth, and Truth is God. A trading community that thrives on deception, fraud, and exploitation rejects God in actual practice, because truth is set aside, and Truth is God. A caste or class that grows and thrives at the expense of other castes or classes is also flouting eternal values and principles in its practice. A nation that subjugates and exploits another nation or people is engaged in the colossal work of atheism by its elimination of true values. For Gandhi, *satyagraha* is the concrete operation of the relative truth through resistance to these evils. Relative truth is the doorway to Absolute Truth. Therefore, *satyagraha*, or the truth-campaign, is the affirmation of the Absolute in the concreteness of daily deliberations, decisions, and the transactions of human beings in society.

Sixth, *satyagraha* upholds and propagates the most precious of human and ethical values: sacrificial love. Voluntary suffering is an essential element of *satyagraha*. Even in the midst of provocation, the *satyagrahi* is expected to love and respect the opponent. The *satyagrahi* also is willing to suffer the consequences of disobedience—including imprisonment, the confiscation of land, the loss of employment, and even physical violence. For the opponent, the repudiation of evil is a painful and humiliating process. The truth in the opponent is concealed by and engulfed in self-centered and self-dominated practices. The *satyagrahi*, voluntarily and out of effective love for the opponent, takes on the pain and suffering the opponent should have endured in the process of uncovering the truth or value in question. *Tapasya* (fasting) is one such exercise of accepting suffering in order to uncover the truth in the other. It is also an act of purification, because untruth in action has polluted society. And it is an affirmation of love for the other, even for the enemy. Gandhi said: "It will be time to fight when we have done enough *tapasya*" (*Harijan*, December 19, 1936).

Seventh, *satyagraha* is a concrete expression of the belief in the existence and value of the transcendent principle in humanity: the soul. Tyrants may oppress, subjugate, torture, and even mutilate the body, but they have no control or power over the soul. This remains unconquered and unbeaten. It reawakens its inner force and asserts its power, without bitterness, without anger or hatred, without feelings of retaliation, through *satyagraha*. The modern erosion of values can be countered only by sustained efforts at practicing these fundamental values.

Finally, *satyagraha* radiates genuine humility. Truth is humility, and humility is truth. Actions and values speak for themselves. The worth of the cause manifests itself. This conviction enables the *satyagrahi* to acknowledge truth wherever and whenever it is met. It paves the way for meaningful exchange and dialogue between conflicting groups or classes. Compromise is an odious term in common parlance. But, for Gandhi, compromise was a sign of the reign of truth. No one has the complete mastery or full perception or possession of truth. Partial truth may be present even in the opponent. The recognition of this fact enables the *satyagrahi* to accept whatever is in accordance with the demands of truth and reject whatever is perceived to be contrary to it. Thus if one finds that one's judgment is proven wrong, it is one's duty to acknowledge it, repent of it, and even do penance for it. Whenever an action or movement went out of control or was shown to be wrong, Gandhi was most willing to withdraw the movement and even acknowledge his decision as wrong. He withdrew a *satyagraha* that had proved to be very successful because violence erupted and vitiated the purity and integrity of the action.

Such demonstration of humility invites opponents to reconsider their stand, change their views, and initiate appropriate actions to rectify the situation. The objective in *satyagraha* is a change of heart and, through that, change of societal structures and value systems. When star-wars, nuclear bombs, ballistic missiles, diplomatic pressures and maneuvers are used to force one view or policy on others, or to gain strategic advantages or economic concessions, *satyagraha* may appear as the weapon of the weak. Gandhiji denied this. *Satyagraha* is the weapon of the strong, for those who are fearless and armed with the power of truth can defy even the mightiest armed force. The morally weak, whose cause is indefensible before the court of human conscience, resort to physical violence, the use of arms, and such methods. What is at stake in *satyagraha* is morality, the value system springing from a true understanding of the human person.

AHIMSA: THE GOAL AND THE CRITERION

When knocked to the ground and hit in the face by a white policeman, Gandhi refused to hit back. When illegally pushed out of the first-class compartment of a train, he refused to give vent to his strong negative feelings. Insulted and abused by a white stage-coach driver on his way to Transvaal, he took the offense with patience and a certain defiance, but never gave way to feelings of revenge. When the agitating crowd lost its self-control and indulged in violence to property and life, Gandhi withdrew the all-India *satyagraha* movement, which had entered a crucial phase. In fact, he went further and imposed a fast upon himself—to expiate for the offense to truth. These instances speak to us of Gandhi's praxis of *ahimsa* (positive nonviolence). All his utterances and elaborations on *ahimsa* came only after he himself had practiced it. By doing he learned, and what he learned he shared with his people, and moved to further practice. This was the pattern of Gandhi's experiment with truth. He insisted upon overcoming all forms of violence by nonviolence. This is now an important tool in the hands of those committed to action for the welfare of the society.

The negative meaning of *ahimsa* is avoidance of any form of injury to anyone. But for Gandhi this was not sufficient. In its positive meaning, nonviolence is active love for all. The metaphysical foundation for this form of love for all is the spiritual oneness of all beings. All have one common origin from the one God, one destiny, and hence one nature. Because of this common origin and spiritual identity, a unique relationship exists among all, especially human beings. It is expressed in many ways: affection, sympathy, mercy, generosity, charity for all creatures, including one's enemy. It calls for service and even self-sacrifice.

For Gandhi, "Ahimsa is the means, truth is the end" (Prabhu 1955, 31). The following reflections spell out the nature and role of nonviolence as a concrete form of love or truth-praxis.

First, nonviolence rejects not only physical but also mental violence; one has to think, speak, and act nonviolently, even under the gravest provocation (*Harijan*, December 19, 1936).

Second, nonviolence has the potential to restructure the present society and reorder the value systems operative in a consumer-oriented society. Violence is built into the very structure of the present society. Exploitation and injustice characterize the social structure, and many forms of violence are due to this. Gandhi says that "where there is possessiveness there is violence" (Gandhi 1969b, 115). Greed breeds possessiveness, and competition and profiteering are the outcome. When given organized and structured form, this trend leads to systematic violence and oppression, exploitation and injustice. The antidote to these evils is nonviolence, which is nonpossessiveness in action.

Third, this understanding of nonviolence is the basis for an economic order that Gandhi based on *trusteeship*. If excessive greed is checked and concern for others is promoted in the economic, political, and other areas of human activity, a better human social order can be created. This order calls for the social utilization of privately owned resources like the land and other economic means. Participation and collaboration and the widest possible service of the people are central to the concept of trusteeship. The needs of one's fellow beings, not profit for oneself, provide the fundamental norm in such a policy.

Fourth, nonviolence promotes a rich humanism because it contains an element of dialogue other forms of confrontation do not embody. Communication with the opponent is an essential aspect of nonviolence insofar as it recognizes the existence of truth in them. The very refusal to do harm, even to the opponent, is an affirmation of the basic identity and of the love on which nonviolence is based. The opponent or oppressor is not a factor to eliminate but a person to win over, so that all work together for the common good.

Finally, nonviolence promotes a high degree of mutual confidence and respect. Gandhi fought against the British, yet the British treated Gandhi with profound respect and regard. In an atmosphere of basic mutual confidence there is a greater chance of reducing passions and prejudices, complexes and hidden motives. Reason and goodwill have a better chance to emerge, and consequently the ethico-moral tone and temper of the culture flourishes unhindered.

Forms of Truth-Praxis

The religious beliefs, practices, social goals of Gandhi coalesce and become one way, the realization of the Absolute through the relative or, in other words, *moksha* (liberation) through *seva* (service). For Gandhi the goal and the means were clear. Both were essentially linked and actualized through praxis. His political involvement, economic programs and policies, and religious experiences were truth-in-action for the attainment of Truth in its fullness. Every area of human concern and popular activity was guided by this perception. It was indeed an integration of vision and praxis.

It was Gandhi's conviction that dependence upon others, especially in the field of economics, is a form of evil and untruth. The equality and basic identity of all people as children of the same Father is vitiated by economic dependence and subservience. Because of the role played by economic activity and relations in human life, Gandhi gave them priority. In opposing the evils generated by unequal economic relationships in the Indian society, Gandhiji advanced a vision of a new society based upon a new concept of economic activity and relationship. The first step, of course, was the overthrow of foreign domination and the liberation of the country from colonial exploitation. For this, an awakening had to be effected among the masses. He initiated it by promoting *khadi*, the village industry, bread-labor, and other such practices. These were aimed at fostering a sense of self-help in each person and thus realizing the objectives of *swaraj* through *swadeshi* (independence through home-marketing). Each individual or family, Gandhi proposed, should produce by its own labor enough food, cloth, and other essential commodities. The same principle could be applied to and made operative at the village, the district, and the state level. To launch an economic revolution with its cultural consequences, he invented and introduced the new symbol: the spinning wheel. Consistent with his integrated steps toward what he called "truth-realization," he made the new symbol a synthesis of religion and economic activity. He said, "Today Rama dwells in the spinning wheel," for "God always reveals to us in some concrete shape" (Gandhi 1969b, 439). According to him one should find God by means of that activity that sustains and promotes life in its fullness. For the economists, it was clear that if Gandhi's proposal was accepted and implemented by the great majority of India's population, the economic structure of the colonial empire would collapse and independence become more speedily attainable. It would also herald a resurgence of culture. Manual labor, village industry, and service are all means toward the same goal. The boycott of foreign clothes, the promotion of native labor and skill, and the concrete economic activities initiated by Gandhi all contained the potential for a great economic and cultural revival. These were subversive steps aimed at undermining a social system that was oppressive and exploitative, under which the spirit of the human person suffered incalculable harm.

SARVADHARMA SAMABHAVANA: RELIGIOUS PLURALISM IN PRAXIS

Gandhi, teacher and practitioner of nonviolence, was struck down by an assassin's bullets when he was in the midst of the crowd that had assembled for the customary evening prayer on the lawns of the Birla House in Delhi. At those sessions he read and explained passages from various scriptures as a way of practicing an ideal he treasured: the unity of all religions in spite of their diversity. Early in his life he had begun responding creatively to the values and riches of other religious traditions. He had been deeply influenced by the Sermon on the Mount. The influence of Jain teaching on his respect for life was quite pronounced. He had supported the Khilafat movement and made vigorous efforts to bring about Hindu-Muslim amity and friendship at various levels. He fasted when communal riots had shaken the country. He fasted on the issue of a separate electorate for the *harijans*, because he thought that would be a retrograde step in a society that was already fragmented by caste and untouchability. He wanted the high-caste Hindus to do penance for the injustices done by them down through centuries, by themselves advocating steps that would eradicate such evil from Indian society. All these actions were based on his conviction that in spite of differences, the fundamental truth of all great religions has to be accepted, honored, and brought to have a bearing on economic and cultural relations.

It is true that the country had finally to be partitioned, thus yielding to the demands of communal forces. It is also a fact of history that lives were lost and blood shed because of communal riots. In spite of these failures, which even Gandhi accepted, the significance of Gandhi's action program to bring about a positive religio-cultural dialogue among religions had many beneficial results.

First, although communal riots are frequent in the country's recent history, yet because of the Gandhian praxis the nation has acquired enough ethico-moral power and resilience to be able to heal the wounds of such conflicts and to absorb the shock. It is this inner resourcefulness of the people that enables them to respond creatively to times of tensions, and Gandhi's contribution to this resilience is remarkable.

Second, the so-called secular character of the Indian Constitution can be attributed to the pedagogy and policy evolved through Gandhian praxis. A formal recognition of the right of each religion to be alive and grow in a particular community without any one particular religion being given a special place is part of the policy of secularism in India.

Third, India's contribution to the international community, through the unique venture known as the non-alignment movement, is a further consequence of the Gandhian principle and practice of religious pluralism. In spite of differences, nations can dialogue, live in peaceful coexistence and contribute to better international understanding.

Finally, Gandhi's practice created the possibility of interaction among the various religions. India enjoys the unique position of being a virtual laboratory of world religions. In the context of the dialogue upon which they seem called to enter, Gandhi's positive and creative response to the many religions of the country and his effort to interpret and organize life in the light of the basic values provided by the religions of the world, are valuable contributions to the cultural revival of the country.

GANDHIAN PRAXIS, THE "SMALL INNER VOICE," AND SCRIPTURE

There is a vital link between the Gandhian praxis and what he called "the small inner voice." His basic attitude was that the past may influence your present and future but should not condition and determine them. Tradition-bound cultures, societies, and religions remain stagnant because the past conditions their present decisions. Gandhi was temperamentally and psychologically made for the freshness and the promises the present brings.

Hence his cultivation of and obedience to "the small inner voice." He attributed the major decisions of his life to that voice within, which he called the voice of God. Through that voice, the will of God, the mind of God, he believed, came to him. Most of the fasts undertaken to bring about peace among the Hindus and Muslims, to fight for the rights and justice of the peasants or workers, or to protest against inhuman policies of the British administration in India, were in response to that distinct and irresistible voice.

For Gandhi, there was also a link between the inner voice and the voice of the people. On the occasion of the Champaran *satyagraha*, Gandhi met large crowds of poor peasants who were oppressed by the Indigo planters as well as by the government officials. After meeting the crowd and listening sympathetically to their grievances Gandhiji reflected over them and wrote the following: "It is no exaggeration but the literal truth to say that in this meeting with the peasants I was face to face with God, Ahimsa and Truth" (Gandhi 1933, 375). He was convinced that though the people were helpless and silent sufferers, unable to assert their rights, capable only of expressing their agony, yet God was present with them and spoke to Gandhi through their pain and humiliation, through their abject and dehumanized situation. He saw God in the faces of the people. He heard the voice of God in the cry of the people. It was truth under strain and servitude that Gandhiji saw and heard in the struggles of the people.

Commitment to truth and involvement with the current problems of the people brought him closer to the face of God and enabled him to hear the voice of God. That voice is from the living God active and involved in history. To listen to that voice, to respond to the tensions and challenges presented by the current phase of history, is as important, or even more important, than being guided and inspired by scriptures. Gandhi stated, "I would reject all scriptural authority if it is in conflict with sober reason or the dictates of the heart" (*Young India*, December 8, 1920). Reason, sanctified by the small inner voice within, was the criterion for accepting even scriptural assertions. It was Gandhi's contention that God speaks and acts today as authentically as in the past, and so the records of the similar experiences of people in the past should always be weighed against the events of the present and the demands of the future.

In this Gandhi is taking a significant stand with regard to the authority of the scriptures, which are normative for the people. He appears to reduce them to mere records of the valuable experiences of those who have already traveled the path. For Gandhi the value in scriptures is not that they are normative for present-day travelers, but that they are inspirational for those who like to undertake their own journey, cutting their own paths and making their own explorations. We are expected to make our own judgment and make our own decisions about our contemporary problems and challenges, guided by our own conscience and reading the signs of the times.

The Story of My Experiments with Truth is the title of the autobiography in which Gandhi summarizes for himself and for the people in general the journey he undertook in pursuit of truth. It was a novel approach. In order to fight against all forms of untruth, he took the vow of truth. He lived simply in order to fight against consumerism and the evils associated with the vulgar display and enjoyment of wealth. He divested himself of all extra clothes and wore one simple *dhoti* because he wanted to identify with the vast majority of India who are poor. He fasted and did penance in order that violence committed by others might be condemned, reparation made, and truth vindicated. He admitted *harijans* into his ashram and started the *Harijan Seva Sangh* in order to expiate the injustices committed against them for ages. Through these actions Gandhi introduced a new methodology and a new pedagogy for India: praxis as the way to truth. Praxis should precede and should be the fountainhead of proclamation. Values are best communicated by interaction and not by mere verbal communication. Possibly Gandhi's most significant contribution to the culture of our times is that humanity felt enriched and ennobled by his life and practice. The value of the human person in India stood at a higher level because of the Gandhian praxis.

THE TASK AHEAD FOR INDIAN THEOLOGY

One of the main thrusts in Christian theology today is its insistence on praxis. The twin demands and challenges faced by the church today are participation in the struggles of the people for a healthy, normal existence, and leadership in a troubled world. Theology itself is being defined in terms of praxis.

The future of theology in India will be determined by its ability to take note of these trends in the country and elsewhere, and to respond to them creatively. India gained political independence, but the economic and social liberation is yet to come. Gandhi initiated schemes capable of achieving these too, but his main concern was the immediate task of gaining political independence for the country.

Part of the success of the Gandhian struggle was due to his ability to integrate the religious values and traditions with his political, social, and economic programs. The religiosity of the country is an essential aspect of the culture of its people. Indian theology will be born when it responds creatively to the challenges offered by the Indian situation. Liberation theology and the Gandhian method of working for the transformation of society provide us with opportunity for a promising dialogue and synthesis, for in both there is the conviction that social transformation will take place when moral, ethical, and religious values are applied to life situations. Doing is the first step in theologizing.

REFERENCES

Chandra, Jag Parvesh., ed. 1946-47. *Gita the Mother*, Indian Printing Works, Lahore.
Gandhi, M. K. 1933. *The Story of My Experiments with Truth*, Navajivan Karyalaya, Ahmedabad.
———. 1969. *The Collected Works of Mahatma Gandhi*, vol. 29, The Publications Division, Ministry of Information and Broadcasting, Government of India.
———. 1969b. *The Collected Works of Mahatma Gandhi*, vol. 32, The Publications Division, Ministry of Information and Broadcasting, Government of India.
———. 1969c. *The Collected Works of Mahatma Gandhi*, vol. 36, The Publications Division, Ministry of Information and Broadcasting, Government of India.
———. 1969d. *The Collected Works of Mahatma Gandhi*, vol. 68, The Publications Division, Ministry of Information and Broadcasting, Government of India.
Hussain, S. Abid. 1959. *The Way of Gandhi and Nehru*, Asia Publishing House, Bombay.
Prabhu, R. K., ed. 1955. *Truth Is God*, Navajivan Publishing House, Ahmedabad.

6

The Liberative Pedagogy of Jesus

Lessons for an Indian Theology of Liberation

GEORGE M. SOARES-PRABHU

Almost everything we know about the Jesus of history comes to us from the gospels, and primarily from the synoptic gospels. And all three synoptics feature teaching as a prominent element in the ministry of Jesus. It is mentioned conspicuously by Matthew in his strategically placed summaries of the Galilean ministry of Jesus, which tell us how he "went around Galilee, *teaching* in their synagogues, *preaching* the good news of the Kingdom, and *healing* every disease and every infirmity" (Mt 4:23; 9:35; 11:1). Mark too likes to show Jesus teaching great crowds on the shores of the Lake of Gennesareth (Mk 2:13; 4:1; 6:34); and Luke has frequent reference to Jesus teaching in synagogues (Lk 4:15; 4:31-33; 6:6; 13:10) or in the Temple (Lk 19:47; 20:1; 21:37).

What was this teaching of Jesus like? What sort of educational model did he follow? Such questions are not easy to answer; the gospels, which alone give us access to the words and works of Jesus, are not biographies in any presently accepted sense of the term. They are not memoirs, reporting a remembered sequence of events or handing down carefully memorized sayings of Jesus in the exact circumstances in which they were originally uttered. Instead, they could be called mosaics, carefully edited compilations of stories about and sayings of Jesus, which circulated as isolated units in the oral tradition of the early church and were put together by the evangelists to give us theological profiles of Jesus (Soares-Prabhu 1974, 112-24,

164-72). The gospels are thus narrative christologies, which spell out for us in story and saying the significance the Jesus-experience in its totality— his life, death, and resurrection—had for the evangelists and their communities.

This imposes severe limitations on any attempt to get to know the pedagogy of Jesus. We cannot, for instance, hope to derive from the gospels a systematic theology of education. Jesus obviously never propounded any such theology. He was not, like Plato, a philosopher elaborating a method for the education of philosopher-kings; he was an end-time prophet announcing God's definitive offer of salvation and urgently summoning people to conversion (Mk 1:14-15). Even occasional sayings that might throw light on his pedagogy are available to us only in the loose collections of the sayings of Jesus that we find in the gospels, and these have been strung together thematically with little reference to the original circumstances in which they were uttered. To discover the original meaning of such sayings is difficult enough; to reconstruct Jesus' theology of education from them is impossible.

Nor do the gospels give us a coherent picture of the pedagogical praxis of Jesus, from which we might derive his educational theory. They do not allow us to follow consistently any major educational project of his, for instance, his formation of the Twelve. The gospels give us only occasional glimpses of Jesus with the Twelve, not always in a chronological order and usually in the form of artificially elaborated pronouncement or miracle stories (like the calling of the first disciples in Mk 1:16-20 or the stilling of the storm in Mk 4:35-41), which have been adapted considerably to respond to the needs of the post-Easter community. We can know little, then, about Jesus' actual dealings with his disciples, and we have no way of tracing the development of his relationship with them.

Yet in spite of all these difficulties, the task of getting to know the liberative pedagogy of Jesus is not an altogether hopeless one. Although the gospels do not supply us with much reliable biographical information about Jesus, they do allow us to encounter him. The accuracy of many of the details they report about Jesus is disputable; but the over-all impression of Jesus they communicate is authentic (Bornkamm 1960, 22-26). The Jesus they reveal is conspicuously a teacher, one whose educational perspective is, I believe, substantially indicated in the three comments the synoptic tradition makes about his teaching: he "went about *among the villages* [of Galilee] teaching" (Mk 6:6); he "taught them as one who had *authority* and not as the scribes" (Mk 1:22); and he taught everything *"in parables"* (Mk 4:33). There is no reason to doubt the historical accuracy of these comments on the teaching of Jesus. If we study them carefully we shall come to know Jesus the teacher and learn a great deal about the pedagogy he used.

TEACHING IN VILLAGES

The teaching *(didaskein)* of Jesus is clearly distinguished in the gospel tradition (explicitly in Matthew, implicitly elsewhere) from his preaching (*keryssein*). While Jesus preaches the "good news of the Kingdom" (Mt 4:23), that is, announces God's definitive offer of salvation as already present, he teaches the "way of God" (Mt 22:16), that is, spells out what our proper response to the proclamation of the kingdom must be. Preaching is thus proclamation, the announcing of the good news; teaching is ethical and religious instruction, an explanation of the form that the conversion brought about by our acceptance of the good news must take. Preaching and teaching are thus complementary aspects of the educational project of Jesus.

A NON-ELITIST PEDAGOGY

This educational project is, according to the synoptic tradition, a public project. The teaching of Jesus is not academic teaching, restricted to the members of a scribal school trained in the Law (as was the teaching of the Jewish scribes of his time); nor is it a secret religious teaching, given only to a select group of initiates who have been admitted into the Covenant of God (as with the Essene sectarians at Qumran) (Vermes 1976, 26). Instead, the gospel tradition shows Jesus going around the towns and villages of Galilee (Mt 9:35; Mk 6:6; Lk 13:22), teaching all who were ready to listen to him, especially "the uneducated, the poor, the sinners, and the social outcastes" (Vermes 1976, 26-27). It is truly the poor (that is, the economically and socially deprived) who have the good news preached to them by Jesus (Mt 11:5; Lk 4:18) (Soares-Prabhu 1985a, 322-46; Nissen 1984, 6-15).

The obscurity of Jesus' constituency is remarkable. Apart from Jerusalem, he appears to have taught in none of the major cities of Galilee or Judea. Neither Sapphoris nor Tiberias, capital cities of Galilee, are mentioned in the gospels as places visited by Jesus. Instead, we find him moving around obscure hamlets like Nazareth, mentioned nowhere outside the New Testament (Mt 2:23; Mk 1:9); in remote fishing villages like Bethsaida (Mk 6:45; 8:22; Lk 9:10); and in small rural townships like Capernaum, which seems to have been his headquarters during his Galilean ministry (Mt 9:1; Mk 1:21; 2:1; 9:33; Lk 10:15). Further, concerning his mission field:

> whenever we have any specific information (as distinct from vague general statements) the terms used are such as to point unmistakably to the countryside.... In so far as we can trust the specific information given us by the gospels, there is no evidence that Jesus ever even entered the urban area of any Greek city. That should not surprise us: Jesus ... belonged wholly to the *chora,* the Jewish countryside of Galilee and Judea (Ste. Croix 1975, 3; Theissen 1978, 47-48).

Jesus, that is, taught in the villages rather than in the cities of Palestine. He was more at home in the rural countryside than in the hellenized (one might say westernized) urban settlements interspersed in it.

The teaching of Jesus is thus far removed from the intellectual elitism of the Academy or the spiritual elitism of the classical Indian theological-schools. These demanded a high level of spiritual and emotional maturity as a necessary predisposition for embarking on the quest for God. But Jesus makes no such demands. To understand him one needs no unusual intellectual ability, no particular moral probity, no special spiritual stature. His teaching is open to, indeed especially intended for, the "little ones," unlearned in the Law, and the tax collectors and sinners, with no moral or religious standing whatever. All that is required is an open heart, for ultimately the teaching of Jesus is not the imparting of doctrine but the communication of love.

A PRAXIS-ORIENTED PEDAGOGY

This message of love is proclaimed by Jesus in word and in deed. Preaching and teaching are complemented by healing in Matthew's summaries of Jesus' Galilean ministry (Mt 4:23−9:35); Mark, quite strikingly, proposes the first miracle of Jesus, his exorcism in the synagogue at Capernaum (Mk 1:21-27), as teaching, for the chorus of acclamation the miracle provokes relates the exorcism to Jesus' authoritative teaching, mentioned immediately before (Mk 1:22). "What, then, is this? a new teaching? With authority he commands even the unclean spirits and they obey him" (Mk 1:27). The exorcism is thus presented by Mark as Jesus' authoritative teaching become deed (Pesch 1976, 124).

This, in fact, is how Jesus understands all his miracles. They are not for him signs from heaven, that is, proofs authenticating his person or his mission, for Jesus consistently refuses to offer such proofs (Mt 4:1-11; Mk 8:11-12; Lk 11:29; Jn 4:48). Rather, they are signs of the kingdom, indicating to those who have the eyes to see that the saving power of God is already at work among them. The healings of Jesus are signs that the kingdom of God is dawning (Mt 11:2-6); his exorcisms, signs that Satan's oppressive rule is coming to an end (Mt 12:24-29) (Soares-Prabhu 1985b, 21-29). And this too is how Jesus understood his table fellowship with tax collectors and sinners (Mk 2:15; Lk 15:1). Such communion with the untouchables of his society, so scandalous to his pious contemporaries, was a proclamation in action, powerfully announcing the wholly unconditional character of God's love (Lk 15:1-32).

Word and deed thus go hand in hand in the teaching of Jesus, and one would be quite unimaginable without the other. In the concrete, action-oriented biblical culture to which Jesus belonged, words without deeds to fulfill them, would have been as empty as deeds without words to expound their meaning. The sharp dichotomies between spirit and matter, soul and body, word and action, preaching and social concern—so characteristic of the post-Cartesian West, and indeed of post-Upanishadic India—would have made little sense to Jesus, whose own teaching avoided both the verbalism of the unauthentic word unable to transform reality, and the activism of frenzied activity deprived of reflection (Freire 1972, 60). Indeed his pedagogy is an authentic example of the fine blend of action and reflection Paulo Freire calls *praxis*.

> Within the word we find two dimensions, reflection and action, in such radical interaction that if one is sacrificed—even in part—the other immediately suffers. There is no true word that is not at the same time a praxis. Thus, to speak a true word is to transform the world (Freire 1972, 60).

This is profoundly true of the word spoken by Jesus.

TEACHING WITH AUTHORITY

The word spoken by Jesus is thus always a performative word or a language event that does not merely inform about, but *transforms* reality (Austin 1962, 1-7). Its effectiveness derives ultimately from the authority with which it is spoken. Authority is a conspicuous feature of the teaching of Jesus as reported in the gospels. The crowds who heard him (whether in the synagogue at Capernaum witnessing his first miracle, as in Mark; or on the mountain in Galilee, listening to his first sermon, as in Matthew) were "astonished at his teaching, for he taught them as one having authority, and not as the scribes" (Mk 1:22; Mt 7:28).

This is a surprising comment, for the scribes were not without considerable authority of their own. They belonged to one of the three dominant classes of the Jewish society of the time, rivaling and eventually superseding both the priestly aristocracy (the "chief priests"), and the lay nobility (the "elders") in their claim to influence and power. Their influence derived not from their birth (as did that of the priestly aristocracy, who belonged to one or other of the four high-priestly families), nor from the wealth they possessed (as did that of the elders, who were either large rural landowners or merchant princes from Jerusalem), but from their learning. "It was knowledge alone," reports Joachim Jeremias, "that gave power to the scribes" (Jeremias 1969, 235). Some scribes, like the historian Josephus, may have belonged to the priestly aristocracy; others, like Johanan ban Zakkai, the restorer of Judaism after the debacle of A.D. 70, may have been prosperous merchants; but most came from the unprivileged part of the population. They were largely artisans—like Shammai, a carpenter, or Saul, a tentmaker—manual workers who owned the tools of their trade, and so belonged to what we would call today the *petite bourgeoisie*. Occasionally they were even proletarians owning no means of production at all, like the great Rabbi Hillel, who, it is said, earned his keep as a day laborer (Jeremias 1969, 233-34).

Yet the scribes enjoyed great authority because of their specialized and even esoteric knowledge of the Torah and of the oral traditions, both legal and religious, which had grown up around it. Such knowledge, acquired through long years of assiduous discipleship in the scribal schools and institutionally recognized by an ordination, equipped the scribes for "key positions in the administration of justice, in government and in education" (Jeremias 1969, 235-37). In a society which was still strongly theocratic, this set them up before the people as prestigious religious leaders with special competence in religious affairs.

How, then, could it be said that Jesus taught as one having authority and not as the scribes? Obviously the point is not that Jesus had authority (for the scribes had authority too), but that his authority was of a different kind from that possessed by the scribes.

A REVOLUTIONARY AUTHORITY

The scribes had authority as custodians of an authoritative tradition, which they had been trained to master, to hand down with meticulous fidelity, and to defend with well-honed arguments derived from the Torah through well-established traditional methods of interpretation. Their authority rested "on a belief in the 'legality' of patterns of normative rules and the right of those elevated to authority under such rules to issue commands" (Weber 1964, 328). Scribal authority was thus strictly institutional.

The authority of Jesus was of a very different kind. Jesus had no official standing in his society. He did not command the power of wealth (he claims to be a homeless, itinerant preacher with nowhere to lay his head in Matthew 8:20); he was academically unschooled (untrained in the scribal schools, as John 7:15 reports) (Jeremias 1969, 236) and he was cultically incompetent (because he was not born into a priestly family but was descended from the royal line of David according to the genealogies of Matthew and Luke). Thoroughly "lay" (religiously and academically) by birth and by upbringing, Jesus accentuates his institutional powerlessness by opting out of the structures of his society and becoming a "wandering charismatic" (Theissen 1978, 8-16). He thus declasses himself, leaving the ranks of the *petite bourgeoisie* into which he was born for those of the propertyless, proletariat. His authority, then, derives not from the traditional institutions of his society, but from his own personal charisma. It is an almost perfect example of what Max Weber calls "charismatic authority," which rests on "devotion to the specific and exceptional sanctity, heroism or exemplary character of an individual person, and of the normative patterns of order revealed or ordained by him" (Weber 1964, 328).

More precisely, the charismatic authority of Jesus is prophetic, similar to that of the Old Testament prophets. His charisma, like theirs, is based not on personal magnetism but on the possession of the spirit. It derives, that is, from a profound religious vocation experience in which "a man is grasped by God, who authorizes him to be his messenger and preacher and speaks through him" (Jeremias 1971, 52). Jesus probably had such an experience at his baptism by John (Mk 1:9-11), for when he is asked by the chief priests and the scribes and the elders (representatives, that is, of the Sanhedrin, the supreme religious authority of the Judaism of his time) to legitimate his teaching, Jesus replies, "The baptism of John, was it from heaven (from God) or from men?" (Mk 11:27-33). This is not an attempt to evade the issue. Jesus is not posing an embarrassing question, which, by reducing his questioners to silence, will relieve him of the need to reply. It is a genuine answer to a question legitimately posed by the religious authorities of his people. By referring to the baptism of John, Jesus is really asking official Judaism whether it is prepared to recognize extra-institutional, prophetic authority, such as that claimed by John (Mk 11:32) and by himself, and he is probably pointing to his baptism by John as the moment of his prophetic calling.

Joachim Jeremias has argued that the baptism of Jesus by John was the occasion for his *"abba* experience"—the overwhelming experience of God as unconditional love, which was to be the basis of Jesus' life and the ground of his mission (Jeremias 1971, 49-68). Jesus' preaching, teaching, and healing were centered on the kingdom of God, and the kingdom (God's definitive saving action) comes precisely in this revelation of his unconditional love. The baptism of Jesus, his act of submission to the Baptist and of identification with sinful humanity, thus becomes the occasion for a foundational experience, homologous to the enlightenment of the Buddha under the boddhi tree or to the call of the Old Testament prophets. Here Jesus becomes "conscious of being authorized to communicate God's revelation, because God had made himself known to him as Father" (Jeremias 1971, 68). The authority of Jesus is ultimately rooted in this experience of God as *abba*.

Such charismatic authority is always innovative. "The genuine prophet," notes Max Weber, "like the genuine military leader and every true leader in this sense, preaches, creates, or demands *new* obligations" (Weber 1964, 361). Indeed, the whole point of charismatic leadership (at least in the biblical tradition) is that it is summoned for tasks that the necessarily conservative institution cannot undertake. Charismatic leaders are raised up (called) to initiate new moments in salvation history (like Abraham or Moses) to counter new threats (like Gideon) or to renew a people grown slack in their observance of the covenant or in their single-minded trust in the Covenant God (like Amos, Isaiah, or Jeremiah). Charismatic authority is thus extra-institutional and as such inevitably attracts the hostility of the institution. The prophet becomes an authorized transgressor. His teaching, like the teaching of Jesus, is inevitably sensed as subversive. "Within the sphere of its claims," Max Weber reminds us, "charismatic authority repudiates the past, and is in this sense a specifically revolutionary force" (Weber 1964, 361-62). How true this is of the authority of Jesus, with his

The Liberative Pedagogy of Jesus

radical critique of Law and cult (Mk 2:23-28; 7:1-23), his revolutionary image of God (Lk 15:1-32), his new and utterly radical demands on his followers (Mt 5:21-48; Lk 10:25-37), needs no elaboration.

A LIBERATIVE AUTHORITY

But if charismatic authority is revolutionary in relation to the larger society in which the charismatic group exists, it tends to be paternalistic and authoritarian within the limits of the group. The charismatic leader, because of his strongly personal charisma, tends to exercise absolute personal control over his followers. This is strikingly evident in the *guruvada* (the way of the guru) which identifies the guru with the deity itself and calls for the total surrender of the disciple to the Master. "The *guru* is Brahman, the *guru* is Vishnu, the *guru* is always the Lord Achutya; greater than the *guru* there is no one whatsoever in all the three worlds," intones the *Yogashikopanishad,* one of 108 Upanishads that are part of the official religious literature of Hinduism (in Shourie 1979, 356-57). As Bhagwan Shree Rajneesh reminds us, "Struggle is not the key with the Master, surrender is the key" (Rajneesh 1975, 8).

The implications of such a Master-disciple relationship have been spelled out by Arun Shourie in his sharp critique of Hinduism:

> The basic propositions here are threefold: first, that I do not have the capacity to find my own way as my current capacities and attainments are limited; second, that it is, therefore, imperative that I should follow the prescriptions of another; and, third, that in order to be able to do so I must completely surrender myself to him, in particular, that I should completely delegate my thinking function to him (Shourie 1979, 372).

How similar these are to the presuppositions of what Paulo Freire has called the "banking system of education" is obvious:

> Education becomes an act of depositing, in which the students are the depositories and the teacher is the depositer. Instead of communicating the teacher issues communiques, and "makes deposits" which the students patiently receive, memorize, and repeat. ... Knowledge is a gift bestowed by those who consider themselves knowledgeable upon those whom they consider to know nothing. ... The teacher presents himself to his students as their necessary opposite; by considering their ignorance as absolute, he justifies his own existence (Freire 1972, 46).

Obviously, teaching of this sort can scarcely be liberative. Instead, it belongs to "the ideology of oppression" (Freire 1972, 46); and it is, as Arun Shourie has demonstrated, an effective means for the "repressive socialization" that creates servile subjects for authoritarian rulers. "An individual who has internalized these notions and has conditioned himself to such *abject* acceptance of authority in the spiritual realm will be equally servile to authority in the temporal realm" (Shourie 1979, 372).

Is the teaching of Jesus of this kind? There is no doubt that we find in it incontestable statements of great power (Mt 5:21-48; Lk 22:25-26), uttered with an authority that goes well beyond the authority of the prophets of the Hebrew bible, who spoke in the name of Yahweh ("thus says the Lord"). It is certain too that Jesus demanded from his followers an unswerving fidelity to his person, outweighing all other values and ties—a demand unparalleled in the history of his people (Lk 14:26-27; Mk 8:38). It is also regrettably true that the teachings of Jesus have been used extensively by the Christian community as a means of repressive socialization. History shows clearly enough how frequently the gospels have been invoked to legitimize feudal oppression, colonial exploitation, anti-semitism, and religious persecution of the most brutal kind. Indeed, since the fourth century at least, institutional Christianity (in comparison, say, with Hinduism) has been remarkably obscurantist and authoritarian. It has consistently opposed all the great movements of intellectual and political emancipation that have swept across the face of the earth, whether we think of the mental revolutions initiated by Galileo, Darwin, Freud, and Marx, which have so profoundly altered our perception of the universe, or of the great social upheavals of our world, which, for all their ambiguity, have taught us to respect human rights, to dream of social justice, to be sensitive to the political autonomy of peoples, and to resist colonial exploitation and racial discrimination wherever they appear. History tells us, alas, that freedom has not been a value much cherished by Christian churches.

But freedom was a value for Jesus, precisely because his teaching was not so much the imparting of sound doctrine as the communication of an experience of love. And there can be no communication of love without freedom. That is why Jesus is so respectful of the freedom of the people he speaks to. There is always a dialogical element in his teaching, an openness to the interlocutor, which is rare in the utterances of charismatic leaders. This appears strikingly in one of the characteristic forms that Jesus chooses for his teaching—his parables.

TEACHING IN PARABLES

The parables of Jesus are possibly the most authentic form of his teaching that we possess. They are so strikingly personal in their style that "we stand right before Jesus when reading his parables" (Jeremias 1972, 12). Not only do the parables bring us right back to the Jesus of history, they also reveal to us a basic dimension of all his teaching. As Mark tells us in his concluding comment on the parable discourse, "With many such parables he spoke the word to them, as they were able to hear it; he did not speak to them without a parable, but privately to his own disciples he explained everything" (Mk 4:33-34).

The meaning of this repetitive and somewhat incoherent passage is best understood if it is assumed that verse 34 is an editorial addition to verse 33, with which the pre-Markan discourse originally concluded (Pesch 1976, 264-66). The addition imposes Mark's own peculiar understanding of the parables of Jesus on to his pre-Markan source. Instead of being an appropriate way of communicating his message to all (so that every one could grasp "according as they were able to understand"), the parables are now seen as confusing riddles (Mk 4:11), which Jesus regularly uses to teach the crowds, while reserving his clear, plain explanations for the disciples, who are instructed "in private" (4:10; 7:7).

Now Mark obviously cannot mean that Jesus taught the crowds (in opposition to his disciples) exclusively in mysterious parables; he shows us Jesus addressing the crowds in other forms of speech (2:23-28; 8:34-38). What he is saying, then, is that there is always a "parabolic" character to Jesus' public teaching. By this Mark may have meant that the teaching of Jesus is always mysterious revelation. It is always the disclosure of "the secret of the Kingdom of God" (Mk 4:11), that is, of the hard and hidden truth (which the crowd cannot grasp) that God's definitive saving action, the kingdom of God manifests itself not in power, but in lowliness and suffering (Boucher 1977, 80-84). But the parabolic character of the public teaching of Jesus to which Mark points can also be understood in another way. It means, I suggest, that all the public teachings of Jesus, his words as well as his deeds, are like the parables—dialogical and critical. They involve the listeners in a creative response, and they put into question the accepted value of their world.

A DIALOGICAL TEACHING

Parables are dialogical. They do not convey information, offer prescriptions, or give lessons to passive and receptive listeners. Instead, by telling a shocking story, they provoke and tease the listeners into a radically new insight into their own situation, which the parable has put before them in story form.

The way this happens is beautifully brought out in the parable the prophet Nathan tells David in 2 Samuel 12:1-7, an unusually clear example of the way in which parables work. Nathan's story of a rich man who owned very many flocks and herds, yet still stole the "one little ewe-lamb" his poor neighbor possessed in order to feed an unexpected guest, provokes David to violent anger. "As the Lord lives," cried the king, "the man who has done this deserves to die"—only to be told with shattering effect, "You are the man." By narrating David's theft of Uriah's wife figuratively, in parable form, Nathan is able to get David to see his situation for what it is. He is made aware of his sin—personally and not just notionally, at gut level and not just in the head. A direct confrontation, say a moralizing sermon by Nathan, full of righteous indignation, would never have achieved this. It would only have made David more defensive. But Nathan's parable is able to bring David to a new understanding of his situation and to induce him to pass a judgment on it. And it is this judgment that provides the lesson of the parable and completes it.

The parables of Jesus are like this. They are not moral stories teaching lessons. Sayings of Jesus have indeed been added to the gospel parables to serve as lessons; for example, a long list of such sayings appears after the parable of the Dishonest Steward in Luke 16:9-13. But these are additions of the early Christian tradition and not part of the parables as they were spoken by Jesus. In original form, every parable of Jesus is a story which "remains 'suspended' . . . so long as the listener has not decided for or against the new possibilities for living opened up in it" (Schillebeeckx 1979, 158). The listeners must supply their own lesson as they hear the parable and feel it strike home. Their reaction is integral to the parable, for without it the parable would remain incomplete. The parable is essentially an open-ended, dialogical form.

For all its authority, then, the teaching of Jesus is not authoritarian. His pedagogy is neither indoctrination nor propaganda. Jesus, in his parables, does not attempt to inform or persuade; he tries only to make his listeners aware. The parables of Jesus are in fact a form of what Paulo Freire has called "conscientization" (Freire 1972b, 51-83; 1973, 3-58), at least in the more general and popular meaning of the word as "awareness-raising."

A CRITICAL TEACHING

The awareness to which the parables of Jesus provokes his listeners is a critical awareness; the parable, as John Dominic Crossan has demonstrated, is essentially a subversive form. As such, the parable is the "binary opposite" of another kind of symbolic story, the myth. For where myth establishes and sustains a "world" (that is, a particular way of structuring and interpreting reality), parable subverts it (Crossan 1975, 54-62).

The parables of Jesus are, in fact, continually subverting the world of his listeners: inverting their expectations, upsetting their accepted attitudes and values. Laborers are paid the same wage for unequal hours of work (Mt 20:1-15); respectable, law-abiding people are said to be less acceptable to God than dishonest tax collectors and shameless sinners (Lk 18:9-14; Mt 21:31); priests dedicated to God's service callously ignore a wounded man lying on the road while a half-pagan Samaritan cares for him (Lk 10:30-37); gentiles are invited to the messianic banquet from which the children of the kingdom are excluded (Mt 8:11-12; 22:1-10). Truly, the listener's world is turned upside-down. Such subversion, Crossan suggests, opens listeners to the action of God (the kingdom) by upsetting the stable certainties on which they run their self-sufficient and self-centered lives. It confronts them with transcendence.

> The parables of Jesus are *not* historical allegories telling us how God acts with mankind; neither are they moral example-stories telling us how to act before God and towards one another. They are stories which shatter the deep structure of our accepted world and thereby render clear and evident to us the relativity of the story itself. They remove our defences and make us vulnerable to God. It is only in such experiences that God can teach us, and only in such moments does the Kingdom of God arrive. My own term for this relationship is transcendence (Crossan 1975, 121-22).

But this, I suspect, is too narrow a way of understanding the parables of Jesus. There is more to them than merely the communication of an individual experience of transcendence. For there is a positive side to the parables underlying their negative function of subversion. The parables of Jesus subvert our world only because they point (figuratively, metaphorically, in a glass, darkly) to another world (the kingdom of God), where relationships are structured not by ambition, greed, and selfishness, but by love.

It is to this world that the pedagogy of Jesus refers us. For the parables of Jesus (paradigms of all his teachings) are parables of the kingdom. But the kingdom of God is not to be reduced (as Western exegesis since Bultmann has tried to reduce it) to personal decision alone. Rather, the kingdom of God stands for God's definitive liberative intervention in human and cosmic history. It leads history to its fulfillment in the end-time community in which all alienations will be overcome and all exploitation and oppression ended (Rv 21:1-5). While it must not be thought of as continuous with human history ("Earthly progress must be carefully distinguished from the growth of Christ's Kingdom"—*Gaudium et Spes,* no. 39), the end-time community is not wholly unconnected with that history either. "For here," Vatican II tells us, "grows the body of a new human family which even now is able to give some foreshadowing of the new age" (*Gaudium et Spes,* no. 39). The kingdom of God thus spells the total liberation of humankind, both individual and societal, and it is this total liberation that determines the thrust of the liberative pedagogy of Jesus.

LESSONS FOR AN INDIAN THEOLOGY OF LIBERATION

All education, Joao da Veiga Countinho points out, is either education for domestication or for freedom (in Freire 1972b, 9). That the non-elitist, experience-based, action-oriented, dialogical, and critical pedagogy of Jesus was highly liberative is evident. Certainly his first followers experienced it as such. "Christ has set us free in order that we might remain free" (Gal

5:1) exclaims Paul. We can still catch in his exultant cry the joyful rush of freedom that must have been experienced by those who were exposed to the liberative pedagogy of Jesus.

This pedagogy is liberative in a double way. Because it is a non-elitist and a dialogical teaching, it liberates people from the restless demons of unbridled competitiveness and insatiable greed by making them conscious of their worth. It teaches them that, as children of God, their value derives not from personal ability, accumulated wealth, or social status, but from the inalienable reality of God's love (Mt 6:25-34). Such a pedagogy leads toward that realm of a wholly unconditioned personal freedom *(moksha)*, which is the goal of the religious traditions of India. Here all greed comes to an end; all aggression is stilled; all illusions engendered by the absolutization of finite values are dispelled. Such unconditioned personal freedom, symbolized concretely in the classless individual of Hinduism (Nikam 1971, 43) — the wholly unattached wandering ascetic *(sannyasin)* who transcends all social categories and is indifferent to all human needs — lies on the horizon of the pedagogy of Jesus.

But the liberative pedagogy of Jesus has yet another dimension. Because it is an action-oriented, experience-based, and critical teaching that subverts the unquestioned assumptions and shocks the stereotyped expectations of its hearers, it frees them from the great manipulative myths that legitimize the oppressive structures (economic, political, social, and religious) of their society, and so allows them to work for a new, non-exploitative world in which men and women will be able to live together as brothers and sisters under their one Parent in heaven, taught by their one Teacher, the Christ (Mt 23:8-10). The societal freedom symbolized by the classless society of Karl Marx also lies on the horizon of the pedagogy of Jesus.

This doubly liberative pedagogy holds important lessons for us in India today. Not only does it challenge the reactionary role that Christian educational institutions play in contemporary Indian society, but it provides a stimulus for elaborating a theology which, while preserving the dimensions of human liberation that have been emphasized by the Indian tradition, will supply those that have been neglected by it. For the pedagogy of Jesus, as we have seen, is a pedagogy of the oppressed, with a strong commitment to societal liberation. But liberation *(moksha)* has been traditionally understood in India not as "the overcoming (of) economic, social, and political dependence," nor even as the building up of "a qualitatively different society" in which the human person "will be free from all servitude ... the artisan of his own destiny" (Gutierrez 1973, 91), but as the emancipation of the individual human being from his or her psychic conditioning. In the Indian tradition, liberation has always been understood as the liberation of the individual from the psychic sources of personal or societal bondage.

These sources of bondage, the three "gateways to hell" as they are called in the *Bhagavadgita* (XVI.21), are listed in the Indian tradition as *kama* (desire), or the passionate craving for pleasure; *krodha* (anger), or the aggressiveness that comes from frustrated ambition; and *lobha* (greed), or the compulsive urge to possess things. Liberation from these leads to a state of *sthita-prajna* (steadfast wisdom) in which the liberated person is *sama* (the same) toward all the pairs of opposites that qualify life: pleasure or pain, profit or loss, victory or defeat (*Bhagavadgita* II.38). The individual thus reaches, in the contemporary description of Jiddu Krishnamurti, a state of psychic freedom in which "there is no fear or compulsion, no urge to be secure" (Krishnamurti 1964, 19). In the Indian tradition, such freedom is the necessary precondition for a liberated society. As the Maharishi Mahesh Yogi has said, "For the forest to be green, the trees must be green" (in Link 1972, 12).

This unwavering insistence on the need for personal freedom in any movement for social change is, I believe, the most significant contribution that Indian religions can make to any theology of liberation. For no genuine societal change is possible without a corresponding personal conversion. "If a million wolves were to organize for justice," asks the Master in one of Anthony de Mello's stories, "would they cease to be a million wolves?" (de Mello 1985, 85). In their anxiety for a radical and much needed societal change, well-intentioned movements of social revolution (like the French revolution in the eighteenth century or the Russian revolution in the twentieth) ended up fashioning tyrannies almost as oppressive as the ones they overthrew—precisely because they forgot that sick people do not make a sane society. The Indian understanding of liberation provides a useful corrective to such one-sided ideologies.

But the Indian understanding of liberation needs correcting too. It is sociologically naive because it imagines that a mass conversion of individuals is possible without preliminary structural changes in the society to which they belong, that individual conversions by themselves can lead to societal change. But a society is not just a collection of individuals; it is also a system of structures, made up of stable patterns of impersonal relationships which determine the distribution of wealth, status, and power among its members. Although such structures are ultimately the objectification of individual attitudes (as the structures of capitalism are the social expressions of greed!), once posited they develop a life and an autonomy of their own. There is, therefore, always a dialectical relationship between an individual and the society in which he or she lives. Individuals do indeed create a society, but a society in turn forms the individuals who belong to it. There can, therefore, be no individual change on any significant scale without previous or concomitant societal change. To make the trees green, one must change the climate of the forest in which they grow!

Genuine liberation is therefore possible only if there is both a change of structures and a change of hearts; if personal conversion complements social change; and if a cultural revolution leavens a sociopolitical one (Soares Prabhu 1981, 605; Pieris 1988, 79-81). This calls for a twofold liberative pedagogy, because there can be no liberation without education. An authentic and enduring liberation of society is never imposed from above. It presupposes the participation of the oppressed people themselves in the process of their emancipation, and this is not possible without their coming to an awareness of the situation of injustice in which they live. But to make people aware of injustice and to awaken them to liberative action is an educational task (Wren 1977, xiii). So too is the task of liberating a person from his or her prejudices and compulsions. In the Indian tradition this can only be done through a guided process of awareness (meditation) that leads to "seeing the Self in the self" (*Bhagavadgita* VI.20). Awareness then, both macrocosmic (conscientization) and microcosmic (meditation), will be basic to any Indian theology of liberation. And it is to just such awareness that the liberative pedagogy of Jesus leads us.

REFERENCES

Austin, J. L. 1962. *How to Do Things with Words*, Oxford University Press, London.
Bornkamm, Gunther. 1960. *Jesus of Nazareth*, Hodder & Stoughton, London.
Boucher, Madeleine. 1977. *The Mysterious Parable*, CBQ Monograph Series 6, Catholic Biblical Association, Washington.
Crossan, John Dominic. 1975. *The Dark Interval*, Argus Communications, Niles, Illinois.
de Mello, Anthony. 1985. *One Minute Wisdom*, Gujarat Sahitya Prakash, Anand.
Documents of Vatican II, Gaudium et Spes, no. 39.
Freire, Paulo. 1972. *Pedagogy of the Oppressed*, Penguin Books, Harmondsworth.
———. 1972b. *Cultural Action for Freedom*, Penguin Books, Harmondsworth.
———. 1973. *Education for Critical Consciousness*, Seabury Press, New York.
Gutierrez, Gustavo. 1973. *A Theology of Liberation*, Orbis Books, Maryknoll, New York.
Jeremias, Joachim. 1969. *Jerusalem in the Time of Jesus*, SCM, London.
———. 1971. *New Testament Theology*, vol. 1, SCM, London.
———. 1972. *The Parables of Jesus*, 3d ed., SCM, London.
Krishnamurti, J. 1964. *Think of These Things*, Harper & Row, New York.
Link, Mark. 1972. *Take Off Your Shoes*, Argus Communications, Niles, Illinois.
Nikam, N. A. 1971. "Individual and Society in Indian Social Thought." In *Indian Philosophical Annual*, vol. 6, ed. T.M.P. Mahadevan, Centre of Advanced Study in Philosophy, University of Madras, Madras.
Nissen, Johannes. 1984. *Poverty and Mission*, Interuniversitair Instituut voor Missiologie en Oecumenica, Leiden.
Pesch, Rudolf. 1976. *Das Markusevangelium*, vol. 1, Herder (Herders theologischer Kommentar zum Neuen Testament), Freiburg.
Pieris, Aloysius. 1988. *An Asian Theology of Liberation*, Orbis Books, Maryknoll, New York.
Rajneesh, Bhagwan Shree. 1975. *The Mustard Seed: Discourses on the Sayings of Jesus Taken from the Gospel According to Thomas*, Rajneesh Foundation, Poona.
Schillebeeckx, Edward. 1979. *Jesus: An Experiment in Christology*, Collins/Fount, London.
Shourie, Arun. 1979. *Hinduism: Essence and Consequence*, Vikas, Shahibabad.

Soares-Prabhu, George. 1974. "Are the Gospels Historical?" *Clergy Monthly* 38.
———. 1981. "The Kingdom of God: Jesus' Vision of a New Society." In *The Indian Church in the Struggle for a New Society*, ed. D. S. Amalorpavadas, National Catechetical, Biblical, and Liturgical Centre, Bangalore.
———. 1985a. "Class in the Bible: The Biblical Poor a Social Class?" *Vidyajyoti* 49.
———. 1985b. "The Miracles of Jesus: The Subversion of a Power-Structure?" In *Jesus Today*, ed. S. Kappen, AICUF, Madras.
Ste. Croix. Geoffrey de. 1975. "Early Christian Attitudes to Poverty and Slavery." In *Church, Society and Politics*, ed. Derek Baker, Blackwell, Oxford.
Theissen, Gerd. 1978. *The First Followers of Jesus*, SCM, London.
Vermes, Geza. 1976. *Jesus the Jew*, Collins/Fontana, London.
Weber, Max. 1964. *The Theory of Social and Economic Organization*, ed. Talcott Parsons, Free Press, New York.
Wren, Brian. 1977. *Education for Justice: Pedagogical Principles*, Orbis Books, Maryknoll, New York.

7

Interiority and Liberation

XAVIER IRUDAYARAJ

In India during the mid-sixties young men and women, especially graduates of cities and towns struck by the awful socioeconomic condition of the rural people, began to move into rural areas. The extensive community development programs of the government in the fifties had failed miserably, and the development decade of the sixties was creating disillusionment.

The move of the ideologically committed young, who wanted to contribute to the reconstruction of the rural areas, gave birth to the so-called action groups—informal groups operating at the grassroots level.

Young Christian graduates entered the field in the seventies. Many of them initiated informal literacy programs and organized the weaker sections, especially the SCs (Scheduled Castes) and STs (Scheduled Tribes). These young people were deeply committed to the gospel message of liberation and were searching to make their faith operative in day-to-day life. In the course of time, some of them distanced themselves from the traditional church.

Besides the Christian and ecumenical groups, there is a multiplicity of other bodies. Some are of Gandhian inspiration; others of RSS (*Rashtriya Swayamsevak Sangh*) inspiration; yet others are inspired by a humanistic ideal, either Marxian or non-Marxian. In addition to these action groups, in the early eighties many groups of intellectuals and professionals have emerged, who have succeeded in creating movements, emphasizing human rights, civil rights, women's rights, and so on.

These people, who are deeply involved in the promotion and organization of people's movements, need an alternative vision, an authentic spirituality, a source of energy and strength, so that their involvement with the oppressed people may be joyful in spite of failures and disappointments, and so they might remain agents of hope in the midst of hopeless situations.

On the other hand, those who are leading a committed contemplative life, particularly in ashrams, feel a certain tension between the traditional ideals (both Indian and Christian) and the present-day challenges (Vandana 1982). Ashrams, such as Shantivanam, Anjali, Divyodaya, are attempting to integrate spiritual freedom and social concerns in their own unique ways.

In this context of a tension experienced by both—those who are socially involved and the spiritually committed—we are called to a deeper understanding of interiority and to interpret it anew with the thrust of liberation theology, for we are aware that we cannot pour new wine into old skins.

In our context, then, the challenge is not to solve the age-old dilemma of action *vs.* contemplation. The demand of the hour is to reinterpret the Indian path of *sadhana* (way of life) and the *yoga* (practice) of self-realization in the light of the theology of liberation.

Before we begin to reinterpret the path of interiority toward liberation, we need to see clearly the characteristics of the two approaches (Indian and liberational) and pay close attention to the insights concerning interiority offered by *Upanishadic* mysticism, which is also prophetic.

TWO APPROACHES

There are many ways of approaching reality. The eastern and the western are usually understood to have their specific differences. Here we take the Indian (Hindu) approach as a model of the eastern, and for the western we focus on the Latin American Christian approach of liberation theology. Of course, the differences are not to be understood as mutually exclusive, but as complementary interpretations calling one another to go deeper through a dialogical encounter.

In the search for reality, Westerners go out of themselves; their tendency is *exteriorization*. In India one enters into one's own being to understand the self. The Hindu approach is therefore that of *interiorization* or getting in touch with what is within.

In short, the western approach is "extrospective"—to coin a word—which results in objectification, research, and scientific progress, while the Indian approach is an introspective search focusing on the *interior identity of the Self*. Very often the Indian search becomes a research object in the West. This is clearly seen in the case of Transcendental Meditation, *yoga*, and others.

The Indian (Hindu) approach is primarily concerned with the personal problem of one's own suffering and the bondage to material conditions. It seeks *moksha* or release from the instability of existence. In this quest it has fixed its attention on the conscious experience of the self (I-hood).

Therefore, in its search for reality, India speaks about awakening and enlightenment (Buddhahood). In short, the Indian is characterized as metaphysico-psychologico-spiritual, while the Westerner is seen as positivo-historico-social.

THE *UPANISHADIC* REVOLUTION

According to the *Upanishads*, the Brahminic talk about an afterlife in the company of the gods has little meaning. Similarly, the concept of temporal life in contrast to eternal life makes no sense; full and authentic life cannot but be one. Hence liberation in the sense of attaining wholeness should mean a radical transformation not simply of life as object, but more especially of the living subject.

One has to break the circular vessel of time to enter the nontemporal sphere. This is the way to wholeness, to true liberation. As long as one is in the net of the temporal, one is in the clutches of death, even if it is postponed for some time. So the oft-repeated Upanishadic prayer: "From the unreal lead me to the Real; from darkness lead me to the light; from death lead me to Immortality" (*Brihadaranyaka Upanishad*, 1.3.28).

The verse makes it clear that the passage from death to deathlessness means passage from inauthentic existence and darkness to authentic life, and light. Here light is a symbol of life, and this light is not from without but an eternal glow from within. "Where the Light shines, everything shines together; by its blaze all this gets illumined" (*Mundaka Upanishad*, 2.2.10).

In the *Upanishads*, light is consciousness. It is a great discovery of *Upanishadic* sages that consciousness alone can assume multiplicity without prejudice to unity. This is a discovery of the person's power of integration, and it is indeed a liberative experience.

The *Upanishadic* seers discovered that in all manifestations of the real, there is a basic oneness, a relative fullness and complementary wholeness, as the following stanza expresses:

> That is full; this is full;
> The full comes out of the full;
> Taking among the Full from the Full
> The Full itself remain (*Brihadaranyaka Upanishad*,
>   5.1; *Isavasya Upanishad*, 1).

The whole enquiry into the nature of reality is carried out by *bringing together epistemic and ontic questions* from which a holistic vision of the world and of individual destiny emerges.

The *Upanishads* express the experience of the Ultimate Reality in two key words: *Brahman atman*, Brahman is the mysterious power in nature. "In the beginning," it is said "this was Brahman, one only" (*Brihadaranyaka Upanishad*, 1.4.11). "This" is the reality in which we find ourselves; this reality is "one only." This is the intuition that underlies all *Upanishadic* thought. In all of us, the universe is originally experienced as a unity. Everything in nature is related to everything else in a cosmic order. In the

Upanishads this principle of unity, this foundation comes into consciousness and is called Brahman.

No words can express Brahman. It is everything and it is nothing. "All this [world] is Brahman" (*Chandogaya Upanishad*, 4.14.1) — "And yet is nothing . . . he is not this, not this" (*Brihadaranyaka Upanishad*, 2.3.6).

In short, the *Upanishads* are the record of human discovery of the self. They seek to answer the question, Who am I? Am I this body, or am I this mind . . . soul . . . or is there something beyond both body, soul in which the real meaning of my existence is to be found?

There is the story of the gods and the demons who came to Prajapati, the creator, and asked him to tell them about the True Self (*Chandogya Upanishad*, 8.7-12). First he told them to look in a pool of water; so they looked in the water and saw themselves (bodily form) and thought that the body was their self.

But then they realized that this was not what they were seeking and so they returned to Prajapati, who told them, "The Self you see in dreams, that is your true self." So they thought that the inner self, the self of thought, feelings and desires was their true self. But they realized that this was not what they were seeking, and so they returned to Prajapati and he said, "The self which exists in deep sleep, that is true self." So they came to see that the self that is beyond both the body and the mind is the true self. But still they were not content, since the self is unconscious. So they returned to Prajapati again, and finally he revealed to them the fourth state (*turiya*), the state beyond waking and dreaming and deep sleep, *the state of awakened self in which one attains to self-knowledge (self-realization)*.

The story is deeply significant. There are three states of consciousness, according to the Hindu tradition: the state of *waking*, the state of *dreaming*, and that of *deep sleep*. Most people think that the real world is found in the external world presented to the senses, such as the thing one sees in a mirror, but when we mature we begin to realize that the inner self, which thinks and feels, is the real self. This corresponds to the dream state. But beyond the waking and dreaming state, there is the state of *sushupti* (deep sleep). Most would think that it is simply a state of unconsciousness and has no significance. But this comes nearest to the real self in the Hindu view.

In *sushupti*, however, there is no consciousness. So it is necessary to go beyond this state to *turiya*. This is the state in which the person awakes to true being, in which one discovers the ground, the source — in pure consciousness. Here is self-realization. This is the knowledge of the self, the atman, the spirit, where the spirit of the person reaches and touches the Ultimate Reality.

INTERIORIZATION OR INTERIORITY

The search in the *Upanishads* is to find reality in one's own self. Reality is encountered in one's own consciousness, which means the awareness of the self. Thus, reality is encountered through the consciousness of the individual self and of the Eternal Self in the individual self. The method of understanding, experiencing, and interpreting the self is called interiorization.

The individual self together with its body is called *jivatman*; in contrast, the Divine Self together with the whole universe is said to be *Paramatman*. The center of the macrocosm is the *Paramatman*, while the center of the microcosm is the *jivatman*. Since the *jivatman* contains in itself the reflection of the *Paramatman*, Brahman in the last analysis is the ultimate center of both macrocosm and the microcosm.

This ultimate center of consciousness cannot be proved; it is experienced by way of *sravanam, mananam,* and *nididhyasanam* (*listening, pondering,* and *realizing*). In the depth of this experience, one is taken from *jivatman* to *Paramatman*. Now the question is, How do we come to this consciousness of the self?

THE WAY TO REALIZATION

Reality or consciousness is known by a process of becoming. To know reality is to become one with it. The *Mundaka Upanishad* explains it thus: "He who knows Brahman becomes Brahman" (*Mundaka Upanishad*, 3.29). So one meditates upon the inner self until one becomes aware of it. Through concentration, one can come to proper self-awareness.

The *Upanishads* describe the experience of the atman in different ways — through different similies and comparisons (*Katha Upanishad*, 2.22-24, 3.12; *Mundaka Upanishad*, 11.2.5.8; *Brihadaranyaka Upanishad*, 4.4.22).

THE STATEMENT OF REALIZATION

Sankara selected four great sayings from the *Upanishads*. They are as follows:

Prajnanam Brahman: Brahman is consciousness (*Aitareya Upanishad*, 3.5.19)

Ayam atma Brahman: This atman is Brahman (*Brihadaranyaka Upanishad*, 2.5.19)

Aham Brahmasmi: I am Brahman (*Brihadaranyaka Upanishad*, 1.4.10)

Tat tvam asi: That thou art (*Chandogya Upanishad*, 6.8.7)

In a sense, the essence of the *Upanishads* in the attempt to unfold the Reality is summed up in the great statement: *Tat tvam asi*. For, Brahman, in transcendence and immanence, is in the spirit of humanity as the supreme Self, as the depth of the consciousness. Hence, in rising to the best in us, we sink to the depth within us, to Brahman, the Ultimate Reality. Brahman, therefore, is at the same time immanent and transcendent, within all and above all.

THE *JIVANMUKTA* MODEL OF INTERIORITY AND SERVICE

Jivanmuktas (freed persons) are gurus in the real sense, because they have been liberated by the realization of the Ultimate Truth in their journey of interiority. Such realized persons do not live for themselves; they become transforming agents. The transformation that has taken place in them as they live by their inner self, makes them a source of energy, a fount of goodness and love. Just as a flower sheds its fragrance all around, a spring shares its waters with all, and the moon gives its coolness to the whole world, the *jivanmukta*, by the very realization, serves humanity and creation.

Significantly enough, the *jivanmuktas* of *Saiva Siddhanta* (the Saivite tradition of the Tamils) are known as *tontar* (servants). Their service extends to the whole creation. Sustained and strengthened by the Lord who lives and acts in them, they spend their lives serving others. Saint Appar, a Tamil poet of the tenth century, sings that it is the duty of the Lord to support him, while his own duty is to spend his life in service (*Tevaram*, 5.19.9). That the bliss experienced becomes the property and possession of the whole of humanity is the heartfelt longing of the *jivanmukta* (*Tirumantiram*, 147).

Hence the *jivanmukta*, who has gone to the depth of self, returns to the world and to society as a liberated agent of service. Regarding the social concern of *jivanmuktas* and their altruistic services, an ancient Tamil poet has the following to say: "They are such unselfish persons that even if that rare and sweet thing, ambrosia, comes their way, they will not enjoy it without sharing it with others."

THE TRANSCENDENCE OF INTERIORITY

True interiority therefore leads to transcendence, which is to see oneself in all and all in oneself.

It is a total identification with all reality, since the realized person becomes one with the Brahman, the self of all beings. It is, therefore, to see, to be moved by, and to act in sympathy toward every creature.

To see all in oneself and oneself in all is a two-way openness—openness to go out of oneself to others in order to identify with them in love and compassion, and openness for the others to come in and feel identified.

SANNYASA: A WAY OF LIFE FOR INTERIORITY

Sannyasa is often understood as "ascetic life," and its meaning is confined to the *ashrama* (fourth stage) of life, a secluded state of a few privileged people. But what is decisive in *sannyasa* is the inner attitude of the person who works in an attitude of genuine detachment from the fruits of the action (*Bhagavadgita*, 6.1). Hence true *sannyasins* live and work out of their experience that "their life evolves in the Lord" (*Bhagavadgita*, 6.31) and their work is participation in the work of the Lord" (*Bhagavadgita*, 4.8).

Sannyasa denotes not only a state of life, but a way of life. It is the outcome of realization. Enlightened through a holistic vision of reality, motivated by service, a *sannyasin* engages in the welfare of all beings; and his or her action is truly liberative.

INTERIORITY IN THE LIGHT OF LIBERATION THEOLOGY

True self-realization or interiority will urge the person toward *lokasamgraha* (welfare of the world). This happens in the life of a true *sannyasin* or a *jivanmukta*. But the dynamic transition from interiority to active commitment has been much limited in Indian tradition to a few illustrious examples like Buddha, Mahatma Gandhi, and Vivekananda.

Dialogue with liberation theology stimulates us to bring to full flowering the social and historical dimensions of an authentic interiority. For, if interiority means living in the depth of the Reality, it must necessarily include the communal and historical dimensions of existence. We are, therefore, called to draw out the full implications of interiority expressed in social involvement and historical struggles.

In this process of dialogue, we begin to see how liberation theology itself enables us to discover the social thrust of interiority, while the Indian insight also unveils the interiority dimension of liberation theology.

First of all, liberation theology challenges us to interpret the meaning of interiority for today in the context of our concern for social justice and commitment to world community. It demands that we affirm and realize not only the self within, but also the self of the society and community, for the ultimate reality of the society too is Brahman. The true self is both the truth of individuals and the truth of the society.

As the changing individuals evolve around the unchanging atman, and as the cosmos revolves around the axis of the reality of Brahman, so too the society in flux has its immutable center of existence. The social sciences today enlighten us more and more on the intricacies of the reality of society. And so today we need to emphasize the social-self and point out that self-realization is not complete unless it includes social-realization.

Thus the liberation perspective of interiority enables us to affirm the reality of the social-self in the context of the *Upanishadic* experience of *jivatman* and *Paramatman*. And the *Upanishadic* insight into the self within further urges us to discover the ultimate or the depth reality of society, together with its social awareness.

This is a significant challenge of liberation theology to *Upanishadic* interiority. It is also a call to make the *jivanmukta*-ideal into an ideology for a movement of social transformation.

On the other hand, the challenge of *Upanishadic* interiority to liberation theology is also significant. Any social commitment must have its own interiority if it is to be rooted in reality. This means the liberation praxis (action-reflection) needs to be interiorized so that it becomes a centered action or a liberative action. The reflection process in the praxis then ought to become a process of purification and enlightenment, so that it turns out to be a realization project. Here the life of the *jivanmukta* or a true *sannyasin* stands as a paradigm to anyone committed to liberation praxis, because involvement in liberative action presupposes a liberative process in the person; only a liberated person can liberate others. The call of the *Upanishads* is to realize (discover) the Self with the help of the self. It is a call to experience the liberative power of the Self in the personal self. This demands a progressive interiorization of action and reflection through *dhyana* (meditation), which is a journey toward the center.

TOWARD A THEOLOGY OF INTERIORITY AND LIBERATION

In their mutual openness to each other, Indian interiority and liberation-praxis become radicalized while keeping their identity and authenticity. Liberation-action with a depth of interiority becomes assuredly potent, as it stands on the very reality of the Truth. So too, an authentic interiority with a liberation thrust becomes truly a transforming service, since self-liberation purifies and frees one to embrace the whole and the total liberation.

The two approaches, interiority and liberation, can be interpreted to offer a mutually inclusive dynamic. The interiority process is widened by the dynamism of active social involvement, while the social concerns are deepened by the inner realization of the unity of all reality. In other words, the mystic experience and the prophetic witness meet and fuse. This approach of mutual interaction between the interiority-process and the liberative-praxis offers us a new way of experiencing the reality without opposing or dichotomizing eastern and western ways.

From the perspective of this integral approach, we can indicate certain implications and consequences with regard to praxis, conscientization, and struggle.

First, the liberation praxis may be integrated with *Niskama Karma* of Hindu spirituality, as taught in the *Bhagavadgita*, for it challenges one to do or involve oneself without craving for the fruits of the actions, that is, to do service without any self-interest or gain.

Such a praxis will prove to be both free and potent. It will be a type of action that will emerge from the truth of oneself and reach toward the truth of all. Thus it leads to becoming a contemplative in action. And only such a praxis could become transformative.

Second, in this approach, the task of conscientization ought to be viewed as the process of awakening to fuller self-awareness, in which one becomes enlightened of the truth of the solidarity of all. Self-awareness and social-awareness are the two poles that constitute the field of our consciousness.

Indeed, one cannot fully become aware of oneself except in social interactions, and on the other hand, social involvement will prove liberative only if it is born of the awakened and enlightened self. Hence conscientization implies both self-realization and social-commitment leading to a total liberation.

Third, the struggles for liberation can be approached as practices of *yoga* and *yajna* (ascetic practices and sacrificial performance). Facing conflicts and tensions (both personal and social) could then become a process of purification and creative self-offering. The inner strength emerging from the true self will empower the person to eschew violence and pursue the struggle for liberation in a nonviolent way. Such a struggle with inner freedom will offer both hope and optimism in spite of external opposing forces and prove itself to be salvific.

For the truth of oneself and the truth of all is realized in this struggle for liberating oneself and the society together, which is the way to integral and total liberation. Truth sets us free.

CONCLUSION

Our consideration of interiority *vs.* liberation has not led us into the traditional opposition or juxtaposition of contemplation/action or transcendence/immanence. But it has challenged us to interpret both interiority and liberation from an integral and holistic perspective that is both dialogic and dialectical.

The life of Mahatma Gandhi provides a concrete model of a hermeneutic circle, in which the interiority and liberation mutually encounter in an open-ended process of experiments. His involvement with the Freedom Movement and his commitment to *satyagraha* throw new light into the experiences of the *Upanishadic* seers. The mystic visions of the seers and their prophetic witnesses find a new birth in Mahatma, in the context of his leadership to free India. The Gandhian experiments inspire us to conduct our own experiments in our struggles for liberation in the India of today. It is in this context that the action groups and the ashramites who are searching for alternatives are called to collaborate and create the path of liberation with interiority.

REFERENCES

Radhakrishnan, S., ed. 1969. *The Principal Upanishads*, London.
Vandana, Sr. 1982. *Social Justice and Ashrams*, Asian Trading Corporation, Bangalore.

8

Outside the Gate, Sharing the Insult

SAMUEL RAYAN

This meditation is an attempt to see caste and untouchability from the point of view of Jesus, as far as this is possible to a disciple who follows him "at a distance" and wishes to follow him closer. First, it takes a quick look at the reality of caste as it operates in India today. Then it seeks to sense the mind of Jesus and, finally, indicates some tasks.

THE REALITY OF CASTE

CRIME, INFECTION, OBSCENITY

If Jesus were born in India, would he be caste or outcaste? high or low? What would be his choice?

Gandhiji said:

> I was in Nellore on the sixth of April. I met "untouchables" there and I prayed that day, as I have done today, that if I have to be reborn, I should be born an untouchable, so that I may share their sorrows, sufferings, and the affronts levelled at them, in order that I may endeavour to free myself and them from that miserable condition. I prayed that if I should die with any of my desires unfulfilled, with my service of the "untouchables" unfinished, with my Hinduism unfulfilled, I may be born again amongst the "untouchables" to bring my Hinduism to its fulfilment. . . . I regard untouchability as the greatest blot on Hinduism (*Young India*, May 4, 1921).

Gandhiji hated untouchability. He worked for its abolition, and already in this birth he sought to identify himself with the outcastes. He allowed himself only the minimum of clothing they were allowed. He swept and scavenged with them. He was convinced that "it is a *sin* to regard anyone born in Hinduism as polluted or untouchable." To do so is *satanic*, he said. To him untouchability was a crime of which the nemesis had overtaken us in the treatment we met with at the hands of the English. "We have segregated the pariah (*paraya*) and we are in turn segregated in the British colonies. We deny him the use of public wells; we throw the leavings of our plate at him. His very shadow pollutes us. Indeed there is no charge that the pariah cannot fling in our faces and which we do not fling in the face of the Englishman" (Gandhi 1954, 4-5).

Bharatan Kumarappa points out that Gandhi, who taught and practiced nonviolence, "could not remain blind to the inhuman violence perpetrated on a section of our population, who were condemned to live *outside* the pale of civilization, without social amenities, made to do the dirtiest work, humiliated to the dust and treated with contempt. . . . No religion worth the name, Gandhi was convinced, could be guilty of such atrocity. . . . So it must be cut out root and branch, or Hinduism would perish" (Gandhi 1954, iii, iv).

Gandhi not only denounced untouchability but rejected the caste system itself. He wrote: "I abhor with my whole soul the system which has reduced a large number of Hindus to a level less than that of *beasts*" (Gandhi 1954, 6). The system was, to Gandhiji, "as devilish as . . . the English system of government in India" (*Young India*, January 19, 1921). Caste, he maintained, had nothing to do with religion. In fact, caste was harmful both to spiritual and national growth (*Harijan*, July 13, 1936). But then Gandhi proceeded to distinguish caste from *varna* and *ashrama*. These he defended. "The law of Varna teaches us that we have to earn our bread by following the ancestral calling. . . . There is no calling too low and none too high. . . . Arrogation of a superior status by and of one Varna over another is a denial of the law" (*Harijan*, July 18, 1936). It was immediately pointed out to Gandhi by reformers like Sant Ramji of Lahore that his distinction between caste and *varna* was too philosophical and too subtle to be grasped by the people:

> For all practical purposes in the Hindu society caste and *Varna* are one and the same thing, for the function of both is the same, i.e., to restrict intercaste marriages and inter-dining. . . . Hindus are slaves of caste. . . . To try to remove untouchability without striking at the root of *Varnavyavastha* [the *varna* system] is to draw a line on the surface of water. . . . To seek the help of the Shastras [the ancient law books] for the removal of untouchability and caste is simply to wash mud with mud" (*Harijan*, August 15, 1936).

To this and similar criticism Gandhi never made an adequate answer. To demonstrations of the ample scriptural basis for caste and untouchability, his reply was to deny the authority of such scriptural passages. In his autobiography Gandhi wrote:

> To remove untouchability is a penance that caste Hindus owe to Hinduism. . . . The purification required is not of untouchables but of the so-called superior castes. . . . I would be content to be torn to pieces rather than disown the suppressed classes. . . . Hindus will certainly never deserve freedom . . . if they allow their noble religion to be disfigured by the retention of the taint of untouchability. As I love Hinduism dearer than life itself, the taint has become for me an intolerable burden. Let us not deny God by denying to a fifth of our race the right of association on an equal footing" (Gandhi 1958).

B. T. Ranadive's comment on this (and on similar passages) follows:

> This passionate protest leaves nothing unsaid. But the equally passionate desire to keep the landlords and Hindu religion intact (untouched and untouchable) reduces the protest to a formal declaration only (Ranadive 1979, 341).

If Jesus were an Indian citizen denouncing untouchability and caste as vigorously as Gandhi and working with Gandhi for their abolition, would he also want to keep the landlords and the religions intact? Or would he insist that the landless fifth of the nation should lay claim to a fifth of the land and wealth of the nation? Would he liberate that group from the religions and gods of the landlords so that they could be free for a God who upholds the rights and the dignity of the oppressed and the outcaste? Kumarappa says that Gandhi indicted untouchability in flaming words, describing it as "gross injustice" and a "device of satan" (Gandhi 1954, iv). Would Jesus too stop short with flaming words, or would he press forward to flaming deeds to deal with the economic basis and ideological legitimation of caste?

Bhagwan Das adverts to the tragic fact that since the advent of freedom in 1947, "this hybrid monster [caste] has been spreading its tentacles all around and taking everything in its *lethal grip*" (Das 1971, 4-7). One tragic aspect of the lethal grip is stressed by Ranadive: "The poison of caste divisions has deeply infected its victims—the masses and the lower orders who further are divided into several castes and sub-castes. Each recognizes the injustice done to it but is not ready to remedy the injustice done to others by its own superior status" (Ranadive 1979, 343).

Tagore lamented India's insult to itself and to God, exercised in its insult to some—many—of its citizens. The strength of a chain is in its weakest link. The honor of India is measured by the dishonor of its outcastes. In the treatment meted out to the untouchables and in the stagnant mire of caste, India meets death. Tagore sang:

> Oh my unfortunate motherland!
> those whom you have insulted
> would drag you down to their same level. . . .
>
> By avoiding the touch of man everyday
> you have insulted the divinity in man.
>
> So the curse of heaven befalls you,
> and you perforce have to share your meal with
> all and sundry at the door of famine. . . .
>
> If you avoid to embrace all
> and shut yourself up within
> the thick walls of pride
> you will be simply courting Death.
> (Ghose 1973, 270)

As long as one man is in chains, mankind is not free, said Karl Marx. As long as a single Indian is outcaste and untouchable, India sits in disgrace, untouchable and outcaste. When Jesus, who takes away the sin of the world, comes to take away the dishonor of our country, to whom will he go first, to the high caste or the outcaste? Where may we look for him? Where will we find him, perchance to join him?

A Pressing Concern

The problem of caste and untouchability is no private problem of any one community or religion. It is not even a domestic problem of the Indian nation. It is a human problem, like racism, apartheid, war, or the mechanisms of underdeveloping and exploiting peoples and lands; it affects world history and touches the dignity of every man and woman. Ranadive is right in insisting that "the question of eliminating the caste system can no longer be presented as a question of Hindu social reform and in isolation from the main struggle of our times—the struggle for agrarian revolution, the struggle for ending the domination of monopolies and imperialist exploitation, the struggle for a state of People's Democracy leading to Socialism" (Ranadive 1979, 347). It is a question of the essence and authenticity of democracy in India, a question of honoring the Constitution, which is vowed to the removal of untouchability, discrimination, and injustice. But it involves more than the honor of the nation. It is a question of human rights and civilization as against barbarism, a matter of humanity, elementary justice, and common sense. To Christians it is also a fundamental spiritual problem touching the very basis of their faith in God, who is the Creator and Father of all men and women, and their faith in Christ, the brother and savior of everyone beginning with the lowest and the least. In our day the problem has become acute and urgent and is claiming the nation's and the world's attention at all levels, socio-cultural, political, and economic. The mounting tensions, contradictions, and conflicts are making it clearer each day that our traditional institutions are inadequate to cope with the emerging situation, which cannot be met without a thoroughgoing cultural revolution.

NON-NAMES

Indian society is constructed like a pyramid on the basis of a hierarchy of castes and classes; the lowest groups bear the burden of the entire edifice. A remarkable fact about the culture of such a society is that it has developed, for the most part, negative terms to refer to the lowest groups. This is perhaps natural, for it is the dominant groups that control culture and shape language, which often is a reflection of domination and dependence. It is natural because the dominant groups make themselves the point of reference and set themselves up as standard groups, as standard humanity. To these upper sectors of society the outcastes are nameless; they have no self and no identity of their own. They do not count, except, of course, when there is work to be done to produce wealth, to create leisure and the conditions for the development of culture, and to keep society healthy. They are *avarnas*, colorless and nondescript; or *pancamas*, those left over as it were after the four castes have been counted; or *antyajas*, last-born, as if they were an accident, an unwelcome appendix, an unwanted tail. Then they were called the *untouchables*, the upper castes missing the irony of the name since it could work both ways; the superior castes now were not completely touchable either. The 1901 census classified Hindus into seven categories, of which the last two were "the unclean castes" and "the unclean feeders," those from whose hands caste people would not accept water.

In the census report of 1921, the downtrodden sectors of the population were called "depressed castes." The name was objected to and provoked a great deal of criticism; it probably exposed some unpalatable truth. In 1931 the appellation "exterior castes" was substituted. Note how the negative connotation persists, and non-people are given non-names; language and culture reflect social realities. Exterior castes could not be served by a brahmin, or by barbers, tailors, and so forth, who served caste Hindus; they polluted caste Hindus by contact or proximity; they were debarred from use of public conveniences such as roads, ferries, wells, schools, as well as from use of Hindu temples; their birth carried social stigma even if they had higher education, high salary jobs, or considerable wealth (Vidyarthi and Mishra 1977, 2-3, 211-12).

No wonder these oppressed masses interiorized the negative valuation in which they lived and breathed for centuries. They lost their self as a result, forgot their name, acquiesced in the system, learned to be thankful for sheer survival, and came to see themselves and speak of themselves as nothing. In 1935 a list of disprivileged castes and tribes was prepared by the government and attached to Orders-in-Council issued under the Government of India Act of that year. To this order was attached a schedule divided into nine parts corresponding to nine provinces. This was, according to Ambedkar, "a very terrifying list"; it included 429 communities, some sixty million Indians, deemed to be untouchables, "whose touch causes pollution to the Hindus" (Ambedkar 1969). Thus since 1936 the term *scheduled castes* took the place of exterior castes; it then got incorporated into the 1950 Constitution of India. Today scheduled-caste people number over a hundred million; along with some forty million Tribals, they constitute the most deprived, exploited, and harassed people, though they are a fifth of India's population and the backbone of the country's agriculture.

So far, then, others have been giving names to the oppressed. Others have been defining their identity for them and informing them of who they are: untouchables, negatives, non-persons, nothings. But now these nobodies are beginning to name themselves, to show a new self-awareness, to find their own identity, and to claim their due place in society. They are beginning to call everybody's attention to their existence. They repudiate the appellations imposed on them. They refuse to be *harijans*, that is, the people of the god of the upper castes and oppressors. They deny upper-caste gods. They call themselves *dalits* (oppressed). That is what they are. That is their truth, and it marks a new accent in the history of their struggle. They are holding up for all to see a terrible truth Indian society has always sought to keep in the dark; India has shrouded in much pious and metaphysical verbiage the truth about the large-scale slavery, violence, exploitation, apartheid, and cruelty on which its proud culture rests. Some of the *dalits* call themselves *Adi* (original) *Hindu*, *Adi Dravida*, or *Adi Andhra* and proceed to organize *Adi Dharma* movements as was done in the Punjab in 1929.

OPPRESSION

The oppressed are all those forced into poverty, deprived of most of human life. In India they comprise those found below the poverty line, estimated in 1978 at 306 million or forty-eight percent of India's population, and an additional 222 million or thirty-five percent of the population who are at the poverty line or just above it. All of them are undernourished, ill-clad, poorly sheltered, deeply exploited, despised, and practically outlawed. The *dalits* belong to this sea of the wretched, only they have to bear the extra burden and pain of an inescapable, irremediable social ignominy attached to their birth. Birth fixes them as objects of free abuse in every sense of the word and disallows all social mobility. They may improve themselves interiorly by working in total submission and silence for the upper castes. L. C Jain points out that seventy percent of India's poverty population and two-thirds of its unemployed are found in seven major states—Uttar Pradesh, Madhya Pradesh, Andhra Pradesh, Tamil Nadu, West Bengal, Bihar, and Maharashtra—and these states precisely have seventy-two percent of India's *dalits*. The description of poverty in these states, and in India in general, is therefore a description of the condition of the *dalits* (Jain 1982, 325).

The *dalits* have little access to education; even bare literacy is low among them. They are assetless, being mostly landless agricultural laborers or small artisans. Without education and assets they stand no chance in the battle for livelihood; the contest is unequal. The poorer the household, the higher the unemployment rate. Wages are arbitrary and pitiably low and fixed by tradition irrespective of the rise in price of essential commodities or enormous profits for the employers. All this drives the *dalits* into indebtedness. The rate of interest is incredibly high, ranging from twenty-five percent to fifty percent. The result of such deepening indebtedness is bondage to which even death brings no end. Endless generations can become bonded labor for a few rupees borrowed by a distant, long-dead ancestor. "In the absence of assets the body of the borrower is mortgaged," says Jain. Agricultural laborers become enslaved, artisans become totally dependent on traders who lend at high interest, sell raw materials at high price, and buy products at low price. "The cumulative effect of all these—lack of education, of assets, employment-opportunities and of institutional credit services on fair terms—is destitution" (Jain 1982, 325, 327). Three decades of development seem to have bypassed the scheduled castes and tribes.

Greater still are the ordeals in store for those who survive the rigors of poverty and inequality. Untouchability persists—its condemnation by thousands like Gandhi and its abolition by the Constitution notwithstanding—because its economic base is carefully preserved and protected. Scheduled castes continue to be denied access to drinking water wells, eating places, particular village roads, certain modes of transport, and even non-traditional institutions such as *balwadis* (creches), youth clubs, *mahila-mandals* (women's associations), and cooperatives. They must do forced labor for endless hours and lay claims to no rights, not even minimum wages. They must surrender their wives and daughters to satisfy high-caste animal lust. Laws are ineffective. "The laws themselves harbour caste prejudices" (Jain 1982, 327).

The Constitution (article 338) provides for a Commissioner for Scheduled Castes and Scheduled Tribes. His task is to be the conscience of the nation in this vital and pressing task of the transformation of Indian society. But report after report of the commission and commissioner bear witness to the helpless and pitiable level to which the political and administrative elite have reduced the status of this conscience-keeper. The annual reports of the commissioner to the president of India are a record of bewailings and beseechings. The commissioner is given neither sufficient personnel nor resources to do his work, and he is treated with indifference and contempt. The reports also list hundreds of examples of district officials, police officials, and higher authorities refusing to take firm and timely action in cases attracting provisions of the Protection of Civil Rights Act (Jain 1982, 328).

CASTE AND CLASS

The question of the relationship between caste and class is intricate. Caste is a burning issue to the ruling class, who own land and capital, employ others, and extract huge surpluses. It is also a burning issue for those who toil and find that their work never wins them an adequate livelihood and that their own organized progress is hampered by the caste divisions and caste wars that exist among them (*Economic and Political Weekly*, February 1979, 223). Hence the debate about the relationship between caste and class. Hence also the questioning of Marxist analysis of Indian society, which is accused of not taking socio-cultural caste as seriously as it takes socioeconomic class. Hence also the discussion on the nature of culture and on the behavior of superstructures.

It is clear that the socioeconomic hierarchy corresponds in general to the caste hierarchy. Thus the whole set-up is "stacked against those whose position is low in the caste hierarchy" (Bhatt 1974, 75). Further, the gap between the upper and the lower castes has widened considerably since British conquest and Independence. This is due to new economic, political, and educational opportunities the upper castes alone could quickly seize; to new and unequal competition; and to consequent uncertainty, all of which act primarily to the disadvantage of the underprivileged.

India has expressed its classes in caste idiom.

> "Today's caste divisions are a carry-over of feudal class divisions. However underpinned caste divisions may be with heredity, ritual, cultural and pollution-conscious practice etc., for the majority of Indians, the material base in relation to land and extraction of surplus from the land is inescapable (*Economic and Political Weekly*, February 1979, 223).

As A. R. Kamath observes, caste is a specific pre-capitalist Indian (Hindu) society, which has "at all times served the dominant social strata as an instrument of economic exploitation, social discrimination and cultural oppression" (Kamath 1979, 354). The vast majority of conflicts and killings relate to disputes over land and wages. The agrarian problem is basic to any discussion on caste and untouchability. Nor is the question of *izzat* (dignity and liberation from insult and sexual abuse) unrelated to the people's economic status. A large number of attacks on *dalits* originate in their refusal to continue to work as serfs, and their demand for the status of modern laborers with settled conditions of work, mobility of labor, 'fair wages, and so on.

Thus the class basis of caste is being uncovered. Both caste and class oppression are sustained by property relations, which lie at the base of the present socio-economic system. It is therefore "sheer deception to think of avoiding untouchability or caste with landlords and monopolists dominating the economy and bourgeois landlord government in power. The caste problem is inevitably merged with the problem of ending the rule of bourgeois landlord class and moving forward to socialism" (Ranadive 1979, 348).

We may say that today it is agreed 1) that caste and class are interlocked realities; 2) that caste has its basis in economics and relations of production and appropriation of surplus; 3) that though a superstructure, caste has its own life and logic and interacts dialectically with its material basis; and 4) that, therefore, as much attention must be paid to the combat against caste as against class. We may even have to deal with the paradox of using caste awareness and caste groupings in order to overcome caste and build up mass organization of all the poor and the exploited across caste lines.

WORLD-WIDE PHENOMENON

The Indian caste system has unique features. But India is not the only place where caste-like formations have taken shape. Social scientists remind us that other societies have birth-ascribed social groups considered to be socially inferior through some permanent stigma. Blacks in the United States, the Eta and the Hinin in Japan, and certain blacksmith tribes in East Africa are examples. The ancient Egyptians, Iranians, and medieval Japanese evolved well-known caste orders. The Prussian Junkers revealed many caste-like traits. The feudal division of medieval Europe resembled superficially the three *varnas* of the *Rgveda*. After the twelfth century entrance into the nobility was only through birth or through royal grace, which was rarely given. Higher clerical offices were preempted by the younger sons of noble families. Church hierarchy was closed to all who were not of noble birth. R. H. Tawney quotes a medieval "theologian" who divided the church into three parts: preachers, defenders, and laborers. He argued that "if one took the service of another and left his own proper work," that would be disservice, contrary to what Christ has ordained (Tawney 1948, 37-38). Such thoughts were repeated as late as 1903 by Pope Pius X, who wrote: "In the order of human society as established by God there are rulers and ruled, employers and employees, rich and poor, learned and ignorant, nobility and the proletariat" (Pius X 1903). Even today such ideas have only been partially overcome among Christians.

The social order in Palestine in the time of Jesus exhibited features comparable to some of the characteristics of India's caste system. It was a hierarchical order descending from a sacred and secular ruling aristocracy at the top through a powerful upper class, also secular and religious, to the poorer masses of peasants, pliers of low and despised trades, the indebted, the unemployed, and the slaves. Much in this hierarchy was determined by birth, much by profession, and much by notions of ritual purity and pollution (Jeremias 1969).

THE MIND OF JESUS

FRIEND OF THE OUTCAST

With a firm hand Jesus set aside the entire system of taboos based on ideas of purity and pollution of races, contacts, and occupations. He associated with outcasts of every sort: publicans, prostitutes, lepers, Samaritans, the common working-class people. He asked no questions about payment of tithes or observance of purity rules. He touched the lepers and let prostitutes and women with hemorrhage touch him. He sat in the homes of tax collectors and sinners, with those whose moral conduct or disreputable profession made them ritually unclean and social outcasts. He ate with them and made them welcome in his own home, to the horror and anger of the Pharisees.

In disregard of a whole tradition of treating Samaritans as untouchables, Jesus asks for and accepts water from a Samaritan woman. Taking food and water with or from untouchables is the last contamination for a caste man in India. That is what Jesus would do, were he here; he would defy social traditions and religious sanctions. We would have to look for him in the huts of the *dalits*, in the colonies of outcasts outside the village. It is from among the poor, the working class, the outcasts, and the sinners that he gathers his disciples and close circle of friends. He thinks that the social rejects, the rejected stones, are the best foundation for a finer future for our world. In his situation, and in ours, his behavior was subversive, disruptive of the old caste-infected mind-set and social fabric, and constructive of a new order of free and equal people. Jesus comes as a new wine pouring itself into the old wine skins of our stupid prejudices and heartless traditions in order to explode them and make room for the new world that free and equal men and women can create. By associating with the "least of these" he set them free; he recognized their humanity, acknowledged their dignity, and affirmed their worth. He awakened their selfhood, rebuilt their pride, and assured them of their status as daughters, sons, and citizens before God. He challenged them to live accordingly in open freedom and to refuse every enslavement.

The ideology of spiritual superiority and holier karma yielding high-caste birth is held up to ridicule. Its hollowness is exposed without pity. Two men went up to the Temple to pray. One was a pure upper-caste man, the other a polluting *candala*. The pure-caste man told God how good he was, how much better than the other man, for unlike the other he knew the *Vedas*, recited the mantras, and revered brahmins. The *candala* stood far away outside the Temple precincts, bowed his head, beat his breast, and confessed himself an impure outcaste due to his evil karma and sought God's mercy. This man God befriended, said Jesus, not the other. Everyone who exalts himself and considers himself spiritually superior, karma-wise higher and caste-wise upper, is, in God's estimate, of low human quality and least promising for the future of the earth. The promises are with those who have known the cruelty of caste and the pain of class oppression and are, therefore, capable of dreaming a new and different dream for humankind. The promises are with those who opt to suffer and struggle with and for the deprived, despised, and rejected outcastes (Lk 18:9-14; 14:11; Mt 23:12; 20:6).

That is why Jesus said to the Pharisees: "Tax collectors and prostitutes are making their way into the Kingdom of God before you." The lowly receive in faith and hope the good news Jesus is announcing. It is in fact to the poor, the lame, and the oppressed, to those who are supposed to have an evil karma, that the good news is directed, offered, given. It is to the little ones, the unlearned, and the simple that the Father reveals his heart and best wishes for our world. From the erudite and clever scribes and from the rich and powerful aristocracy God keeps these things hidden (Mt 11:1-4, 25-28; Lk 4:18). The little ones are the socially powerless and defenseless, who have no status, who do not count, who are not allowed the freedom that is everybody's birthright. Significantly, in the Lukan infancy narratives, it is the most despised of outcasts, the shepherds, who are chosen to be the first to hear and see what kings and prophets have longed in vain to hear and see.

INVERSION

The last shall be first. Reversal is a major theme in the Christian scriptures. Even before the call of the shepherds is narrated, Luke presents in the Song of Mary a succinct theology of subversion, which then overarches the rest of the story till the Crucified is appointed Lord and Lifegiver. In this song, sung by a working-class woman whose son was oppressed and killed by the ruling class for the stand he took on behalf of the outcast masses of the people, God is shown as standing the world on its head and turning the social order upside-down. God is one who dethrones the ruling classes and high castes and puts the *dalits* in charge of history. God brushes the aristocracy aside and concerns himself with the wretched of the earth. God and history bypass those who make a dash for seats of honor, or rush to reserve for themselves seats of prestige and power in the kingdom, or start a dispute as to who is the greatest, noblest, holiest, or high caste. We disputed among ourselves furiously in Kerala, in Tamilnadu, in Gujarat, in Bihar. Jesus called a *paraya* and a *chamar* and said, if you do not become converted to the side of these little ones and the promise they hold, you shall never see your humanity completed. They brought some *bhangis* and *dusadhs* to Jesus, and we the upper caste said, "No, do not educate them, educate us; do not give them land, they will pollute it, give it all to us." Jesus was angry and he said . . . But who heard what he said?

When, therefore, you give a party for the wedding of your dentist son, on the occasion of your ordination as priest, or the anniversary of your episcopal consecration, or the golden jubilee of your profession as religious, do not invite all the priests and brahmins, the commissioners and the collectors, the well-fed neighbors and silked and scented angels; rather, invite the poor, the (socially and physically) crippled, the blind, those who cannot invite you back, who are not allowed to draw water from the village well or to wash and clothe themselves decently (Lk 14:7-11; Mk 9:35-37, 10:35-40; Lk 9:46-48, 1:51; 16:15). To welcome a little outcaste is to welcome me, says Jesus; it is to welcome God. A hard saying, surely; rude and offensive language; unacceptable. But that is what Jesus is saying.

DEMOLITION OF A MYTH

The myth of pure ancestry too is unmasked. Even if the claim to biological purity of blood were true and demonstrable, what human value does it have for history and what spiritual value in the sight of God? When a crowd sitting around told him that his mother and brothers were standing outside and asking for him, Jesus made a reply that carries a profound challenge to anybody, Hindu or Christian, who thinks in terms of purity of race or nobility of birth. Anyone who does God's will is, to Jesus, brother and sister and mother. The given, the biological-natural is set aside and transcended. The historical commitment to the doing of God's will on this earth alone counts as a basis of relationship to Jesus and to God. In such historical commitment to overcome what is antihuman and to build up people from their physical, material basis upward, all the oppressed can cross the dividing lines created by erroneous thinking and socio-religious mystification; they can unite in God's kingdom as God's family sharing his Bread of life (Mk 3:31-35; Mt 25:36-46, 6:9-13).

In John 8, some of Jesus' Jewish listeners decline the offer of freedom Jesus makes through the gift of his word and truth. They decline it on the grounds that as descendants of Abraham they have always been free. Once more Jesus shifts the argument from the plane of natural relationship to the plane of historical relationship. Abraham's true descendants are those, and only those, who stand in the line of Abraham's obedience to the will of God. Those seeking to kill Jesus because of his obedience to God in serving God's dispossessed people could not be Abraham's descendants but the devil's.

We must appreciate the fact that it was not easy for the early Christians to understand and follow the mind of Jesus; neither is it easy for us. A clear enough grasp of his mind after his death is presented in the Acts as a fresh and shocking revelation. One noon Peter, hungry and looking forward to his meal, had a vision of all sorts of animals, accompanied with a word that bade him kill and eat. He refused because he had never eaten anything unclean and profane. (We know that the animals refer symbolically not to food but to people.) Jesus had indicated that food has nothing to do with the goodness or badness of the human heart. It is words and actions that spring from the heart that spell out the quality of the human. Jesus had also befriended and moved with people generally considered impure. The point Jesus makes is that God has made and declared all men and women pure. And now Peter lands on the same conviction. "You know it is forbidden for Jews to mix with people of another race and visit them, but God has made it clear to me that I must not call anyone profane or unclean.... The truth that I have now come to realize is that God has no favorites, but that anybody of any nationality who fears God and does what is right is acceptable to him" (Acts 10 and 11). This Christian position cuts the root of casteism and racism and inaugurates an open universal history.

BREAKING THE CULTURE OF SILENCE

Like all oppression, caste also creates and imposes a culture of silence. The outcastes may not only not complain of torture, exploitation, and rape, they may not speak at all. They are prevented from talking, from expressing their dissent or their creativity, from singing their own songs or telling their own story. A significant part of Jesus' work was an attack upon this culture. He loved to touch the eyes, the ears, and the tongues of people with physical impairments in order to unlock them and enable them to see reality, to hear people's cries, and to speak up. It is when people are possessed, owned, bonded, enslaved, and oppressed by satanic social forces and their human agents that they lose their identity and their name, lose their vision or have their eyes punctured and sealed, lose the use of their mind and their tongue. Jesus breaks into such situations with exorcism and liberation followed by the sound of new human voices rising in protest, claiming rights, affirming life, and celebrating community. This was Jesus' praxis of liberative education, and it poses questions to our practice. The vital question is: Whom are we equipping with word and voice, and with what social results?

A LOWLY SLAVE: AN OUTCASTE

We must pass beyond what Jesus taught and stood for. We must consider what he *became* in our world and is becoming now. In our society, infected by caste and class, Jesus becomes a slave, an oppressed person, an outcaste. An ancient Christian hymn, which Paul quotes, speaks of Jesus emptying himself of high, divine status and glory, and assuming the condition of the lowliest in his society, living at that level the weakness of our earthly existence, and accepting death by crucifixion, the ignominious death of a criminal or slave. We could say he refused to grasp at power, prestige, privilege, and profit; he refused to side with their votaries. Instead, he chose to be a *dalit*, a *paraya*, the lowest among the outcastes. And as such he was wantonly insulted, harassed, and killed by the landlords' hirelings. Is such language offensive? We know that the proclamation of a crucified Messiah and of salvation through the cross has always been a scandal to the Jews and stupidity to the Greeks. To those who have faith, however, Jesus and his humiliated people are God's saving wisdom and power. God raises them on high. He gives a name to the nameless. In their hands he places our history, and in the heart of their death he lets our earth's future unfold (Phil 2:5-11).

THE REJECTED STONE

The destitute of India, almost half the population, and the untouchables in particular, together with the deprived tribes, the bonded laborers, and the prisoners of our jails and brothels are the rejects of society. Their rejection is structural and permanent, and it is renewed daily, thus increasing and refining the cruelty of our ancient exploitative system. These human beings are used daily for profit and pleasure, and daily discarded. The experience of rejection, central to their life, is central to the life of Jesus too, so much so that John's gospel includes it among the main themes in his prologue: "He came to his own domain and his own people did not accept him." The synoptics too emphasize this theme from the start. Jesus came to his hometown and taught in the synagogue, but the people would not accept him. They found him too ordinary; they knew him as a carpenter; they knew his mother, his brothers, and his sisters. At one point in their discussion with him, "They sprang to their feet and hustled him out of the town," intending to throw him down a precipice. Jesus was deeply affected by this rejection. He could work no miracles there. He reflected that a prophet is only despised in his own country and his own house. "So they seized him and killed him and threw him out of the vineyard" is a line in one of his parables; it is likely that in his mind he was himself this killed and thrown out son. For, immediately afterward, he recalls a word from a psalm about "the stone rejected by the builders that became the keystone" (Jn 1:11, 5:43; Lk 4:16-30; Mk 6:1-6, 12:1-11; Ps 118:22-23).

OUTSIDE THE CAMP

Rejected and thrown out of the vineyard and out of the town, Jesus finds himself outside the walls where the untouchables are forced to live and suffer. He finds himself among the external groups, those pushed out of society and excluded from its wealth and culture which, however, they have worked to create. "So Jesus suffered outside the gate to sanctify the people with his own blood" (Heb 13:11-12). This is witness of special interest and relevance to our situation. In Jewish worship animal blood was brought into the sanctuary by the high priest for the atonement of sin, while the bodies of the slaughtered animals were burned outside the camp. The "camp" meant Jerusalem (Buchanan 1972, 234-35). It meant the establishment. It stood for the power of the nobility and the orthodoxy of the religious elite. It represented what was deemed sacred, pure, and favored by God. That is why carcasses, which caused defilement, had to be taken outside the city and burned. The Christian witness is that Jesus in his suffering life and death does not belong with the holy city, its nobility, purity, and orthodoxy. He belongs to the realm outside; he belongs to the region of carcasses and of defilement, which is a realistic description of the life of many an outcaste group. He suffered as an outcaste, cast out of Jerusalem as a polluting carcass, as a blasphemer, a sinner, a seducer, a breaker of sacred traditions and purity laws, a friend of publicans and harlots.

Jesus suffered outside the camp in order to disclose, proclaim, and affirm the inborn dignity and the native purity of all our castes. All who would participate in the freeing and life-giving love and struggle of Jesus will have to seek him outside the city, with the lost, the lowliest, and the least. With Jesus we go out of the old cities and establishments of self-righteous poses, frozen orthodoxies, and oppressive power. We go out of debasing conceptions about God and humans, and about untouchables and touchables. We quit the old bastions of religious legitimation for antihuman economic and political systems. In fact, we leave behind all the ancient religiosities with their temples, sacrifices, and priests with their arrogance and ambiguities and "almighty gods," and go to join Jesus outside the camp to discover in him a new, surprising God, an outcaste, crucified.

BECAME FLESH

In the light of all this, the witness of John's gospel about God's word becoming flesh takes on new significance. In biblical tradition flesh may mean the body, the soul, the heart, or the human being; it can denote all living creatures as well as humanity. But every time these realities are called flesh, an accent falls on their weakness, fragility, and transitoriness (1 Kgs 2:27; Ps 6:1, 84:2, 136:25; Is 40:5-7; Gn 6:12-16; Mt 24:22; Mk 13:20). Flesh or flesh-and-blood may also mean various natural relationships such as woman (Gn 2:23), family (Gn 2:25), township (Jdg 9:2). This suggests the social nature of *flesh*, which can therefore signify corporate personality. Flesh carries the idea of special social bonds with the weak brother, as in Isaiah 58:7, to clothe the man you see to be naked and not turn from your own flesh (kin). Thus flesh also comes to signify sensitivity, the opposite of hardness and stubbornness, the ability to register and respond to human or divine reality. One of God's great promises is to remove from our bodies the heart of stone and give us a heart of flesh instead (Ezek 11:19, 36:26). Caste is a heart of stone. Jesus has a heart of flesh. He is flesh, sensitivity, and loving compassion, carrying in his corporate personality all flesh, all who are weak and vulnerable, the powerless multitude of the wretched of the earth. That is the Word of God become flesh.

The self-emptying and the scandal consist not so much in the Word becoming a human being but that the Word became a powerless, rejected human being, that this outcast is the disclosure of a suffering and oppressed God who is one with the untouchables and outcastes of all times everywhere. *Flesh* in John's prologue is not only a theological word; it is a sociological term giving historical content to theology. There are no socially neutral human beings in history; human beings are ruling or ruled classes, agents or victims of injustice, and high or low caste or outcaste. John is here expressing the same thought as Paul expresses in Philippians 2 and 2 Corinthians 8. The word was made flesh; Christ made himself poor; he assumed the condition of a slave. Matthew's witness to the same truth is in his story of the Magi, where Jesus is, from the start, a condemned person and a refugee. Luke's symbols for the same faith are the manger in which the infant Jesus was laid because there was no room in the inn, in the poverty of his Temple presentation, and in the prophecy about his rejection and his mother's anguish. John too frames the flesh-becoming of the Word in the context of rejection. His basic witness may be rendered in our context thus: And the Word was made an outcaste, a *candala*, a *paraya*; he lives in the *jhuggis* outside the village and in the hovels in the slums of our city; we have experienced his presence and his greatness, the unique greatness of God's son, which consists in the authentic graciousness of identifying himself with the wretched of the earth and the judgment passed thereby on the power structures that so degrade the children of God.

When, therefore, Jesus presses us to eat his flesh and drink his blood, his meaning may go beyond acceptance of his revelation and beyond ritual eucharistic practices. It may mean further, and more pointedly, the necessity of assimilating vitally and making our own his entire person enfleshed or embodied in his historical-social options; that is, we must identify ourselves with his powerless and rejected condition; we must live and struggle with and for the millions to whom life is scarcely permitted, whose bread of life is daily taken away and who are massacred and burnt at the slightest sign they show of movement, growth, or dignity. Jesus made their cause his own and worked so that they might have life and have it in all its abounding fullness. In his commitment he becomes their bread of life.

Sharing His Insult

The insults heaped on Jesus are symbolic of the permanent load of insult to which the poor and the untouchables are subjected in our society. When Jesus declared sins forgiven the scribes said he was blaspheming. That accusation will be repeated again on various grounds. When he mingled with the common people and the working class and tax collectors, he was criticized and implicitly charged with defilement. If he did not fast according to rule and custom, as in fact he did not, he was questioned and required to explain himself. And not grasping his answers, his critics called him a glutton and a drunkard. For pointing out the human meaning of the sabbath and using it to make broken people whole, he was threatened with annihilation (Mk 2:5-7, 15-17, 18-19, 23-28, 3:1-6; Mt 11:18-19). When Jesus freed people from the grip of alienating forces and evil spirits he was painted as an evil magician in league with Satan. His enemies never scrupled to hurt him with calumnies. They said Jesus himself was possessed by unclean spirits. "You are a Samaritan," they said, "and possessed by a devil. . . . We know for certain that you are possessed" (Mk 3:22-30; Jn 8:48-52). They plagued him with tricky questions to test him, hoping to catch him in some unguarded word, and questioned his credentials for acting as freely as he did. The rulers despised Jesus as an untrained rabbi and objected to him as an irregular teacher who had received no instruction from any recognized master (Jn 7:14-18; Brown 1966, 316). The crowd, however, was divided in their estimate of Jesus. Some said that he was a good man. Others said that he was leading the people astray. And many said that he was raving, and called him a mad man (Jn 7:11-12, 20, 10:19). And finally the Pharisees declared Jesus a sinner and an imposter. The case of Jesus is but an example of the calculated insults and false charges the established system hurls at the socially defenseless in order to repress them when they begin to express new thoughts and suggest changes in social and property relations. The experience of the outcastes and the experience of Jesus coincide. In them, Jesus is still being insulted, persecuted, and tortured.

Godforsaken

The high point of such coincidence of experience is the experience of godforsakenness. The history of the *dalits* gives little or no evidence of God's love, concern, justice, presence, or existence. The dispossessed outcastes of India have known no god who is good, awake, or blissful, who is truthful, thoughtful, and hope-giving. They have been dominated and destroyed by utterly heartless and cruel gods. They are determined to wipe all such gods off the face of the earth—all Molochs and Mammons who fatten on human life and establish their thrones on human helplessness and misery. And in that Jesus is their ally. A major part of Jesus' service is work for the abolition of all antihuman gods, all those monsters that are more interested in magnificent temples for themselves, with elaborate priesthoods and expensive sacrifices, rather than in the plight of slaves, the dignity of outcastes, land for the landless, food and tenderness for children, and hope of a more human future for all.

Jesus shares in the historical experience of godlessness common to all the oppressed. In the last hour of his life, as he hung on the cross, rejected by his people, he realized that the God he had loved and served all his days, in whose name he had spoken and taken sides, had now abandoned him. He cried out, "My God, my God, why have you deserted me?" Nothing less than that anguished cry can represent the experience of India's millions of untouchables. Within that experience, all the classical, traditional ideas of God die and disappear. Good riddance! The old gods and religions have to go or be abolished for their crimes against the *harijans*. These gods are unworthy and incapable of the future of the outcastes. But within this barren godlessness, the lineaments of a new divine Face begin to show, the Face of the Crucified God, the oppressed God of the oppressed, whose very agony undermines and shatters the thrones of Powers and Dominations. There, in the heart of death and triumphant injustice, a fresh hope — a vision of a new earth founded on equality and freedom and love. That means in the heart of godlessness a new faith comes to birth. The atheism of Jesus was the place of a new revelation, the womb of a new faith. So it is now in India with the godlessness the *dalits* experience. That is why we must leave the old behind and go out to Jesus and to all those outside the camp, sharing in their degradation no less than in their godforsakenness, but with the unspeakable hope of being met by the Father who raised the outcast Jesus from the dead.

THE TASK

Conversion

The fact that Jesus is one of the oppressed, and God in him is made an outcast, pleads with our hearts to be converted from caste practices and be cleansed of caste mentality. Let our mind and spirit reflect Jesus', "Who did not cling to his equality with God but emptied himself to assume the condition of a slave."

Jesus chose to be an outcast not to approve the system, not to legitimate *varna*, not to give it any divine sanction. Quite the contrary. Jesus became one with the outcasts in order to awaken them to the fact that he was challenging the system, to enable them to join him in setting aside the rules, to create within their own mutual relationships an exchange of recognition, affirmation, and honor, to show them how God was with them, to stimulate them to discover the revolutionary meaning with which their suffering was replete, and to summon them to stand together on the basis of their shared suffering in order to say a clear no to oppression, relativize all human powers, authorities, rituals, and laws, and stand as a sign of the liberation God wills for the people. The method of Jesus was not sidereal but incarnational, not metaphysical-absolute-idealist but concrete-historical-social. He worked from within the situation to be transformed.

REVOLUTION

In thus challenging the existing social order and in working for its radical transformation, we are only linking up with and reinforcing meaningful historical movements within the country. Protest movements against caste have been frequent throughout Indian history. M. N. Sriniwas says,

> These rebel sects, rejected the idea of brahminical supremacy, the performance of elaborate rituals and the punctilious observance of rules of pollution and purity, and they instead emphasised the love of God and right conduct as indispensable to salvation. It is not surprising that protest sects attracted followers from a wide range of castes, from rebel brahmins to untouchables. . . . Caste and anti-caste are both parts of a single phenomenon and those who wish to root the idea of human dignity and equality in Indian soil would do well to go to these historical sources of protest and build on them

Solidarity with the downtrodden is an essential constituent of the Christian church. It is in choosing to be identified with them that the coming kingdom is discerned, met, and served. It is in their life, suffering, and struggles sincerely shared that we meet Jesus. Without participation in their pain, we scarcely keep the memory of the Lord's death in the scriptures and in the Eucharist. For the untouchables are the passion of Jesus. They are the Good Friday we grieve over with reverence and hope. They are the crucifixion of the Son of Man, the Son of God, today. No Christian faith is possible in India today without identification with them and commitment to their resurrection from the tombs in which they are now held, guarded by the musclemen of the ruling castes and classes according to the law and otherwise. Let us then go to Jesus and to all those outside the camp, bearing his and their shame, instead of running after those whom God shuns, those who use their power, science, religion, and high birth to oppress, enslave, and then legitimize it all. That these great ones were bypassed by the Jesus movement in its earliest formation and in its life for some two to three centuries is a fact to be pondered; it is of theological significance and of practical consequence.

By the deliberate act of God these people were called to become the core of the world's greatest redemptive revolution. The existing things, including people "of substance," were nullified precisely by these despised nothings (Orr and Walther 1976, 161).

THE LANGUAGE OF THE CROSS

The untouchables and the destitutes of our country are the crucifixion expressed. The suffering of the outcastes is immense. It can break them completely and crush their spirits. But it can also be a healthening and strengthening experience historically necessary to build up the unity, vitality, and courage of the oppressed as a whole. Historically, providentially, their suffering is the fire in which the bricks of tomorrow's finer society are baking, in which its steel is tempering. The signs are that this is happening. Suffering has been maturing the oppressed, who no longer see their plight as intractable fate but as human creation, something they can tackle, and use, and forge into a sword with which to sever the chains that hold them in bondage. How do we Christians and our organized churches view and relate to the sufferings of outcast people? How do we relate to their new awareness and to their firmness of purpose and the dangerous forward steps they are taking? Are we anxious at the prospects of losing material for proselytism for Christianity? Or at the prospects of a revolution that will sweep away our bourgeois institutions and the bourgeois culture in which we nestle? Or are we glad their liberation is at hand? Are we ready to repent, and receive the good news, and support their struggle, and underscore the Christ-meaning of their suffering?

ACTION

Biblical thought, which shocks Indian society by confronting us with a God who is one with outcastes has consequences for social practice. It summons us to press for fundamental alterations in patterns of social relations, and therefore in relations of production, in ownership of land, in industrial policies, in the designing of national education, in the distribution of social power. It is within action for such changes and the resultant beginnings of new relations that God's will is done and his reign keeps coming.

The resources of the church, however limited, precisely because they are limited, have to be mobilized for the service, defense, sensitizing, and organizing of the most deprived and despised sectors of the population. It has to muster up all its faith resources to make a clear preferential option for the outcaste, to withdraw from institutions, commitments, and services that consolidate the class and caste structure of a repressive and unjust social tradition. We need to gather all our spiritual strength to stand by the Crucified in the conflictual situation his gospel creates without anxiety about minority status, or the future of proselytism, or acceptance by upper castes and classes. We believe that the cross is the place where the new humanity begins to bud. It is the cross of the outcaste that bears the promise of the new earth and the new India with a human heart, a heart of flesh, sensitive to the all-encompassing Brahman, and realizing collegiality at all levels of life and relationships.

REFERENCES

Ambedkar, B. R. 1969. *The Untouchables*, Bharatiya Boudha Shiksa, U.P.
Bhatt, A. 1974. "Caste Class and Politics: An Empirical Profile of Caste Classifi-

cation in Modern India." Delhi. In J. Maliekal. 1981. *Caste in India Today.* CSA Publications, Bangalore.

Brown, R. 1966. *The Gospel According to John*, vol. 1, The Anchor Bible, Doubleday & Company, New York.

Buchanan, G. W. 1972. *Epistle to the Hebrews*, Anchor Bible, Doubleday & Company, New York.

Das, Bhagwan. 1971. In B. R. Ambedkar, *Annihilation of Caste*, 3d ed. (first published 1936). Bheem Patrika Publications, Jullunder.

Gandhi, M. K. 1954. *The Removal of Untouchability*, Ahmedabad.

———. 1958. *The Story of My Experiments with Truth*, Navjivan Publishing House, Ahmedabad.

Ghose, S. 1973. *Socialism, Democracy and Nationalism in India*, Bombay.

Jain, L. C. 1982. "Emancipation of Scheduled Castes and Tribes: Some Suggestions," *Economic and Political Weekly* 16 (February 28, 1982).

Jeremias, J. 1969. *Jerusalem in the Time of Jesus*, SCM, London.

Kamath, A. R. 1979. "The Emerging Situation," *Economic and Political Weekly*, February 1979.

Orr, W. E., and J. A. Walther. *1 Corinthians*, Anchor Bible, Doubleday & Company, New York.

Pius X. 1903. *Motu Proprio "Fin dalla Prima."* In *All Things in Christ: Encyclicals and Selected Documents of Saint Pius X*, 1954, p. 208.

Ranadive, B. T. 1979. "Caste, Class and Property Relations," *Economic and Political Weekly* 14 (February 1979).

Sriniwas, M. N. 1979. "Future of Indian Caste," *Economic and Political Weekly* (February 1979).

Tawney, R. H. 1948. *Religion and the Rise of Capitalism*.

Vidyarthi, L. P., and N. Mishra. 1977. *Harijan Today: Sociological, Economic, Political, Religious and Cultural Analysis*, New Delhi.

9

Toward an Indian Theology of Liberation

SEBASTIAN KAPPEN

There is as yet no distinctive school of thought among Indian Christians that may be called a theology of liberation. Instead, there are gropings toward a new interpretation of the gospel prompted by the Second Vatican Council and the exigencies of organized action for social justice. No attempt has been made to define the specificity of the Indian approach to liberation theology. The present essay, therefore, is bound to be more prescriptive than descriptive; that is, it explores the lines theologizing must take to be fully contextual and truly responsive to the challenge of transformative action on society.

A CIVILIZATIONAL CRISIS

Profound changes are taking place in the Indian sub-continent affecting its social institutions, culture, and world-view. With the advances of science, technology, and modern education, the world above of the sun, the moon, and the stars has shed its aura of divinity and has collapsed into the human world below. The same fate has befallen the earth, the trees, the rivers, and the waters of the sea. From being deities of fertility, these have become mere raw materials for human labor, thereby also part of human history. Much in the same manner, social and cultural institutions have lost the status they have hitherto enjoyed of being divinely willed, immutable realities. They are being recognized for what they are: humanity's handiwork which people can remake or unmake at will. This new awareness created the mental climate for popular struggles against oppressive social structures. Such struggles at once presuppose and generate the consciousness in the masses that they are the creators of their own future. Involved here is the historic transition from cyclic to historical time. Temporality begins to follow the rhythm not of cosmic processes but of human decisions. This mutation in self-awareness and world awareness is a universal phenomenon affecting people all over the world. What is specific to India is the telescoping of historical processes that elsewhere took centuries to reach maturity, so that the future becomes present before the present has receded into the past, resulting in an anguishing conflict between the old and the new.

The absorption of natural history into human history and the transition from cyclic to human historical time carry with them a revolution in the way humans conceive the Divine. They can no longer look for it in a mysterious world above or around. They must seek it in history, in temporality to which they themselves give name and form.

This, admittedly, is an anticipatory extrapolation. The common people by and large still cling to traditional conceptions of the Divine. Besides, since cyclic time will never be fully absorbed into linear, and since the cosmic will always maintain a certain residual autonomy in relation to the human, the religiosity proper to the former will not entirely vanish; it will be both negated and preserved.

But where in history do we encounter the Divine? The Divine comes to us both as gift and challenge. As gift, in the experience of beauty, love, friendship, and togetherness. Though confined within the bounds of the here-and-now, such experiences open a window into that which is beyond the beyond. The Divine confronts us as a challenge when through historical situations it demands that we break loose from all fetters and march forward to the unknown, hoping against hope. Both theophanies are mediated by history and call for an appropriate answer. The gift requires that we safeguard and preserve it for the future; the challenge must issue in transformative action that re-creates ourselves and the world. The two responses complete and enrich each other. The person who has not experienced the absoluteness of beauty, love, and community will seldom revolt against conditions of ugliness, oppression, and the fragmentation of the human. Similarly, whoever ignores the challenge of creating the future is likely to miss the annunciation of the Divine in the present. The twofold response of humans we call *theandric practice.* In it are blended contemplation and action, celebration and creation, safeguarding and subverting, memory and hope, self-transformation and world transformation. It is in theandric practice and what it brings into being that the gift-call of the Divine becomes flesh. If so, revelation is, in a sense, humankind's historical task. Humans have as much to create the truth about the Divine as they have to discover it.

Lest I introduce too complex a perspective, in what follows I shall focus on the transformative character of theandric practice.

THE CRY OF THE POOR AND THE MARGINALIZED

In order to further define the call of the Divine at this critical juncture in our history, it is necessary to examine the social system as a whole and the conflicting forces at work in it. Since a detailed social analysis is not possible here, I shall confine myself to pointing out the main problems facing the country.

What we have in India is a form of dependent capitalism characterized by vast concentration of the means of production (agricultural and industrial) in a few hands. Though it has contributed to the development of the productive forces, capitalism has created wide disparities in income and opportunity, which have only increased since Independence. While the top ten percent of the population live in relative affluence, forty-seven percent are doomed to live below subsistence level. Economist Ranjit Sau sums up the results of capitalist development thus far:

> Nine-tenths of India's population are left behind in economic backwaters. Mass poverty is on the rise; the net availability of the most basic human necessities per capita such as foodgrains and clothing is scarce; rural indebtedness has multiplied; unemployment and underemployment have reached the level of 20.8 million person-years (Sau 1981, 77).

To this must be added the proliferation of slums, the marginalization of tribals and the outcastes, the destruction of traditional handicrafts, and the ecological ravages wrought by profit-oriented production.

On the political front, the affluent classes—the landlords, the rich capitalist peasants, and the medium and big bourgeoisie—are able to use democratic institutions to their own purposes. They manipulate elections, create powerful lobbies in the assemblies and the parliament, corrupt the bureaucracy, and control local self-government bodies. What is more, political power has become highly centralized, reducing people's participation to the minimum and denying states and ethnic groups their legitimate autonomy.

Deeper than the economic and the political is the cultural crisis, which has its matrix in the conflict between tradition and a bourgeois modernity transplanted here from outside. At one extreme of the cultural spectrum is the traditional casteist culture coupled with an obsolete religiosity; at the other is bourgeois modernity in its pure form patronized by sections of the westernized urban elite. In between is a hybrid culture that combines the worst elements of tradition and the capitalist values of private interest, competition, aggressivity, and consumerism (Kappen 1984). It is this monstrous un-culture that holds sway over the vast majority of the Indian people. It has vitiated the well-springs of societal life and has ushered in an era of moral decadence and universal corruption. Under its spell every social reality begets its evil, grotesque shadow. White money has its counterpart in black money, genuine goods in adulterated ones, true ownership in false ownership, bourgeois democracy in mafia politics, the written law in the unwritten law of might and manipulation, genuine religion in the worship of spurious god-men and god-women.

The challenge that faces the Indian people is clear: to restructure the economy in such wise that production for profit is replaced by production for social needs; to give power back to the people so that they mold their own lives; to create a counterculture consonant with the dignity of the human being and with the positive values of tradition. This last task must receive the highest priority in the Indian context, where no genuine sociopolitical revolution is possible without a preceding cultural revolution. But who will bring about these changes? Gandhism is a spent force today and has degenerated into all but a mere cult. The parties of the left have been absorbed into the politics of power and into the bastardized culture in vogue (Kappen 1985a). It is to fill this political vacuum that grassroots groups have sprung up all over India. Once in the field, the Christian activists among them experienced the contradiction between commitment to the unconditional call of the Divine enfleshed in the historical situation and the kind of theology they had inherited. Liberation theology in India is an attempt to solve that contradiction.

A FOUNDATIONAL THEOLOGY OF LIBERATION

The self-revelation of the Divine made concrete in the contemporary historical situation is addressed to all, irrespective of religious affiliation. Hence the possibility of, and the need for, a foundational theology of liberation that cuts across the barriers of religions and ideologies. Understood thus, theology is committed, critical reflection on the historical self-manifestation of the Divine as gift-call, and on the human response to it. Let me explain the terms. The theme of theology is not God. *God* is a loaded word implying a personal supreme being. As such, it is a product of earlier theology. Hence the term *the Divine* is preferred as it can better express what is neither personal nor impersonal but transpersonal. But the theme of theology is not the Divine as it is *in itself* but as it reveals itself to men and women in history and bodies forth in theandric practice. Seen from this angle, all genuine theology is liberative, as the divine gift-call and the human practice it provokes issue in freedom *from* every alienation and freedom *for* love, communion, and creativity.

On this ongoing theandric practice theologians are called to *reflect*. Reflection involves a conceptual element. This is not so much theologians' strength as their weakness, for their theme can more adequately be expressed in the multidimensional language of symbols (poetry, drama, music, painting, sculpture, dance, etc.) than in the unidimensional language of concepts. Hence future theology will have to recapture the poetic-symbolic language of parables of Jesus and the dialogues of the Buddha and the *Upanishadic* seers.

Reflection must fulfill a *critical* function, for human beings do not come on the scene with empty minds but with symbols, myths, conceptions, and biases deriving either from their own religious background or from other beliefs and ideologies encountered in day-to-day life. Such presuppositions are generally ambivalent. They may either illumine or throw a veil over reality. Hence the need for criticism aimed at verifying whether the divine gift-call and the human response to it have been correctly interpreted or have been misconstrued due to wrong preconceptions.

Besides being critical, reflection must also be *committed*. The theologians cannot remain neutral in respect to that which they are reflecting on. Doing theology is itself part of the human response to the divine gift-call mediated through history. It is a form of subversive-creative action and is more akin to prophecy than to science. For the same reason the theologian cannot escape the destiny of the cross.

The theology of liberation whose bare outlines I have just delineated is foundational and universal. It is foundational because the revelation of the Divine in the here and now of individual-collective existence and the theandric practice it provokes have an immediacy that revelation in the past does not have. As such, it is the ultimate criterion by which all earlier theologies have to be judged. It is universal, because its theme is accessible to followers of all religions, and even of secular ideologies like Marxism. It is on the basis of this underlying unity that religious and theological pluralism has to be understood.

INDIAN CHRISTIAN THEOLOGY OF LIBERATION

The reflections thus far enable us to define Christian theology of liberation as critical, committed reflection on the gospel in the light of theandric practice and on theandric practice in the light of the gospel. Before elucidating what this means concretely, let me make two preliminary observations.

It is generally believed that the Indian Christians are beings apart, having little in common with Hindus. Such a perception is, in fact, jealously instilled in them by the churches from early childhood. But, anthropologically, they are first Indian and only then Christian. They are children of the soil as much as any Hindu. The deeper recesses of their being reverberate with the collective unconscious of the Indian people. To cite but one instance, though fanatically fond they may be of Christian liturgical music, what strikes the deepest chord in them is often the *gayatri* (hymn to the Sun sung at dawn) peeling forth from the nearby temple. More, from early childhood they are exposed to the symbols, myths, rituals, and conceptions proper to other religions. This makes the average Indian Christian a cross-cultural, cross-religious being. The same holds true of the average Hindu or the Muslim, though to a much smaller degree; they have in varying ways and degrees assimilated ideas, values, and symbols from the Christian tradition. This symbiotic relation among many religions is the living context in which the Indian Christian carries on theological reflection.

My second observation concerns the relation of theologians to the theandric practice they reflect on. In countries like Latin America, where Christians form the majority, theologians and the human community on whose practice they reflect all belong to the Christian fold. That is why Gustavo Gutierrez could define liberation theology as "critical reflection on Christian praxis in the light of the Word" (Gutierrez 1973, 13). This makes little sense in India where the agent of theandric practice necessarily has to be a broader community comprising men and women of different religions and persuasions. It is as one inserted in such ecumenical communities that the Indian Christian does theology. This is not a matter of expediency but is rooted in shared commitment to the humanization of society. In fact, the stirrings of a new theology can be found only among theologians and Christian groups who have broken loose, at least mentally if not also physically, from the ghettos of church institutions and have cast anchor in the secular world.

FROM THEANDRIC PRACTICE TO THE GOSPEL

The first task of any liberation theology in India is to critically reflect on the gospel in the light of our contemporary theandric practice. But the gospels are read by the average Christian with the spectacles provided by tradition. Hence tradition too needs to be critically examined. Theandric practice will help us to distinguish between elements in tradition that are perennially valid and those that have become obsolete, and to criticize away the interpretative accretions that have either covered up or distorted the true meaning of Jesus' life and message. The following are a few important areas where a rethinking is necessary and is already taking place in India, though timidly and gropingly.

1. The intuition that the Divine reveals itself in the challenges and experiences of secular life explodes the notion of a God who spoke his last word two thousand years ago and then, so to speak, retired from the scene. It also subverts the hegemony of the past over the present and confers theandric value on the strivings of our people for a more humane society. Besides, the recognition that the Divine continues to confront humans signals the return of prophecy, which the institution had all but smothered.

2. Theandric practice calls for a revolution in our discourse about the Divine. Traditional theology speaks of God as though it were a subject already known to which predicates may be attributed, as when we say, God is love, God is truth, God is the defender of the orphan and the widow and so on. But this manner of discourse becomes problematic upon realization that the truth about the Divine is what humans have *yet to create* in the course of history. The Divine can be known only as a predicate of the human, as the depth dimension of human history in the making. What we encounter are no more than pointers, invitations to the Divine. This perspective requires that we reformulate our earlier statements and say, Love is divine, Truth is divine, Caring for the widow and the orphan is divine,

and so on. In doing so we are rejoining Gandhi, who wrote that for a long time he used to say, God is truth, but subsequently came to realize he should rather say, Truth is God (*Young India*, December 31, 1931, 427-28). This manner of theological discourse will put an end to the arrogant wordiness of Christian theologians and set the Divine free from the dead concepts in which it has been encapsulated. Further, it will restore to theology its lost credibility. Tell the slum-dwellers of Bombay or Calcutta that God is the defender of the poor, and you are lucky if they don't lay hands on you. Not so if you tell them that when you love one another, when you strive to shake off your shackles, you are under the grip of the Divine.

3. If the self-revelation of the Divine continues in history, the conception of Jesus as definite revelation needs to be revised. Jesus will be seen from now on for what he really is: a unique, intense, hitherto unparalleled manifestation of the transcendent in the immanent, in the flow of history, a sure way and guide to humanity's ultimate future. The metahistorical "Christ" seated at the right hand of the Father will give way to Jesus the Wayfarer on the road to Jerusalem. With that, the worshippers of "Christ" will become once again disciples and followers of Jesus. Putting Jesus back where he belongs, in history, will bring to a close the ideological imperialism Christianity has exercized over non-Christians, because it was the concept of Jesus Christ as the fullness of revelation that begot the theology of conversion and the missiology of conquest. It also served to legitimize colonialism and the imposition of the so-called Christian civilization on other peoples and nations. Not until Christians relinquish their customary stance of self-righteous intolerance will they be able to engage in concerted action for a better world in a religiously pluralist society like India.

4. The standpoint of theandric practice alone can throw light on the personal destiny of Jesus. Experience shows that the struggle against injustice and oppression inevitably exposes one to reprisal from the powers-that-be. The Christian involved in transformative action is therefore better attuned than the worshipping Christian to perceive the truth that Jesus did not just die but was murdered by those intent on maintaining the status quo in Palestine. It was a perverse theology that converted that murder into death, and death into a ritual, and the ritual into a mere steppingstone to resurrection, itself ritualized. It begot a Christianity that for all practical purposes eliminated the cross and the Crucified, a Christianity suited to the affluent West that has "risen and ascended" into the heaven of overconsumption.

5. Only Christians who harken to the Divine's call to march forward from slavery to freedom can grasp the original character of the church as the community of disciples, conscious, like Jesus, of the mission to preach good news to the poor. That community was truly ex-centric, having its center outside itself in the absolute future of humankind. Only those who sought first the kingdom of God and its justice and were prepared to contest the forces of injustice and oppression had a place in it. In contrast, the

current notion of church as a community of worshippers of a Christ who remains supremely neutral before the slave and the master, the exploiter and the exploited, has no foothold in contemporary theandric practice.

6. Since the Second Vatican Council many Christians—priests, nuns, and lay persons—have taken to politicizing and organizing slum-dwellers, the rural poor, and the tribals. In the process they have found it necessary to form wider groups including Marxists and people of other religions. In such groups, members share the same sociopolitical and humanist goals but derive inspiration from different sources, religious or secular. These activist groups already enjoy theological legitimacy insofar as they constitute a response to the Divine call conveyed through the concrete situation. However, Christians cannot but ask whether they have any foundation in the teachings of Jesus. A positive answer may be found in that gospel narrative where, pointing to the crowd that came to listen to him, Jesus said, "These are my mother and my brothers. Whoever does the will of God is brother and sister and mother to me" (Mk 3:34-35). What Jesus envisions here is a community based not on discipleship or on any set of doctrines, rituals, and laws, but solely on doing the will of God which, for him, meant loving one's neighbor in deed. Since its focus is on the reign of God to come, one might call it a basileic community. In religiously pluralist societies like India such communities are a necessary mediation between the Jesus community and the reign of God to come. In truth, the primary mission of the ecclesial community is to create basileic communities.

7. Theandric practice calls for a reappraisal of authority in the church. Where the Divine reveals itself through events and situations, it at the same time *authorizes* those who respond to it. This is authority in its most original, unconditional manifestation. Of it institutionalized authority is but a historical concretization. The latter must derive from and serve the former. More, institutionalized authority can bind and loose only insofar as it lets itself be bound by the call of the kingdom. The same applies to the sacramentality of the ecclesial community. It is sacramental—that is, it signifies and communicates the Divine—only insofar as it, in obedience to the Divine, takes a stand against the forces opposed to the reign of God and is committed to the total liberation of humans. Sacramentality is not a magical prerogative but an ethical quality of the community of believers. Nor is it exclusive to Christians. Basileic communities too are sacramental, even more so than ecclesial communities because they alone constitute effective agents of transformative action.

8. Encounter with the Transcendent as immanent in history undermines the dualism of the sacred and the profane, of the material and the spiritual, which provided the official churches with both a convenient alibi for sordid involvement in the affairs of the world and an excuse for culpable inaction in the face of manifest inhumanity (Kappen 1985b, 97-122). Contemporary Christians are impelled by their secular experience of the Divine to return to the gospels and recapture the holistic perspective of Jesus, who saw the

inbreaking of the kingdom in the visible, tangible realities of history: the blind see, the deaf hear, the oppressed are set free, and the poor take possession of the earth.

We have thus far reflected on some aspects of the gospel and tradition in the light of theandric practice. We shall now reverse the process and direct the searchlight of the gospel to the Indian reality. Here too we must be on guard against certain presuppositions that might vitiate the approach.

FROM THE GOSPEL TO THEANDRIC PRACTICE

Our starting point here must not be just orthodoxy but the gospel already reinterpreted along the lines indicated above. It is here that academic theologians go wrong. They often start out with the assumption that Christianity is a cultic religion and then proceed to integrate into it elements from Hindu rituals.

Thus the estrangement of the prophetic movement of Jesus into a cultic religion as that movement spread to the Greco-Roman world is further accentuated on the Indian soil. As a result, Christianity loses its identity, having nothing specific to offer which Hinduism cannot. Similarly, those theologians who take it for granted that theirs is a religion of individual salvation will end up singing hymns to the notorious religious individualism of the Hindu. Here, again, the specificity of the revelation of the Divine in Jesus is given the go by. It is equally misleading to approach the Indian reality from the standpoint of the so-called mystical Christ. This theological construct along with the notion of "anonymous Christians" enabled Christians to integrate whatever is true and good in non-Christian religions and peoples into their own religious universe. This is Christian imperialism under a new guise, seeking to annex the non-Christian world through an act of ideological aggression, as though to offset the bankruptcy of the theology of conversion. At least so it will be construed by the Hindu population.

We should also get rid of the notion that the gospel is an essential prerequisite for transformative action on Indian society. Long before Christians took the initiative in organizing popular struggles, Indian communists had done so for decades, particularly in Kerala, Andhra, and West Bengal. Hundreds of men and women have laid down their lives in the cause of justice, and only a few among them were Christians. The majority drew inspiration from the situation of oppression itself or from other religions or ideologies. What is essential for transformative action is obedience to the unconditional call of the Divine, though one might not name it so. This is not to devalue the Christian presence in India, but to see it in the proper perspective. What the gospel can bring to the scene is its own power to illumine and to inspire. Its role is one of reinforcing the energies of the new age that are already fermenting in Indian society.

Academic theologians often entertain the notion that secular society follows the cyclic rhythm of institutional life, where nothing new happens. They, therefore, fail to see that society and culture in India are undergoing rapid changes under the impact of science, technology, and the spread of capitalism. Taking the religion of the written scriptures for lived religion, they engage in the futile attempt to salvage traditional elements Hindus themselves have long since left behind. They are even worse off when they take the Sanskritic tradition for the whole of Indian tradition, whereas the former is largely the creation of the dominant castes to protect their own interests (Lobo 1985, 16-28). The temptation is all the greater when the theologian's own standpoint is that of a Christian faith which has itself degenerated into an ideology of the status quo.

With these caveats in mind, let us examine the creative response of the Indian people to the liberating challenge of the Divine from the standpoint of Jesus.

First, the light of the gospel will enable the Christian and the Hindu alike to discern better the working of the Divine in contemporary history. That humankind's self-creation in time-space has a theotic dimension is not something obvious to the average Indian, who is inclined to look for the Divine either in natural phenomena or in the mythical universe of gods and goddesses or in the realm of the metaphysical. If more and more Hindus are beginning to recognize that human history has a religious dimension and religion a historical dimension, it is largely due to the influence of the gospel. In the same way, it is the historic contribution of Christianity to have reminded Indians that authentic religiosity has a social thrust and involves loving one's neighbor irrespective of caste or creed. It has inspired Hindus to start service institutions like hospitals, orphanages, and schools. One may hope that as Christians become progressively radicalized and take up the cause of the exploited, it will open the eyes of Hindus to the realization that authentic belief involves struggle for a humane social order.

Second, the gospel also helps distinguish between authentic and spurious responses to the historically revealed Divine will. Jesus' teaching that where the Divine presents itself in time and space, there the hungry are filled, the thirst for justice quenched, and all shackles fall to the ground, shows that humanization of the world is the only sure index of its divinization. The response of the community bears the stamp of authenticity only if it results in the free and full development of each individual in the community. Theologians will, therefore, be wary of all attempts at social transformation that rely on violence and hatred, that use the masses as mere tools to power, or that sacrifice the individual to some estranged collective will in the hope that society can be restructured through dictates from above. Their sympathies will rather lie with the Gandhian way of nonviolence; this, however, does not rule out organized resistance to unjust structures of power and wealth.

Third, taking the Indian tradition as a whole, the Christian theologian will find a point of insertion for Jesus and his message not so much in the Brahminic scriptures or in the lifestyle of the upper castes as in the tradition of dissent (Kappen 1983; Pieris 1988). The scriptures do contain a theology of liberation (*mukti*). But, at best, what they envisage is the liberation of the individual. They know nothing of the liberation of the human community, much less of nature and history. In this perspective the world of human creation has no ultimate value. Further, that from which liberation is sought is *papa* (sin) or *samsara* (bondage to the cycle of existence), or *avidya* (ignorance). In the Hindu scriptures there is no mention of liberation from social sin in the form of unjust structures or institutions. As to the manner of liberating oneself, the dominant tradition speaks of *karma marga* (the way of action), of *bhakti* (devotion to a personal God), and *jnana* (gnosis). Since structural sin is not recognized, there is no recognition either of collective human striving, let alone struggle, as a valid liberative practice. On the contrary, the scriptures in their present form are geared to maintaining male supremacy and the caste system of institutionalized inequality. They promise human freedom in some heaven above or on the plane of transcendental being, while ignoring the fetters here below.

A refreshing contrast to all this is the dissenting tradition in India, whose earliest and most powerful spokesman was the Buddha, who flourished in the sixth century before Christ. Though there is much that is enigmatic and mystifying in his teachings, it is remarkable that in many respects he anticipated the concerns of the prophet from Nazareth. This great Asian was the first to repudiate the hierarchy of caste and the supremacy of the Brahmins; the first to denounce the worship of gods, goddesses, and spirits, good and evil, along with the superstitious practices accompanying it; the first to point out the economic roots of violence and social anarchy; the first to remind his fellows that each must be a light unto himself or herself; the first to project a future society in which the rule of kings will give way to the rule of *dharma* (ethics); the first to preach universal love and compassion as the eternal law of life. The Buddha also founded communities that were to mediate between the present age of sorrow and the kingdom of righteousness to come (Kappen 1983, 37-41; Ling 1981).

But this powerful upsurge of the Asian spirit toward love and freedom could not maintain its original radical thrust; Brahminism managed to absorb it and thereby neutralize it. But the energies Buddhism released were to reemerge once again in medieval India, this time in response to increasing feudal exploitation and oppression. Its spokesmen were the saints of *bhakti*, who directed their attack against the caste system and formalistic religion and for that reason were persecuted by the priestly class (Kosambi 1962, 31-36). But devotional religion too eventually succumbed to caste Hinduism, itself assuming the form of caste. Again in the eighteenth and nineteenth centuries, at the height of colonial exploitation, there arose messianic movements among tribals and outcastes, some drawing inspiration from Christianity, some from folk traditions regarding the Golden Age

(Fuchs 1965). But they were all ruthlessly suppressed by the colonizers, who were often in league with the local ruling castes. Leaving aside the innumerable peasant struggles that broke out in the beginning of this century spearheaded by the Communist movement, we come to the Independence movement under the leadership of Gandhi. In him the Buddhist doctrine of nonviolence, a reinterpreted Hinduism, and the message of the gospel blended to form a powerful ideological weapon to fight colonial rule. It was the unifying power of religious symbols that enabled him to rally around him the peasant masses. He is second only to the Buddha in laying the foundations for a theology of liberation. His genius consisted in harnessing religion to liberative political praxis. However, Gandhism failed in radically restructuring Indian society, mainly because an irrational commitment to the unity of Hinduism based on the disunity of caste and an ambivalent attitude in regard to capitalism prevented it from recognizing the reality and the necessity of class struggle (Unnithan 1979, 85-112).

Even this cursory overview of history shows that the Jesus tradition must merge with the radical currents in the Indian religious tradition and with the positive insights of Marxism. It is from out of such a symbiosis that the new Asian Christian theology of liberation will take shape. Its breeding ground will not be closed Christian communities but *basileic communities* engaged in the struggle for a fuller humanity.

REFERENCES

Fuchs, Stephen. 1965. *The Rebellious Prophets*, Asia Publishing House, Bombay.
Gutierrez, Gustavo. 1973. *A Theology of Liberation*, Orbis Books, Maryknoll, New York.
Kappen. S. 1983. *Jesus and Cultural Revolution: An Asian Perspective*, a BUILD Publication, Bombay.
———. 1984. "The Dialectic of Tradition and Modernity," *Negations: A Journal of Culture and Creative Praxis*, nos. 11 and 12, Trivandrum (the publication of the journal has since been discontinued).
———. 1985a. "Indian Communism and the Challenge of Cultural Revolution," *Negations*, no. 13.
———. 1985b. "Church, Liberation Theology and Marxism," *Vaidikamitram* 18. (This article is a comprehensive reply to the recent Instruction of the Sacred Congregation for Doctrine of Faith on liberation theology.)
Kosambi, D. D. 1962. *Myth and Reality*, Popular Prakashan, Bombay.
Ling, Trevor. 1981. *The Buddha's Philosophy of Man: Early Indian Buddhist Dialogues*, Dent, London.
Lobo, Lancy. 1985. "Towards an Inculturation in the Non-Sanskritic Tradition," *Vidyajyoti Journal of Theological Reflection* 49.
Pieris, Aloysius. 1988. *An Asian Theology of Liberation*, Orbis Books, Maryknoll, New York.
Sau, Ranjit. 1981. *India's Economic Development—Aspects of Class Relations*, Orient Longman, New Delhi.
Unnithan, T. K. 1979. *Gandhi and Social Change*, Rawat Publications, Jaipur.

10

Liberation as an Interreligious Project

MICHAEL AMALADOSS

If I situate the following reflections on religious pluralism in the Indian context, it is because I am an Indian, not because it is a peculiarly Indian phenomenon. However, India does offer a good example for a case study, because there religious pluralism is not merely a fact, but a problem. Why is it a problem? Unlike the other countries surrounding it, which have Islam (Pakistan) or Buddhism (Burma) or Hinduism (Nepal) as a state religion, India has opted constitutionally to be a secular democracy that commits itself to secure to all its citizens: *justice,* social, economic, and political; *liberty* of thought, expression, belief, faith, and worship; *equality* of status and of opportunity; and to promote among them all *fraternity* assuring the dignity of the individual and the unity of the Nation (*The Constitution of India*, Preamble).

India is secular, not in the sense of being antireligious or even a-religious, but in treating all religions with equal honor and allowing them equal liberty. This attitude is manifested, for instance, in the freedom given to religious groups to "establish and maintain institutions for religious and charitable purposes" (*The Constitution of India*, 26, 1) and at the same time the assurance that "the State shall not, in granting aid to educational institutions, discriminate against any educational institution on the ground that it is under the management of a minority, whether based on religion or language" (*The Constitution of India*, 30, 2). Even then, religious pluralism in India is a problem because the open spirit enshrined in the Constitution has not yet been fully appropriated by the people. Communalism based on religion has been a problem from the beginning. The division of the subcontinent in 1947 into two nations on religious grounds, leading to the founding of Pakistan as an Islamic state, has challenged the secular basis of India at its very inception. It has given the nearly eighty-five million Muslims in India, the third largest group of Muslims in any country in the world, a permanent minority complex. It has also been instrumental in creating a desire in the hearts of some of the Hindu majority that India be a Hindu state. Hindu-Muslim riots have become a recurrent feature in some areas in India. Though clashes between Hindus and Christians are rare, Christians have the experience of being considered somehow "foreign." The Sikhs today are violently agitating for a separate state in the name of their religious identity. That such waves of religious fundamentalism are not peculiar to India today makes the problem more acute and intractable.

In this manner, in spite of the dream of the fathers of the Constitution, religion in India still seems to be a cause of division, at least of mistrust, rather than of union. That is why any effort to build up a new humanity of freedom, fellowship, and justice in India has to take into account the fact of religious pluralism and seriously examine whether it can only be an obstacle to be overcome in a public life that should become totally areligious, or whether it can also be a positive influence on the collective project of liberation.

I should like to make three further preliminary remarks before taking up the topic of liberation as an interreligious project. First of all, I am not going to elaborate primarily a theology of interreligious dialogue dealing with the problem of the relationship among religions as religions. I am not going to raise questions such as ultimate truths, inclusive and exclusive perspectives of salvation history, the tension between mission and dialogue, the uniqueness of Christ and even of Christianity. It is not that these problems are not real or that they are not important. But my purpose in this contribution is to start with religious pluralism as a fact of experience and explore the impact of such pluralism on societal life, with special reference to any movement that promotes social change leading to greater justice and fulfillment. My focus is therefore practical. Certainly any authentic practical attitude will have to seek its roots in theological approaches, but I hope that practical questions provoke new insights in the ongoing reflection on faith-experience.

Second, any discussion on the relationship between religion and society tends to slip into an enquiry into the relationship between the church (institutional religion) and the state (institutional society). It may further be specified in terms of priesthood and politics (Webber 1986). Moreover, the discussion is often confined to one particular religious tradition—Christian or Islamic, for instance. But this development has been challenged in recent years by religious radicals of the right or the left. The emergence of a pluralism of religions coexisting as such within a single state raises new kinds of questions, unfamiliar to a social tradition that has been dominated by a single religion. A recent study has pointed out that even an open document like the Second Vatican Council's *Church in the Modern World* spoke of the other religions simply as forming part of the world that the church is facing. It was not aware of religions together facing the world (Phan Tan Thanh 1986, 381-88). This multireligious awareness being rather recent, my reflections tend to be prospective, structural, and theoretical, even if the questions that provoke such reflections are real enough.

My final preliminary remark is that I shall be reflecting throughout as a theologian, as a Christian believer. I do not claim to approach the topic from a purely sociological or phenomenological point of view that rules out a priori any transcendent reference. I do not feel the need to defend the claims of religion. I take them for granted, though not uncritically. My Christian belief does not prevent me from placing myself in an open dialogical perspective with regard to other religious believers. I do not think that a neutral perspective in the area of religious faith is necessary or even possible.

I shall develop my reflection in three stages. First, I shall attempt to understand the role of religion in society and its relationship to other realities like culture, ideology, society, and politics. As a theologian trying to understand my experience and seeking an appropriate conceptual framework I shall borrow—sometimes eclectically—from social scientists. The twofold criteria for such borrowing is its heuristic utility and the consistency of the over-all heuristic system. At a second stage, in the light of this general theory, I shall reflect on the experience of religious pluralism and especially the impact of such pluralism on a society that is in a process of transformation toward greater justice. Finally, I shall try to spell out the practical implications of the theoretical perspectives that I develop. Here I shall focus attention particularly on the conditions that would facilitate the needed praxis rather than offer detailed plans for the praxis itself.

THE ROLE OF RELIGION IN SOCIETY

Based on the evidence of the history of the great religions, *religion is not simply a product of society*. While the conditioning of social, economic, and political forces is inevitably there, and while this influence tends to be structural and hence unconscious, culture and especially religion have a twofold influence that makes them break out of the shackles of conditioning. The production of culture is not instinctual. Humans, being creative, free agents, do challenge tradition in the light of experience—at least some creative leaders do it. Revolutions and revolutionaries are not phenomena that emerged only after Marx. Second, many great religions believing in a special moment of divine intervention in revelation do claim to have another source that challenges their present experience and its limitations in the name of a just order that is seen both as primordial and as eschatological and which needs to be pursued. By pointing out also that the injustice is not only due to the unconscious forces of the mode of production but to the conscious choices of individuals and groups that are sinful, religion also points to the need and possibility of conversion on the one hand

and a conscious process of change on the other. This aspect of individual and collective sin also points to the possibility of deliberate creation of unjust structures or the abuse of neutral ones or the exploitation of potentially good ones. But what is deliberately chosen can also be deliberately changed.

It is this transcendent element of religion that we have to emphasize in the face of others who reduce religion to a necessary integrative function in society. These people tend to call any socially integrative structure religious. Marxism or national socialism is for them a religion or quasi-religion. Some talk of the civil religion of the United States of America. We have to say that at least believers are aware that religion, while it does play a role of legitimation and integration, has also a transcendent element that makes it something more than a force for integration. One anthropologist speaks of the phenomenological and the transcendental complex in religion (Mandelbaum 1966, 1174-91). Religion is not simply an otherworldly affair. It aims at providing meaning for what happens in this world. In this effort it is very closely allied to culture. The myths seek to explain all phenomena—natural, human, and social—in terms of symbols and spirits. The whole cosmos is seen as a unity. Even at this level rites of passage and rituals of *"communitas"* point to a better world, which the community is called to become, going beyond the limitations imposed on life by humans and their own evil desires (Turner 1969). Humanity's persistent quest for meaning, however, leads it beyond the cosmos to a transcendent world.

The emergence of this transcendent world on the one hand roots this world in something beyond itself and on the other makes this world relative. While the growth of science has progressively replaced the simpler explanations offered by cosmic myths, it leaves untouched the ultimate questions or the metacosmic dimension (Pieris 1980, 75-95), where the great religions claim to receive these answers from a revelation from above. It is this transcendent dimension that sets religion apart from culture. Forgetting the correlative nature of this transcendence to our life and experience, one can make it an element of alienation. But at the same time it is the distance and the difference that makes it an element of prophecy and a basis of hope. In Hinduism, for instance, of the four ends of human life: *artha* (wealth), *kama* (pleasure), *dharma* (righteousness), and *moksha* (fulfillment), the pursuit of *moksha* without the other three is alienating except as a prophetic role played by the *sannyasi* as an integral member of the wider community. The pursuit of the first three ends not ordained to the last is materialistic and meaningless with regard to the ultimate end of life. Similarly, in the Christian tradition the kingdom is at once immanent and transcendent; stressing either aspect one-sidedly is an alienation.

The process of secularization has further strengthened this distinction between culture and religion. Secularization has led to a greater differentiation between the various elements that constitute society. It has demonstrated the autonomy of the sciences, politics, arts, social relations, and even of culture as a world-view. But at the same time it has not done away with religion. It has, rather, specified the place of religion in human and social life as protecting the ultimate ground without which life will be merely mechanical and utilitarian. That people are distancing themselves from institutional religion or choosing to live at superficial levels is no indication that they ignore this ultimate ground as the basis of values.

The dialectical relationship between religion and culture is important. It is like the relationship between the body and the spirit. Religion needs to be inculturated in order to be relevant and effective. But then it runs the risk of becoming over-institutionalized, domesticated, rigidly determined. It can be made into an ideology and a bondage. Religion must also keep its transcendence in order to remain inspirational, prophetic, and eschatological. Cut off from life it can become alienating, an "opium." It is a potential and a challenge for change precisely because it can speak of another world as realizable here and now. Its myths and rituals make it a realistic hope. Its charismatic leaders and saints render it a dynamic presence. Its call to commitment and praxis makes it a concrete duty. Only human response can make it a reality. Sometimes one hears a distinction between religion and faith. Faith without religion is disincarnate; it is powerless and useless, because it is not human without symbolic and social self-expression. Religion without faith is oppressive.

The phenomenon of secularization, therefore, has deprived religion of its claim to be a universal meaning system. It would be a mistake also to take it as one among the other meaning systems at the same level. On the contrary, religion has become aware of its metacosmic identity, while losing its image as cosmic superstructure. This is why the confessional state is no longer meaningful. The church learned this the hard way. The Second Vatican Council with its *Constitution on the Church in the Modern World* and the *Declaration on Religious Freedom* formally recognized this situation, though the strong institutional structure of the church may render this awareness ambiguous. Many Islamic states too are engaged in interpreting Islamic tradition in the context of the modern situation (Donahue and Esposito 1982). The various fundamentalist movements across the globe, big or small, show that differentiation is still in process (Wilson 1981). Perhaps it will be a process in every age. The weakening force of religion as institution does not mean that religion is becoming a private affair. This may be inevitable where its public expression is strictly controlled, if not prohibited. But precisely because religion is becoming a more personal, conscious project and because it has to do with the ultimate meaning of life, it cannot but have a public impact, though new forms of such impact may be evolving (Hammond 1985).

RELIGION IN A MULTIRELIGIOUS SOCIETY

What role can religion play in the process of liberation and fulfillment in a multireligious society? One easy answer is to dismiss the question itself as meaningless. Many who take secularization seriously think that religion must be totally private. Religious belief is a personal matter and must not be allowed to play any role in public affairs. This position is certainly unacceptable to a person who believes that religion is not only relevant to life but is also a prophetic force. Without this challenging force of religion in the public sphere, society tends to acquire an absolute character and to become a sort of civil religion with its own myths and rituals. The basis could be an atheist ideology, or the profit motive, or efficiency. Ethical considerations yield place to self-interest often hidden under noble ideals. Might becomes right. What works is what is needed. The state becomes a technocracy intent on managing the country, its economics, its power, and its influence, ready to sacrifice principles and people. An amoral society, even if it does not tend to become immoral, misses the inspiration, dynamism, and prophetic force and vision that religion can bring to the task of building a new society.

A second point of view sees the link between religion and society as so close—especially seeing religion as an integrative force—that it is not able to understand how a multiplicity of religions could contribute to a real cohesion. The solution then is a culture and a society shaped and animated by *one particular religion*. Religion is made to serve the interests of society. The religion serving this role is, of course, the religion of the majority. It would be tolerant of other religions. Human rights would be protected. But basically the society is Christian, Islamic, Hindu, Buddhist, and so forth. This model is more widespread than it would appear to a superficial observer. Where Muslims are in a majority it is taken for granted, except in Indonesia, where a constitutional effort is being made to promote coexistence among various religious groups. Most countries in Europe and America are Christian in this sense, even if some governments may have a secular stance or appearance.

In spite of its Constitution, most people think of India as a Hindu country. It has been said that Indian traditions are basically Hindu, and this fact cannot be ignored (Shah and Rao 1965). From this point of view, religious pluralism becomes a problem regarding the treatment and protection of minorities. The challenge of building a secular, multireligious, democratic society is sidestepped. For example, in a *society* that is experienced as primarily Hindu, though open to other minorities, one might at best accept or at least tolerate a secular *state* as defined in the Constitution (note the distinction between society and state here). Here we have a clash of world-views, attitudes, and ideologies that is bound to be a continuing source of tension. A secular state cannot really survive effectively unless the society also becomes secular, with an awareness of itself as a multireligious society.

THE INDIAN TRADITION

What does this awareness of being a multireligious society imply? The Indian tradition suggests a third point of view. This is not a new problem, but an old one faced by Emperor Asoka in the third century B.C.E:

> The faiths of others all deserve to be honoured for one reason or another. By honouring them, one exalts one's own faith and at the same time performs a service to the faith of others. By acting otherwise, one injures one's own faith and also does disservice to that of others. ... Therefore concord alone is commendable, for through concord men may learn and respect the conception of *Dharma* accepted by others (Rock Edict XII in Nikam and McKeon 1962).

Asoka, a convert to Buddhism after the shock of a bloody war, is not only tolerant of other religions, but honors all of them. He has undertaken to propagate *dharma*, which in Indian tradition and according to the use made by Asoka himself means righteousness or right behavior seen as an integral human way, including religion and morality. He sees this as common to all religions.

In India's history we had to wait twenty-two centuries before a similar ideal surfaced again in an integral — that is socio-political-religious — context. Concluding his autobiography, *The Story of My Experiments with Truth*, Mahatma Gandhi writes:

> My uniform experience has convinced me that there is no other God than Truth, ... that a perfect vision of Truth can only follow a complete realization of ahimsa. To see the universal and all-pervading Spirit of Truth face to face, one must be able to love the meanest of creation as oneself. And a man who aspires after that cannot afford to keep out of any field of life. That is why my devotion to Truth has drawn me into the field of politics; and I can say without the slightest hesitation, and yet in all humility, that those who say that religion has nothing to do with politics do not know what religion means (Gandhi 1966, 282-83).

In another passage Gandhiji places this ideal in an interreligious context. As he is preparing to meet Muslim leaders on the occurrence of communal violence between Hindus and Muslims, he writes:

> My Hinduism is not sectarian. It includes all that I know to be best in Islam, Christianity, Buddhism, and Zoroastrianism. I approach politics and everything else in a religious spirit. ... I may not leave a single stone unturned to achieve Hindu-Muslim unity. God fulfills Himself in strange ways. He may, in a manner least known to us, both fulfill himself through the interview and open a way to an honourable understanding between the two communities (de Bary 1958).

Once again Gandhi's vision and praxis are as remarkable as Asoka's. Gandhi's Truth replaces Asoka's *dharma*. Commitment to fullness for everyone, conversion, purification, love, nonviolence, openness and respect for the other, dialogue, and a sense of God's transcendent action in us are not empty ideals for him; he practiced what he preached.

THE MUSLIM VIEW

A similar open approach to collaboration with other religious believers in common nation-building is also found among Muslims in India. S. 'Abid Hussain proposes to the consideration of Indian Muslims the following facts:

> The secular Constitution of India has given to the Muslims, as to the followers of other religions, complete freedom of religious faith and practice and of teaching and propagating it. This Constitution has recognized a number of Islamic values like the freedom, brotherhood of man without distinction of race, of colour and legal, social and economic justice as fundamental rights, and adopted them as the most important ideals of the Indian State. Under the present circumstances in the world and specially in India, there can be no better political organization from the Muslim point of view than a secular state and they should, instead of merely tolerating it in a passive way, support it actively and zealously (Hussain 1982).

Another Indian Muslim scholar, Syed Vahiduddin, shows how the Koran itself supports such an open perspective:

> Every community of mankind has been prescribed a pattern of belief and behaviour which it has, and the differences which are therein have a sanction in the divine planning. So what matters is not the outward pattern but the works that one does. "To each of you we have appointed a right way and an open road. If God had willed He would have made you one community, but that he may try you in what is given to you. So be you forward in good works; unto God shall you return altogether and he will tell you of that wherein you were at variance (Q 5,48)" (Vahiduddin 1986).

POPE JOHN PAUL II

In the light of this longstanding Indian tradition, however unfaithful we Indians have been to it, it is not surprising that Pope John Paul II chose the occasion of his pilgrimage to India to stress the need for interreligious collaboration in the pursuit of a better world. In his talk to leaders of other religions in Madras the pope said:

> By dialogue we let God be present in our midst; for as we open ourselves in dialogue to one another, we also open ourselves to God.

We should use the legitimate means of human friendliness, mutual understanding and interior persuasion. We should respect the personal and civic rights of the individual. As followers of different religions we should join together in promoting and defending common ideals in the spheres of religious liberty, human brotherhood, education, culture, social welfare and civic order. Dialogue and collaboration are possible in all these great projects (Vahiduddin 1986, 598).

I use quotations not only because they place our reflections in the twofold tradition of India and Christianity, but also because they bring out so succinctly and well the points that I want to make. In any society that is committed to liberation the role of religion is one of providing inspiration, prophecy, challenge, and hope in terms of the ultimate. In a multireligious society the various religions play this role together; that is, believers must not be satisfied in rooting themselves and in being challenged by their own religion. They must in dialogue seek to provide a common religious grounding that would inspire collectively the community committed to liberation. Gandhi used to try to achieve this by reading passages from various scriptures at his prayer meetings. But believers should do more than this. They must be able, on the one hand, to challenge others to grow out of the limitations of their historically and culturally conditioned religion in a pilgrim state. Religious persons must also be ready to face the same challenges from other believers, to go out of themselves and to grow.

Such mutual enrichment is more than simple dialogue by which we try to understand each other and live in harmony. It is more than finding a common ground. It is mutual inspiration, challenge, and enrichment. It is a converging movement in which each one is growing toward fulfillment — but a fulfillment that is not simply a religious reality, which is but only one aspect albeit the deepest one — of the common community of freedom, fellowship, and justice that is being built up. One can enrich others and be enriched oneself only insofar as one remains oneself. Hence there is no question of losing one's identity, but rather of achieving unity in pluralism. *The principle of unity is precisely the praxis of liberation.* This means that interreligious dialogue must descend from the level of experts to that of the ordinary people, the poor, who are struggling together for liberation and fulfillment. It will be shown more in symbols and gestures and common activity rather than in abstract discussions. It will be the dialogue of life and struggles.

THE THEOLOGICAL FOUNDATIONS

What are the theological foundations for a Christian for such interreligious collaboration? They are twofold: All peoples are called to be and are pilgrims toward the fullness of the kingdom; and, in the mystery of God other religions too have a positive role in this pilgrimage, however qualified.

The first and really basic perspective is that God's plan for the universe is one and that God's universal salvific will embraces all human beings. The *Declaration on Non-Christian Religions* of the Second Vatican Council speaks of a common human vocation. All human beings form a single community whose origin and goal is God. "His providence, His manifestations of goodness, and His saving designs extend to all men" (*Nostra Aetate*, no. 1). The *Constitution on the Church in the Modern World* draws out the consequences: "Therefore, if we have been summoned to the same destiny, which is both human and divine, we can and should work together without violence and deceit in order to build up genuine peace in the world" (*Gaudium et Spes*, no. 92).

Pope John Paul II affirms in his encyclical *Redemptor Hominis* that the Spirit is working "outside the visible confines of the Mystical Body" (no. 32). Commenting on and drawing out the implications of the symbolic gesture of the leaders of all religions praying for peace in Assisi, he says:

> There is only one divine plan for every human being who comes into this world (cf. John 1,9), one single origin and goal whatever may be the colour of his skin, the historical and geographical framework within which he happens to live and act, or the culture in which he grows up and expresses himself. The differences are a less important element, when confronted with the unity which is radical, fundamental and decisive (*L'Osservatore Romano*, December 22-23, 1986).

In the context of this basic unity of all human beings and the universal salvific will of God the other religions are not seen as evil or as merely human, but as somehow mediating the action of the Spirit of God. The Asian bishops have affirmed: "We accept them (i.e. the other religions) as significant and positive elements in the economy of God's design of salvation. . . . And how can we not acknowledge that God has drawn our peoples to himself through them?" (Asian bishops 1974, nos. 14-15).

Besides the one plan of God for all human beings and the positive significance, however qualified, of the other religions, another important element is the freedom of God and of the human person. The *Constitution on the Church in the Modern World* declares: "Since Christ died for all men, and since the ultimate vocation of man is in fact one, and divine, we ought to believe that the Holy Spirit in a manner known only to God offers to every man the possibility of being associated with his paschal mystery" (*Gaudium et Spes*, no. 22).

I think it is proper for us to respect this mystery without pretending to know and much less to judge all the mysterious ways of Divine Providence and the sovereign liberty of the Spirit of God, who "blows where it wills." Corresponding to the liberty of God is the liberty of the human person. The *Declaration on Religious Freedom* underlines not only the freedom of every human person to follow his or her conscience in the pursuit of truth, but also the legitimacy of giving expression to this search socially in the various religions.

> Every man has the duty, and therefore the right to seek the truth in matters religious. Truth, however, is to be sought after in a manner proper to the dignity of the human person and his social nature. . . . The social nature of man itself requires that he should give external expression to his internal acts of religion; that he should participate with others in matters religious; that he should profess his religion in community (*Dignitatis Humanae*, no. 3).

Jesus proclaimed the kingdom of God as present and active in the world. But the kingdom, God's rule, is cosmic, from the beginning of the world, and will reach its fullness only on the last day. The church is not the kingdom, but its sacrament and servant. In the light of all that we have said above, it would be easy to understand that other religions too belong in some way to the realization of God's kingdom in this world (Amaladoss 1990, 43-60).

In seeking to establish this kingdom on earth we are called to collaborate with other believers and all people of goodwill. All of us are called to conversion. All of us are called to confess our sins. All of us are called to be open to enrichment by others. All of us are called to a common commitment. We are not here talking of interreligious dialogue leading to the enrichment of each other's faith, but we are asking for a common action in the pursuit of justice and fullness for all human beings. We are called to do this without in any way being disloyal to our faith.

A meeting of a group of Asian bishops in Madras, India, convened to consider the problems of dialogue between Hinduism and Christianity in Asia, stressed this common commitment as the place of dialogue:

> Since the religions, as the Church, are at the service of the world, interreligious dialogue cannot be confined to the religious sphere but must embrace all dimensions of life: economic, sociopolitical, cultural and religious. It is in their common commitment to the fuller life of the human community that they discover their complementarity and the urgency and relevance of dialogue at all levels, socio-economic and intellectual as well as spiritual, among the common people in daily life as among scholars and people with deep religious experience (Asian bishops 1984, 199).

CONDITIONS FOR INTERRELIGIOUS COLLABORATION

Some efforts have been made to work out how concretely Hinduism and Christianity in India could complement each other in this pursuit of a new humanity (Amaladoss 1983, 67-76). A similar effort could be made with regard to Islam and other smaller Indian religions. In the spirit of authentic dialogue, it is for each believer to witness to the riches that he or she brings to the community and say what is received from the other. This sharing of riches must take place not in the abstract, at the level of ideas, but in the concrete, in the context of a common struggle for a better humanity. Besides, given the variety of religions in India, it would be unfair to point to two or three of them, however important they may be in terms of the number of their followers.

Nevertheless, one could talk about the conditions necessary to make such a collaboration among religions possible and successful — conditions that could be created. First of all we should all commit ourselves to nation-building. I often wonder whether we are not hidden, perhaps unconscious, communalists. Talking only of Christians, we still seem to have a minority complex, very defensive of our rights. There is nothing wrong, of course, in being sensitive to one's rights. That is part of democracy and is necessary. But any action from the public or government that we think affects us unfavorably draws more reaction from the Christian community and from our leaders than the more serious injustices suffered by other people.

In a complex society, even in a democracy committed to majority rule, the rights of the minority have to be protected by law. Given human nature, one cannot always count on the spontaneous goodwill of the majority. But we should not allow such self-defensive attitudes to become a way of life. When we start thinking of ourselves as Indians, we will start defending human rights more readily than Christian rights; that is, we will defend our rights, not so much as Christians, but as human beings.

A more difficult problem is that of awareness. I think that for the ordinary Indian, a Christian appears as a follower of a foreign religion, even though Christianity has been in India for two thousand years, ever since the time of St. Thomas. The problem is not one of history (Divarkar 1986, 176-84). The problem is the kind of image we project through our style of life, ways of worship, organization, dependence on foreign funds, extensive foreign contacts, and training abroad. We are not yet really inculturated. A more serious problem is whether we have not ourselves interiorized these structures of dependence, the more powerful because they are the more unconscious. The only way of getting out of this situation is to get involved with other people in common action programs for the benefit of all. That is why we must rethink such strategies as Basic Ecclesial Communities. We have, of course to keep our identity as Christians. The best occasion for this seems to be the eucharistic assembly. Since the special characteristic of the Basic Ecclesial Communities is precisely their political awareness as compared to other Christian groupings, it seems advisable that we do not have political groups based on a particular religious identity in a multireligious country. Politics and religion is a dangerous mixture that we can do without in India. We should rather think of *Basic Human Communities* insofar as smaller groups of people provide an ideal ground for conscientization and concerted action.

The second condition is that we be truly religious. Our religion should neither be alienating nor become an ideology. We cannot really enter into dialogue till we are fully and deeply rooted in our own faith and in that very experience learn to respect the deep faith commitment of the others. Real rootedness and real openness are not opposed to each other. It is when one is not really rooted that one becomes defensive and aggressive. Besides, dialogue is not the search for the lowest common denominator on which we can easily agree, but the common search for the Truth, to which we bring all our riches and enrich each other. It is in this way that we realize our own limitations and respond to the prophetic challenge of the other. Thus we will move toward mutual fulfillment.

Third, we should become more secular. S. 'Abid Hussain says:

> As it is the constitution of a democratic state, it gives to Muslims, as Indian citizens, the right and opportunity to try to change anything in the national constitution or national life which appears to them to be in conflict with Islamic values and to advocate the recognition and adoption of more Islamic values. But their effort in this direction can only be effective if they speak to the Indian nation not in religious, but in secular language and argue their case for the reforms which they think are necessary, not on the basis of religious authority and tradition, but on that of observation, experience and reason. Muslims firmly believe that Islamic teachings are in harmony with the fundamental urges of human nature and can stand the test of reason, observation and experience. They should, therefore, not find it difficult to express the need for the desired reforms in secular terms and to prove it by rational arguments (Hussain 1982, 170).

The same would be true of Christianity too. We are not speaking of a secularism that would be antireligious. We are thinking of a secularism that treats all religions equally, offering them appropriate liberties, but at the same time supports the rightful autonomy of science, politics, ideology, and so on. Even when our religious faith is relevant to our day-to-day experience, it has no immediate solution to all problems. The religious level is different from the moral. The legal is different from the political. The absolute demands of religion—like "love one another" or "thou shalt not kill"—have to be mediated by appropriate knowledge of the situation and practical judgment before we can enunciate a concrete course of action. Knowledge and judgment, however, are very much influenced by one's culture, world view, tradition, sentiment, ideology, and so forth. We should be aware of all these different levels and how they interact and at the same time know that they are different and that the relationship between them is not a logical deductive one from general principles to conclusions.

Secularization and the differentiation it has introduced into society is a gain for pluralistic societies of all kinds (Kuitert 1986). While secularism of this kind is essential at the level of the religions relating to the state, when the religions meet among themselves at the level of dialogue, they must be able to go beyond the merely rational level and share also perspectives of religious faith and seek a convergence at that level of faith. This would be particularly possible and even advisable when we are speaking together not as faith meeting faith in individuality, but faiths committing themselves together to promote justice.

Politics and the state must play a very limited role in the life of the community. The various freedoms of the people, of course, must be protected from people who seek to abuse them. But law must play a minimal role that conserves a free space for the people. The people themselves must be encouraged to participate at every level, whether of policy or decision making or of execution. It is not the role of the state or of the law to help implement anyone's religious convictions. One should promote these, of course, but by persuasion and not compulsion. One wonders whether contemporary democracy based on party politics and rule by majority is an ideal structure to protect these freedoms. The majority could easily turn oppressive of the minorities. Governments with absolute majorities in parliament can turn autocratic. One should explore alternative structures of promoting people's participation at the grassroots, solidarity, and subsidiarity. Maybe these are dreams and ideals, but they are worth pursuing in all societies, especially in a pluralistic one (Raj 1986; Claver 1985, 316-23).

This secular spirit means that religion as an institution may have visibility and play a public, social, and even political role. But if within a government we ask for proper distinctions between the executive, the legislative, and the judicial functions, and we would not like the military to get involved in any of these, it is only proper that the religious power should keep its specific role in society. It can be prophetic and constructive, especially in political matters, only insofar as it keeps its freedom of reflection and action. Institutionalized religion (the church) and institutionalized society (the state) are bases of religious and political power, and it is better for both of them and for their interaction that they remain separate as power roles in the community. This is not to say that religion should be apolitical and politics should be amoral. They cannot be and should not be. But it is not advisable for the same person to hold offices in the church and the state, not because the church is sacred and the state is profane, but because they are two functions in society that are better kept separate. If this is the need in every type of society, it is very much moreso in multireligious societies in which religions should keep their independence in order to collaborate better, and the state should not be linked to any one religion.

The central piece of the whole picture is the human person. Everything else is condition, context, instrument, structure. They are all for the person. It is the people as community who are going to use all these and build a better future for themselves. Pluralism is not a problem but a richness, because it is primarily a pluralism of persons and communities (Panikkar 1979, 197-230). Interreligious dialogue must not remain an activity of the experts centered on "spirituality." It must become the activity of the poor arising out of interreligious praxis for liberation and fulfillment.

CONCLUSIONS

My first conclusion, following from the last point regarding the centrality of the human person, is that interreligious collaboration is not between religions, but between believers. The obstacles in the way of interreligious collaboration do not always come from the side of religion. Often they are economic, socio-psychological, historical, cultural, political. We have not analyzed these areas here and their impact on interreligious collaboration. It is good to keep this in mind. Very often religion is only a cloak to hide other more or less worthy reasons, which may be sometimes unconscious or implicit.

Second, if our praxis includes interreligious collaboration even at the level of faith, and if theology is reflection on faith experience, this would also give rise to a sort of interdenominational theology—like the ecumenical theology that we sometimes come across (Pieris 1988, 87-110). One would also raise questions about the rigid boundaries that we have set up around our institutions, scriptures, and rituals.

In countries with a variety of little cultural traditions these are integrated in the course of history into a great tradition, of which the little traditions become folk traditions. Between the great tradition and the little folk traditions there is constant osmosis. In India this great tradition at the moment is based on Hinduism. Islam and Christianity have remained unintegrated, "foreign." Hence there is the tendency to identify India with the Hindu: Muslims and Christians have a minority consciousness. But if inculturation has any significance there is no reason why a religious minority should be a cultural minority or, much less, a political minority. But then we have to refashion our great tradition. We need a new one adapted to our contemporary needs and sociopolitical institutions. It will be pluralistic, secular, open to science and technology. It will integrate them in a holistic perspective of integral humanism. What we are witnessing today in India is the search for identity and the self-assertion of various little traditions that feel threatened by other little traditions or by the present great tradition. When this search turns into a struggle, it takes communal overtones. I think that the only solution to this problem is the conscious development of a new pluralistic great tradition. The Constitution has already given us a political framework. But the various cultural forces are not allowing it to function. So what we need is a cultural transformation, and this can only be an interreligious project given the central role of religion in any culture.

If praxis is at the root of reflection, then the multireligious action groups committed to the promotion of justice that seem to be emerging in some parts of India may really be "harbingers of hope" (Wilfred 1985, 539-64). Because the ideologies that animate them see in religion only an obstacle to the pursuit of justice, religions in these groups are often privatized. From privatization to dissatisfaction and disappearance may seem inevitable unless we can restore the relevance of religious faith to liberation even in multireligious situations, thus making liberation an interreligious project. In India this would not be totally new, but something dreamed of and occasionally, however haltingly, practiced. It is this tradition—sometimes manifested as religious tolerance—that is a real sign of hope.

REFERENCES

Amaladoss, Michael. 1983. "Towards a Culture of Wholeness," *Vidyajyoti* 47.
———. 1990. *Making All Things New*, Orbis Books, Maryknoll, New York.
Asian bishops. 1974. "Evangelization in Modern Day Asia," Statement of the Plenary Assembly of the FABC. Taipei. In *For All the Peoples of Asia*, vol. 1, IMC Publications, Manila, 1984.
———. 1984. *For All the Peoples of Asia*. Manila.
Bary, William Theodore de, ed. 1958. *Sources of Indian Tradition*, New York.
Claver, Bishop Francisco. 1985. "The Church in Asia: 20 Years After Vatican II," *East Asian Pastoral Review* 22.
Divarkar, Paramananda. 1986. "A Call to Conversion: Reflections on the Papal Visit," *Vidyajyoti* 50.
Donahue, John J., and John L. Esposito. 1982. *Islam in Transition: Muslim Perspectives*, New York.
Gandhi, M. K. 1966. *The Story of My Experiments with Truth*, 2d ed., Ahmedabad.
Hammond, Philip E. ed. 1985. *The Sacred in a Secular Age*, Berkeley.
Hussain, S. 'Abid. 1982. "Indian Muslims in a Secular State." In Donahue and Esposito, *Islam in Transition*.
Kuitert, H. M. 1986. *Everything Is Politics, But Politics Is Not Everything: A Theological Perspective on Faith and Politics*, London.
Mandelbaum, G. David. 1966. "Transcendental and Pragmatic Aspects of Religion," *American Anthropologist* 68.
Nikam, N. A., and Richard McKeon, eds. 1962. *The Edicts of Asoka*, Bombay.
Panikkar, Raimundo. 1979. "The Myth of Pluralism: The Tower of Babel—A Meditation on Non-Violence," *Cross Currents* (Summer 1979).
Phan Tan Thanh, Joseph. 1986. "Religion and Religions in the Second Vatican Council," *Christ to the World* 31.
Pieris, Aloysius. 1980. "Towards an Asian Theology of Liberation: Some Religio-Cultural Guidelines." In *Asia's Struggle for Full Humanity*, ed. Virginia Fabella, Orbis Books, Maryknoll, New York.
———. 1988. "The Place of Non-Christian Religions and Cultures in the Evolution of Third-world Theology," *An Asian Theology of Liberation*, Orbis Books, Maryknoll, New York.
Raj, Sebasti L. 1986. *Total Revolution: The Final Phase of Jayaprakash Narayan's Political Philosophy*, Satya Nilayam Publications, Madras.

Shah, A. B., and C.R.M. Rao, eds. 1965. *Tradition and Modernity in India*, Bombay.
Turner, Victor. 1969. *The Ritual Process*, London.
Vahiduddin, Syed. 1986. *The Islamic Experience in Contemporary Thought*, Delhi.
Webber, Robert E. 1986. *The Church in the World: Opposition, Tension, or Transformation?* Grand Rapids.
Wilfred, Felix. 1985. "Harbingers of Hope. Action Groups in India," *Vidyajyoti* 49.
Wilson, Bryan, ed. 1981. *The Social Impact of New Religious Movements*, New York.

11

Liberation in India and the Church's Participation

FELIX WILFRED

Not long ago in Surjgarh, a little village of Rajasthan, Kanna, a 37-year-old man belonging to the untouchable Bhils axed his four children to death and killed himself. Was he an eccentric? The villagers testified to what a conscientious person and loving father he was. Why did he, then, do what he did? It was simply because, impoverished as he was, he could not bear the cry of his four children for food anymore (Saint 1987).

Even as India was celebrating its fortieth anniversary of independence on August 15, in another village, an undernourished and emaciated little girl of 10, Tulsi by name, lay in a hut battling for life. Her parents had died, and she was brought up by her uncles, poor peasants who were struggling just to survive. Trying to save Tulsi's life, a doctor injected a needle into the frail body to let in saline intravenously. But the needle pierced through her flesh and came out; her frail and dehydrated body did not have flesh enough even to hold the needle. Nothing could save her. Little Tulsi died, not having reached even the age to ask why she should die (*Indian Express,* September 1987).

The deaths of Kanna, his children, and Tulsi, and the dismal living condition of millions in India who envy the dead, can leave no conscientious woman or man unmoved. They haunt and torment our conscience, shake up our being, and raise very fundamental questions about ourselves and about the society in which we live. What happens in India is a kind of holocaust. Innumerable men, women, and children are daily tortured and consigned to a slow process of death through heartrending forms of oppression and through the indifference and callousness of fellow human beings.

In an India confronted with massive poverty, oppression, hunger, and death, where does the church figure? What liberation does it bring?

Actions of any individual, group, or institution are set in a particular context of relations, history, power-structures, and sociopolitical processes. It would be a mistake, therefore, to believe that any one individual, group, or institution in India can develop people and save them from their woes, while failing to interact with the country's present complex situation. This applies as well to the church. As for Christian involvement, we have to also take into account the dominant image of the church in this country as an alien body, a proselytizing institution and a legacy of colonialism (Panikkar 1953). In spite of it, the church can and ought to play a liberative role. But her role needs to be circumscribed and defined in relation to the larger context of the liberation process that is taking place in the country. The church should understand its role only as a *participant* in this movement of liberation, and not as one who directs, much less monopolizes it.

This participation should flow from the acknowledgment that the ideals of God's kingdom and the power of the Spirit are active in the aspirations and struggles of the poor for greater humanity; it should be based on the conviction that the kingdom, which is promised to the poor, is "already taking shape in our history" (*Gaudium et Spes,* no. 39); that it is at work in a mysterious way over which the church has no power and control. In this way, the participation of the church in the process of liberation will correspond to its vocation to be a pilgrim church, following God's call coming to it through the challenges of history.

ANTYODAYA (AWAKENING OF THE LEAST) AND THE CHURCH

The first and most significant impetus for liberation derives from the quest of the oppressed themselves for fuller life and humanity. Despite all odds placed in the way of the marginalized, there is a spurt of new consciousness among them and a growing determination to overcome the present antihuman arrangements of the political, social, economic, cultural, and religious order. This is particularly significant against the background of the situation in India, in which the poor have become the unwanted lot, considered a burden by the dominant classes. The poor have become, in a word, redundant and therefore easily dispensable. This is the most inhuman aspect of the oppression in the Indian society, controlled by an elite pressing forward on the path of technological modernity and by a government trying to catch up with the technological and scientific advancement of the western world.

And yet it is the poor—the landless laborers in the rural areas, the slum and pavement dwellers in the cities, child laborers, and over a hundred and fifty million untouchables of India—who contribute to the economic growth of the nation through their sweat and blood. They do the hardest and the most menial work under the most trying conditions. Without their labor the economy of the rural and urban areas would come to a standstill. It is through their poverty and misery that the others become rich; through their votes, the politicians wield power; and through their work, the villages and cities are maintained. To these rural and urban poor, we should add three other groups who belong to "the least" in India: tribals, women, and bonded laborers.

Among these groups restlessness has set in as they search for fuller life and dignity as human beings. A sharper awareness of the present unjust situation is permeating them. They are learning to identify the forces manipulating their lives and call into question systems and structures that have legitimized their marginalization and oppression. Consequently, there is a vigorous affirmation by the oppressed of their rights (Thomas 1980, 10-20 and 1978b). The emerging new consciousness among the oppressed has begun to lead them to protest and revolt against all those forces that have kept them in bondage. This *antyodaya*, the rising of the least, represents the overcoming of fatalistic views about their situation. The deep-rooted attitude of resignation is giving way to the conviction that things can and ought to be different; the feeling of helplessness is being replaced by a feeling of growing self-confidence.

The new awakening manifests itself at three interrelated areas. There is, first of all, the awareness about their right to the basic necessities of life—food, shelter, health care, and so on. It should be noted that the rights of the poor are not exactly the same as the civil rights and liberties of the liberal tradition, which has as its focus the freedom of thought, freedom of movement, the right to marry, to form associations, and so on. These rights are, however, closely linked to the rights of the poor, in such a way that any choice between bread and freedom is bound to result in a dehumanizing situation. The attempt to suppress freedom with the promise of bread, as was done during the Emergency (1975-77) in India, could not hold out for too long.

The second area of the awakening of the least relates to *samata* (equality). Traditional Indian society is unequal, having caste as its basic social structure. Inequality and hierarchical thinking permeate every aspect of life. Intimately connected with caste are the feudal and semi-feudal systems still very much prevalent in India. Industrial capitalism, which is pervasive, reaching every nook and corner of the country, even villages where there may not be drinking water facilities, has contributed to the traditional inequality deriving from casteism and feudalism. As a result, there is an overlapping of high castes, rich landowners, and top classes, although this overlapping is slowly being disrupted by new forces (Beteille 1971). Correspondingly, there is an overlapping of low castes, the landless, and the lowest economic classes.

The most affected by this growing inequality are those who by their low birth bear the stigma of untouchability. They are looked down upon as inferior to all others. Untouchability was abolished by law in 1947, but it has ceased to exist only on paper; it continues in practice, giving lie to the belief that social changes can be effected by legislation. In everyday life discrimination is practiced against the untouchables in various ways; for example, they may not draw water from the same wells where the high castes draw water, walk with sandals on through the streets of caste people, or enter temples. Their women are raped, their huts burned, and so on.

The new ferment of thought and consciousness seeping among the traditionally discriminated against groups, especially the outcastes, has brought to sharp focus the problem of inequality as a great challenge facing Indian society (Kananaikil 1983). The discrimination practiced against the outcastes is only one expression of it, albeit the most obvious. But there are many other forms of inequality in areas like land-ownership, educational opportunities, and so on. The oppressed have begun to raise their voice against all kinds of discriminations.

To the above two areas of awakening we should add a third one; namely, the awareness of the oppressed that they are not masters of their own destiny, but that their life is determined and controlled by others who dictate terms. They are deprived of the necessary power to shape and mold their own lives; they are puppets in the manipulative hands of the rich and the powerful—landlords, the merchants, politicians, business people, and so forth. The power structures in Indian society—for example, the high castes and landlords acting in collusion with modern higher social classes in control of industrial and technological power—have reduced the poorest segments of the society into totally powerless groups. From such a situation is born the protest of the powerless against the traditional and modern power structures responsible for their present plight.

The aspirations and yearnings of the least are crystallized into various movements and organizations as they seek liberation from economic, social, political, cultural, and religious bondage. These movements and organizations, such as the *dalit* movement of the untouchables and the *jahrkand* movement of the tribals, have become forces to reckon with in Indian society today. The stirrings of protest from the least have in recent times manifested themselves in actions such as boycotting political elections, fasting, agitation, and so on. Such a protest is directed also against religion when it discriminates against the poor and the untouchables, and worse still legitimizes this discrimination by appealing to sacred texts. Frequently the poor and the marginalized have protested by changing their religion. There have been several cases of conversion of the untouchables from Hinduism to Islam, as well as from Christainty to Islam (Augustine 1981, 51-57; Raj 1981, 58-66).

How has this whole awakening of the poor and downtrodden come about? How are we to explain the movements of protest and liberation emerging from the people? There is no simple answer, for they are the results of the confluence of various complex factors and forces. Nevertheless, certain elements can be highlighted. First of all, the poor and the downtrodden have been driven to an extreme situation of bondage, poverty, and deprivation. Such a situation has emboldened them to take steps and measures that otherwise they would never have imagined. It is the art of survival. Today, instead of being broken under the weight of oppression, the victims are coming out of their ordeal stronger than before. The grain has fallen on the ground, and it is going to bear fruit.

There is also the role of charismatic leaders who have generated awareness among the people about their plight. We could here think of Ambedkar, the leader of the *dalits;* E. V. Ramasami Nayakar, popularly known as Thanthai Periyar (father, great man), who spearheaded the movement of liberation among the Tamils by making them aware of their glorious heritage and the present sad plight of bondage to which they are subjected; Gandhi, who through his magnetism mobilized the masses for the struggle for independence; Sri Narayana Guru, who created self-confidence among the Eazhavas in Kerala; and numerous tribal leaders. Further, if the tradition of the oppressors and those who wield power has been, by and large, individualistic (for example, the Brahminic great tradition centered on the *moksha* [liberation] of the individual), the tradition of the oppressed has been basically communitarian (for example, with the tribals). The experience of extreme oppression and the role played by the leaders have brought to the fore the deep-rooted sense of community among the powerless; this sense of community was channeled to energize the movements of liberation. Finally, the developments on the global level toward greater humanization, the universal awareness of the dignity, freedom, and rights of human beings gaining momentum all over the world (which are all themselves the result of micro-level, grassroots liberational praxis) have struck a responsive cord among the poor of India.

How is the church to respond to this general awakening of the downtrodden and their forging ahead on the path of liberation? What contribution can it make to the project of liberation that God is bringing about through the least, the last, the marginalized, the rabble of our society? The response will depend on how the church views this awakening. The church can assume a defensive posture to the serious detriment of its own credibility. This is what the history of the relationship of the church to the various social movements in the West teaches us (WCC 1978).

The whole present Indian situation challenges the Indian church. The challenge must be faced in all its implications and consequences. The first thing expected of the church is a deep sensitivity to peoples' movements and the burning questions they raise. Issues relating to bread, equality, and self-determination are not alien to the gospel and Jesus' vision of the kingdom, but rather belong to their substance. The church must dialogue with the situation and the various socio-historical forces shaping it. And a genuine dialogue is possible only when the church inserts itself, roots itself, into the lives of people struggling for liberation. Here we understand truly the significance of local church and inculturation. Local church is not simply a realization in a geographical locality of an abstractly conceived church, but a community that lives Jesus' vision of the kingdom in dialogue with the life-realities of the people, especially the oppressed and downtrodden among them. It is through dialogue with the poor that a church which claims to be sign and instrument of the kingdom can be built up (Asian bishops 1974), for in Jesus' words, the poor inherit the kingdom of God. But what is dialogue with the poor if the church does not share their hopes and dreams of freedom from bondage.

Therefore, in reality, in the movement of the poor and the oppressed for liberation in India, the Indian church is confronted with its own deeper mystery as a local church. Sensitivity to and rootedness in the world of the poor and dialogue with the situation will make the church truly inculturated. An inculturation that is not liberation-oriented can become church-centered and not kingdom-directed. One of the major reasons why the church has not been able to respond sensitively to the oppressed and their movements of liberation is that it has been over-institutionalized from the time of the missionary enterprise during colonial times. The dominant image of the church since then is that of a powerful organization with a large network of structures, institutions, and services. This image has been maintained even today with some cosmetic changes. The church runs so many educational, medical, and other institutions to the benefit of the elite in society that very often it is identified with such institutions in the public mind. These institutions are controlled by the clergy and the church leaders. The shape and the structure of the present Indian church is fundamentally geared to this role in society. Therefore, when the church wants to work for the poor, it very often runs into contradictions deriving from institutional constraints. When contradictions and conflicts arise, it is prone to give up the cause of the poor and their liberation in exchange for the welfare of the institutions.

Another important factor that inhibits the church in its commitment to the liberation of the poor is the perception of its self-identity. In a society with an overwhelming population of Hindus, Muslims, and other religious groups, the church tends to differentiate itself from the rest. It construes its identity not in terms of relationships with others but in contradistinction from others. That dovetails with the institution-oriented character of the Indian church. All this is markedly different from Jesus, whose divine identity was in identification with the human. It was an identity in terms of relationships and not differentiation. "The Word became flesh and dwelt among us" (Jn 1:14). This perception of self-identity leads the church to act in practice as a narcissistic church and progressively acquire the characteristics of a ghetto group.

In all fairness, it must be recognized, however, that the Indian church did engage itself in the liberation of the oppressed at certain periods of its history. In fact, the majority of Christians in India and Asia at large belong to the poorest sections of the society and hail from the lowest castes and social standing. The conversion of the fishermen along the Pearl Coast at the time of St. Francis Xavier meant freedom from the Muslims who had been oppressing and harassing them, though this was not the directly intended goal of conversion work, but its consequence (Schurhammer 1977). Similarly, the church played a well-known role in freeing the tribals of the Chotanagpur region from the clutches of unscrupulous landlords and rapacious moneylenders (de Sa 1975; Oddie 1979).

But today circumstances have changed profoundly. Today, the church is not leading the work of liberation; rather, the people themselves are struggling for their liberation, and the church is called to respond (Puthanagady 1986). But the important thing is for the church to be attuned to the stirrings of liberation in the country, which is not possible as long as it remains in its pattern of thinking, mode of action, way of life, and in its structures and ministries a foreign church. To the extent the Indian church becomes truly a *local church* it will also be an instrument of liberation, capable of joining forces with all those who struggle for the liberation of the poor and the oppressed.

THOSE ACCOMPANYING THE MASSES IN SOLIDARITY AND THE CHURCH

The struggles of the marginalized for life, freedom, equality, and self-determination have found an echo among peoples and groups at various levels. Those who respond to the plight of the downtrodden, though small in number, are very articulate. They want to be in solidarity with the suffering masses and stand by their side in their afflictions. They belong to various professions, religious traditions, and educational backgrounds. Among them are groups of intellectuals, judges, and lawyers who are involved in public-interest litigations, trying to interpret law not simply as an instrument of order but as something in service of the poorest and the weakest; there are journalists and mass-media men and women who expose issues of oppression and investigate incidents of injustice and discrimination.

To these we should add a whole range of voluntary organizations, the so-called nongovernmental organizations (NGOs). For over one hundred and fifty years they have been engaged in social reform movements as well as in welfare, relief, and other developmental works. The point to note about these voluntary organizations is that many of them have tried to shift their focus from welfare and developmental works to more liberative involvement in an effort to eradicate the roots of oppression and inequality at the micro as well as at the macro level.

New voluntary groups are springing up all over the country in response to wide-ranging concrete situations of exploitation and injustice. Among these are the so-called *social action groups*, which consist of educated young men and women who opt to live among the poorest segments and groups of society and participate in their struggles. There are also initiatives such as movements for civil liberties, for democratic rights, and movements concerned about the ecological question, so vital for the survival of depressed groups as well as of the tribals and fishermen. All these initiatives, groups, and organizations constitute a grassroots movement in favor of the marginalized. And these grassroots movements are engaged in developing new thinking and in evolving alternatives to the present system from out of their deep involvement with the masses in their struggles.

These groups and organizations are taking up the cause of the poor — opting for the poor — at a time when even institutions that are to be dispensers and guardians of justice are turning against the poor and the downtrodden. The state and its machinery is geared to sustain and protect the interests of the traditional landlords and modern wealthy business houses and enterprises with economic policies that seriously damage the welfare of the poor and infringe upon their basic rights. The judiciary and the police are prone to favor the rich and the powerful and ignore the perpetrators of gross injustices and crimes, who if arrested are acquitted for money and favors. A short visit to any Indian prison is enough to convince anyone of this grim state of affairs. How many among the hundreds of prisoners are unjust landlords, corrupt businessmen, officials, and bureaucrats? It is a fact that almost all the prisoners belong to the poorest strata of Indian society. Very often they were led to commit their crimes by situations characterized by injustice. The really big criminals, those who exploit the poor and the powerless and strangle justice, are outside the walls of the prison, going about free.

Against this Indian setting, groups supportive of the struggle of the downtrodden sprang up spontaneously. Such grassroot activism reinforces the emerging *loksakti* (the power of the people). Today the movements are fraught with serious problems. There is, for example, the effort of divisive forces and vested interests to split one group of the poor from the other. The grassroots activists play a role in helping the people to overcome these divisions and organize themselves. Nothing can have greater liberative potential than when the downtrodden stand together against exploitation. This was clearly proved in the effort of Gandhi to unite the peasants of Champaran. The peasants who were unjustly taxed by the colonial authorities were visited by Gandhi, who told them: "It is true that the collector is going to attach your property, your plots, if you do not pay the land revenue dues. Your plots will be auctioned. But what can he do if no one bids at the auction? Tell the collector when he next time comes to your village that he should put your plot in his pockets and take it to England!" (Shourie 1982, 205).

The supportive groups and organizations cannot and should not substitute the struggle of the oppressed for their own emancipation; instead, they can help the poor pool their energies and resources. Often, when members belonging to the lower castes and classes have moved ahead on the economic, social, or political ladder, they turn against their own. Hence it is important that not only the supportive groups, individuals, and organizations opt for the poor, taking up their cause, but also the poor themselves ought to opt for other poor and downtrodden. All this calls for an educative process, a systematic understanding of society and its working—tasks in which the supportive groups are involved with the people.

Where does the church come into the picture? In what direction could its contribution lie?

SOLIDARITY WITH THE POOR

The first and most fundamental thing for the Indian church is to be in deep solidarity with the least and marginalized and to align itself with those forces that have taken up the cause of the poor. In the concrete sociopolitical and historical circumstances of India, the option for the poor is not a matter of academic debate, but a question of dead seriousness since lives of many millions are at stake. In this regard the community of the disciples of Jesus has only to look to the life, teaching, and example of its Guru.

The gospels present clearly the predilection of Jesus for the least, the small, and the lowly—the little mustard seed (Mk 4:30-32), the few coins of the poor widow (Lk 21:1-4), the lost sheep (Lk 15:4-7), children (Mt 11:25-30). Parables such as the one in which the owner of the vineyard pays all laborers equally, even the very last ones who arrived for work, manifest Jesus' concern "unto the last" (Mt 20:1-16). His love and compassion for the suffering and the outcasts knows no bounds. His proclamation of the poor as blessed (Lk 6:20) and the statement that the kingdom of God is promised to the least (Mt 10:42) flow from his solidarity and total identification with the least: "Truly I say to you, as you did it to one of the least of these brethren, you did it to me" (Mt 25:40). By their practice everyone is ultimately judged.

This powerful challenge of the life and teaching of the guru Jesus urges the Indian church to reach out to identify itself with the slum-dwellers facing eviction, the tribals driven out of their lands; to make her own the traumas of the bonded laborers and the humiliations of the untouchables; and to be the friend of all the unwanted in our society. The aspects of Jesus as God in the poor and the lowly, and as the suffering one—symbolized by the cross—have been most appealing to the millions of Hindus in this country. It is this identification with themselves and their sufferings the poor and the lowly expect from the church. So that the Indian church may go all the way where this solidarity leads it, following Jesus outside the gate to Calvary, it is important that the church constantly look at the world through the eyes of the poor, the suffering, and the humiliated— through the sunken eyes of the starving child, through the weeping eyes of the helpless mother, through the expectant eyes of the youth frantically in search of a job. This would radically change the perspective of the Indian church on many urgent issues and make its message credible. The world is bound to appear very different when looked at from the perspective of the oppressed. Looking at the world from the continuous way of the cross of suffering human beings is bound to have a deep transformative effect on the church's mode of being in society, on its priorities, and its thinking. Even more, the church itself will be converted to the gospel through the experiences of the poor.

A Source of Inspiration and Power

The church could also become an inspirational force among all those who have taken up the cause of the downtrodden. She could become truly a much-needed moral and spiritual power to sustain them. The path of liberation is an arduous one, full of conflicts and contradictions, demanding perseverance, selflessness, a spirit of sacrifice, and inner freedom.

In India only a church that has deep faith in humanity could be a force of inspiration and sign of hope to the struggling poor and those who accompany them in their journey toward liberation. The wellspring of this faith is the humanity of Jesus and his own faith in humanity. In him the church will find immanent the transcendence it wants to live and proclaim. Faith in humanity is for the church to follow the path of the Word, which embraced the human, the immanent as its own, with all the ambiguities and risks it carries with it, knowing full well that this is the only form in which transcendence can be encountered.

Unfortunately, the Indian church has, by and large, kept aloof from the ferment of liberation movements and has clung to its traditional activities and services like educational, medical, development, and relief works. Far from playing a role of inspiration, the involvement of Christians in grass-roots movements is frowned upon, if not opposed, by a large number of church leaders. The lack of comprehension on the part of church leadership alienates those working at the grassroots.

Building Community

A third area where the church can be an active contributor is in building up a sense of community. The loss of the sense of community and the assertion of individualism and competitiveness are root causes for the oppression of the poor. The sense of belonging in the villages, where traditionally even the least were taken care of through spontaneous measures of social justice, is fast disappearing.

There were many fringe benefits the poor enjoyed in village communities. For example, the hides of dead animals were left to the outcastes; common forests and lands were preserved in villages where the needy could collect fruits and firewood; clothes and food were given free to the poorest on certain occasions such as marriage. Today these practices have become rare since everything is increasingly valued in terms of money and profit.

Capitalism and individualism reposing their trust on quick money and profit rather than on human beings and their welfare have made deep inroads into the fabric of Indian society, breaking it, infiltrating it with seductive consumerism, pitching groups against each other, fragmenting communities, fellowship, and togetherness. The inherent weaknesses of the traditional society are exploited by capitalism to pursue its own ends.

The recovery of a deep sense of fellowship and togetherness is of paramount importance, but it cannot be achieved without the establishment of justice. The being of the church is in communion; its mission is to create fellowship. Therefore the Indian church is called upon to contribute to the creation of a free and fraternal community by releasing its moral and spiritual resources in the midstream of Indian life. The Indian church can fulfill a meaningful role when it relates to peoples and groups as a builder of community, while remaining deeply committed to the issue of justice. The church can play an important role also by promoting a sense of community among the groups and movements working for the liberation of the masses.

The contribution of the church as a promoter of fellowship and as a builder of community assumes particular importance in the context of communalism, with which India is beset today (D'Cruz 1987, 213-27; Engineer 1989). The conflict, violence, and riots that mar the relationship among the various ethnic, linguistic, and particularly religious groups, have deep historical, psychological, and, above all, economic roots. Beneath the surface of apparent religious strifes, conflicts, and rivalries there lies submerged a world of oppression and domination. Almost every communal conflict is the symptom of a situation of bondage or of a longstanding injustice that has not been redressed. The liberative role of the church should, therefore, go below the surface level to the underlying causes. The real proof of the church as an agent of unity and communion is precisely in its ability to respond to the situation of bondage and injustice. The church cannot promote communion, amity, and harmony among the various groups without itself committing to justice and liberation.

These brief reflections on the contribution of the church as an agent of unity will not be complete if I do not refer here also to an unfortunate handicap of the Indian church that raises critical questions about its witnessing to fellowship—I mean the deeply entrenched caste discriminations within the Christian communities themselves (Forrester 1980; Wilfred 1983, 320-33). Even today in some churches of South India lower castes are assigned a separate place, and they are not to sit with high castes. Among Syrian Christians of Kerala outcastes are discriminated against; they are also forced to have separate churches called *pulayan palli* (Koilparampil 1982). In Tiruchirapalli there is a Christian cemetery where a huge wall is erected separating the tombs of the lower castes from those of high castes. Inspired by the words of St. Paul, with reference to Jesus as the one who "has broken down the dividing wall of hostility" (Eph 2:14) between Jews and the Greeks, two priests and some committed Christians literally broke down the wall one night, only to find it rebuilt more strongly within days by infuriated high-caste Christians with the support of other priests!

The anti-Christian character of caste-division was addressed by the bishops in 1982. At their general meeting they declared:

> We state categorically that caste, with its consequent effect of discrimination and "caste mentality" has no place in Christianity. It is, in fact, a denial of Christianity because it is inhuman. It violates the God-given dignity and equality of the human person (CBCI 1982, 45).

These words have not had much effect among Christians as they know that caste mentality and practice are deeply at work among church leaders, priests, and religious themselves. It is this sad situation of a caste-ridden Christian community that made Ambedkar, when contemplating the conversion of the outcastes to a religion that would accept them as equals, give up the idea of turning to Christianity. Instead he and his *dalit* followers embraced Buddhism.

Finally, a word must be added on the ritual conflicts in the Indian church (Wilfred 1988, 249-65). In the Catholic communion in India there are three rites: Syro-Malabar, Syro-Malankara (the Orientals), and Latin. None of the three rites was born in India; all of them were imported into India, the Oriental rites from West Asia and the Latin from the West. Unfortunately we cannot claim that there exists an authentic and effective communion, understanding, and collaboration among the three rites. The conflicts and rivalries that mark the relationship among the three rites certainly does not contribute to the mission of unity and communion the Indian church is called to play in a precarious and volatile communal environment.

ACTIVITIES AND SERVICES

Another area where the church is challenged to be a liberative force is to reorient radically its traditional activities and services and gear them toward establishment of justice. Its complex of institutions and services, contrary to the general impression, has in actual practice benefitted the well-to-do and the middle class, leaving those at the very bottom of society untouched. Schools, colleges, and hospitals run by the church and religious congregations in the cities cater by and large to the elite of society. Further, church institutions are concentrated in the cities, whereas the heart of India pulsates in the villages. In establishing institutions of service, rural areas are shunned. How can we justify all this? The functioning of church-run institutions blatantly contradicts any serious claim on its part to be in service of the masses or to have opted for the poor.

How strange it is that in a country with a majority of rural population and millions of agricultural laborers, we do not have—to my knowledge—a single religious congregation which has as its charism the mission among landless farm laborers, while most religious congregations (there are hundreds of them in India) have as their charism the running of educational institutions. How are we to explain that in a country in which almost two-thirds of the population is illiterate the activities of the church and religious societies should be heavily concentrated on formal education with almost total neglect of informal education? Such contradictions and inconsistencies show that the Indian church has a long way to go before it can claim that it is truly a local church, a church that creatively responds with liberative action to the summons of God coming to it through the cries of the downtrodden.

The awakening of the masses for their liberation and the supportive forces in their liberation challenge the church to reorient its traditional institutions and services for the work of liberation. This implies that the educational, health, and social welfare works have as their target-group the most marginalized, and that social consciousness and education for justice are instilled through church-run institutions. The challenge to the church today goes even further. In the light of what we said above concerning the task of creating community, the church in India should try to cooperate with other faiths and other movements in offering educational and other services, with the poor and oppressed as the target group. The church should move into new areas, avenues open to the liberation of the oppressed, such as legal aid to the poor, to vindicate their rights.

RENOUNCING POWER AND PRESTIGE

Finally, for the church there is the challenge of *kenosis* (self-emptying). There is an intimate relationship between the material poverty and poverty understood as detachment. The poverty and misery of the teeming millions is the result of egotism and greed embodied in various social structures and operating at various levels. The fight against material poverty requires that individuals and groups be liberated from acquisitiveness and possessiveness. Truly liberated persons will be able to stand by the poor and sustain them in their struggles.

Self-emptying, or *kenosis*, has an immense liberative potential; in the Indian tradition true detachment is also the mark of true spiritual existence.

The contribution of the church to liberation will depend upon the degree of its self-emptying, of its renouncing of power and prestige. In a land where the poor do not own any land at all, where the struggle for bread is the fundamental problem, a rich church with extensive landholdings, elite institutions, and affluent religious houses presents a sharp contrast. Some questions are then inevitable. To what use are the possessions of the church put? Whose interests do they serve? To what extent do they help the church be the voice of the poor and an agent of liberation? In this connection, we have to reflect also on the continuous dependence of the church on foreign funds to establish and maintain expensive structures and institutions, which all go to reinforce further the impression that the church is an alien body with its roots and sustenance in the West.

QUESTIONING THE PRESENT ORDER

In one of his poems the great Indian poet Tagore prays to God in these words:

> This is my prayer to thee, my lord—strike, strike at the root of penury in my heart. . . . Give me the strength never to disown the poor or bend my knees before insolent might (Tagore 1918, no. 36).

There is an intimate relationship between "owning the poor" and refusing to surrender before the powers that be. For those who have opted for the poor, there is no budging in the face of what dehumanizes people. This is a grace we need urgently in India today, and it is beginning to manifest itself. The liberative movements are slowly building up into a strong force at the micro and macro levels; they challenge the deeply entrenched forces of exploitation. The present functioning of the political, economic, and social systems, along with their assumptions, are being called into question. The poor peasants refuse to part with the land they have been cultivating for years; women in large numbers carry empty pots and break them in front of government offices as a sign of protest against the indifference of the authorities who fail to provide drinking water to the people in the villages; the *dalit* youth refuse to get down from the bicycle when they pass through the streets of the higher castes; slum-dwellers boldly face the bulldozers sent to raze their huts for beautifying the city. In sum, the oppressed and those who accompany them in their liberation refuse to conform to an unjust order that represses their life and mortifies their spirit.

The upper classes, higher castes, landlords, and exploiters of every type feel threatened by this tide of liberation. They unleash violence and terror on the poor and the marginalized. Those who organize the people and support them in their legitimate demands become particular targets of attack. Terrorism by the powerful has become a serious problem. *Ghoundas* (thugs) are hired to assault, harass, torture, and even kill innocent people for the sole "crime" of having claimed their due—human dignity, equality, and freedom. In some parts of India wealthy landowners keep *bhoomisena* (a private army) to attack the poor and their supporters.

What is most deplorable is that the government, which one would normally expect to defend the poor and the weak, is not only on the side of the rich and the powerful, but is actually controlled by them. In effect, in some of the states of India we have not a government but a political mafia. In the post-colonial period in India, as well as in many other parts of the Third World, the role of the state has changed considerably. It has come to occupy progressively greater space in the life of the society. On the other hand, it has become an instrument of the elite and the economic and social power groups. The result is that the state itself has become a force of oppression (Kothari 1986, 210-16; Thomas 1978a)

No wonder that a state falling in line with the dominant sections of the society has come more and more under questioning; the masses who feel that their welfare has been compromised protest against a state that is hand-in-glove with the rich and powerful. It is against this background that Jayaprakash Narayan, a follower of Gandhi and of the *Sarvodaya* ideal, gave the call for *"total revolution"* (Raj 1986). The situation has not substantially changed, nor have the protests died out. More than the opposition parties, which have become almost a nonentity, the wave of protests from the bottom questions the way the state functions, its corruptions, and malpractices.

This situation of resistance and questioning followed by repression and terrorism presents a whole set of challenges to the church. It is a challenge basically to its message of loving one's neighbor as oneself and the proclamation of the poor and the hungry as blessed. The church is challenged to give a political expression to its faith. Politics and faith are not opposed to each other.

In the ocean of misery, induced poverty, and deprivation of the masses, the church cannot take shelter in the islands of affluence, nurtured and cultivated by the dominant classes; it has to throw itself right in the midst of raging sea and tempest where the drowning poor are desperately looking for some support. Instead, the church has given the impression of accommodating, compromising with the powers that be, rather than taking up a prophetic stand in defense of the poor and the marginalized.

Is the church ready to place not only in theory but *in practice* the interests of the poor and the marginalized before its own institutional interests? This is a crucial question. Blatant injustices and inhuman exploitations go unheeded by the church, which fears losing benefits from the dominant sections in the society. Their support is necessary for the church to run its elite institutions. It is not as though the church is not concerned about the poor. It is very much concerned about them, as amply testified by its humanitarian work in favor of them. But the test of this concern is to be seen in *conflictual situation* where the liberation of the oppressed clashes with the interests of the powerful classes and castes. And here the church tends to side with the powerful rather than commit itself to liberation. As one atheist committed to the liberation of the poor put it in a recent meeting in Madras, "The Church is with the rich, but with a lot of devotion to the poor!"

Similarly, any questioning or critical posture in relation to the state is studiously avoided for fear of losing the minority rights guaranteed by the Indian Constitution. To this we should add the fear that the state may curtail the flow of foreign funds on which the church continues to depend. Such fears and anxieties have worked as a strong deterrent to keep the church from becoming involved in the task of liberation, thus deluding the hope the oppressed pinned on the church. A glaring instance has been the almost total silence of the church at the time of the Emergency, when the state perpetrated all kinds of human rights violations (Roekaerts 1980; *Religion and Society*). The church protests against the state—and does this vigorously—when its institutional interests are at stake or when its minority rights are called into question or violated.

It is a welcome sign that in recent years in certain areas of the country and on certain human rights issues, Christian groups engaged at the grassroots have, with the conviction of their faith and the hope for a better tomorrow for the poor, protested against incidents of exploitation of the weaker sections of the society. These efforts have had in some places the effect of at least loosening the grip of the dominant classes and castes over the powerless. Any initiative to liberate the poor and establish justice is interpreted by the affected power groups as an attempt to convert the poor. These narrow power groups are joined in their chorus by Hindu fundamentalist groups, who also belong to the upper castes and classes.

We should be aware that, of late, the grassroots activism inspired by Christian groups has come under attack also from civil authorities. Efforts to help the poor to withstand injustice have come under suspicion, and the people and groups involved have undergone harassment. Sporadic incidents are generalized to create a general impression that grassroots activism is disrupting law and order. In this context, there seems to be a calculated attempt to drive a wedge between the official church and the activists. Government officials assume that the official church is on the side of the civil authorities, and that it does not endorse liberation theology.

In these circumstances it is highly important to state unambiguously that Christians, whether church leaders or those working at the grassroots, while being firmly committed to nonviolence, cannot abdicate their duty to denounce injustice. It is a responsibility flowing from their faith in the gospel "which is by its very nature a message of freedom and liberation" (Sacred Congregation for the Doctrine of the Faith 1986, no. 1). This should appear clearly to civil authorities and to vested interests of all kinds. The necessity of commitment to justice and liberation comes through very clearly in recent church teachings.

The Vatican *Instruction on Certain Aspects of the Theology of Liberation,* while warning against certain deviations, does not leave any doubt on the validity of liberation theology. It states, "In itself, the expression 'theology of liberation' is a thoroughly valid term" (no. 3). The Instruction, sensing the possibility that the correctives given by the Vatican to liberation theology could be interpreted as an excuse to harass those involved in the struggle for liberation, declares:

> The warnings against the serious deviations of some "theologies of liberation" must not at all be taken as some kind of approval, even indirect, of those who keep the poor in misery, who profit from that

misery, who notice it while doing nothing about it or who remain indifferent to it. The Church, guided by the Gospel of mercy and by the love of mankind, hears the cry of justice and intends to respond to it with all her might (no. 11).

Indian church leaders, therefore, would be seriously failing in their duty if they showed indifference or opposition to the task of liberation and disowned the priests, religious, and Christian laity engaged in this task. The practice of liberation is evidently wrought with ambiguities, contradictions, and limitations. These matters have to be sorted out between the church leaders and those concerned, avoiding outright condemnation of actions for justice. Interestingly, in not a few places today, civil authorities have begun to exert pressure on church leaders to curb the activities of priests and religious and obtain their transfer. This situation should be an invitation to church leadership to reflect more deeply on the question of justice and liberation and its concrete implications.

In India *conversion* has become a despicable word, conjuring up images of colonial times when the missionaries are alleged to have converted large numbers of poor people from Hinduism to the Christian faith with the support of money and material benefits. Therefore any association of liberation with conversion is bound to provoke widespread reaction and condemnation. In fact, the whole talk about liberation in Christianity is seen by the extremist Hindu groups as a subtle new way of pursuing the same old work of conversion under changed circumstances! The church should not be cowed by these allegations and attacks. It is only by the tenacious and disintereted practice of liberation that the church can gain credibility as a true friend of the poor and the marginalized, and thus correct the pervasive image of a Christianity associated with the poor only to proselytize them.

Another source of opposition to Christian participation in the task of liberation derives from some sections of the Christian community itself. Those who oppose the work of liberation are mostly the well-to-do and the upper castes within the Christian community, while in the same community the poor and the scheduled outcastes look up to the church as an agent of liberation. Here again, instead of siding with the dominant castes and classes and letting itself be an instrument for them, the church should direct its attention to a serious educational process of sensitizing the whole Christian community regarding issues of human rights, justice, and liberation.

AN IDEOLOGICAL FRAMEWORK FOR INDIAN LIBERATION AND THE CONTRIBUTION OF THE CHURCH

In order to be effective the project of liberation calls for a certain ideological framework. Ideology is not a mere statement of principles. It offers a vision and interpretation of humanity, society, and history, and also provides practical strategies for social change (Lambino 1982, 10-32). It is able to bring together various forces in a society or nation and give a certain cohesion and direction to its life and action. An integrating and unifying ideological framework is needed in India, made up of so many and varied linguistic, ethnic, cultural, and religious peoples and tribes.

In modern times, the most widespread movement for liberation was the struggle for independence from the British colonial power. And what sustained this movement was the confluence of many streams of thought. There were three main components: 1) the nationalistic ideology oriented to political independence and to the revival of cultural and religious heritage; 2) the democratic liberal and secular ideals and values; and 3) a reinterpretation of religious sources like the *Bhagavadgita* in terms of liberation.

The struggle for national independence culminated in the establishment of a democratic secular and social country. This was envisaged as the framework for the unity of the country and its programmed development. After forty-three years of independence we have come to realize that this ideological framework has been tearing apart all along. There has been a serious erosion of democratic and secular ideals and institutions. Democracy has become simply a huge blanket spread over the nation under which rapacious wolves have been preying on defenseless lambs. The failure of democracy and secular institutions to protect and defend the weak, allowing the dominant classes, castes, and extremist religious groups to rule has resulted in a crisis of fragmentation of the country and in the escalation of communalism and communal violence, death, and destruction. Why have democracy and secular ideals failed to take root?

I think there are three major reasons. First of all, the democratic rule and parliamentary systems were introduced without taking into account the gross disparity and imbalance of power among the various traditional groups in India. The result was that the traditionally dominant groups have also come to instrumentalize the democratic system by turning the masses into a vote-bank to be manipulated during the elections. This is something which the western observers and writers often fail to understand. While there is the exterior appearance of democracy, in reality the masses are not able to participate effectively and freely in the democratic process.

Second, the whole secular, liberal, and democratic tradition was losing at the world level the spiritual elan and humanism it had embodied at the time of its emergence in the West and has, in conjunction with capitalism, progressively banished from public life all ethical perspectives. These institutions introduced into India at a degenerated stage, in interplay with the traditional Indian power groups, have put out even the flickering flame of ethics and have immersed public life in total darkness where corruption and bribery rule.

Third, in the present form the democratic system and secular institutions are the fruit of the historical evolution of European history and society; they do not correspond to Indian culture and ethos, though the substance of these ideals has not been absent in the Indian tradition. Some of the national leaders already at the time of independence had expressed reservations about projecting democratic and liberal ideals as a unifying framework for the whole nation.

At this juncture of the evolution of the Indian nation, we can observe four ideologies at work, each one claiming to redeem the poor and the downtrodden. These four ideologies are the legacy of four great personalities: Nehru, Gandhi, Ambedkar, and Marx.

Nehru was an ardent advocate of secularism, modernization, and industrialization. In his vision these would lead India on the path of progress, abolish poverty, and ensure a bright future for the poor. Through the process of education and modernization social evils like caste-discrimination and inequality would disappear. These high hopes have been belied. And yet this ideology has many votaries all over the country.

The second ideology is the Gandhian path of *sarvodaya*, the welfare of all. Gandhi was sceptical of large-scale democratic systems where individual freedom and growth could be easily submerged. Gandhi's ideals for the welfare of all was the *swaraj* (self-rule) by which every village would be self-governed and economically self-reliant (Iyer 1973; Chatterjee 1983). This may appear an anachronistic attempt. But Gandhi with his ideology of *sarvodaya* stands, in reality, not on the side of the pre-modern but on the side of the post-modern. He sensed the inherent weakness and detected the seeds of destruction in modern society, its political and economic systems. Hence he projected a post-modern society of small communities intended to safeguard freedom and independence. This vision of society is increasingly turning Gandhian ideals into an attractive alternative.

Both the secular democratic ideology of Nehru and the *sarvodaya* ideal of Gandhi differ from the ideology which has as its main focus the powerless and outcastes. According to Ambedkar, the foremost representative of this ideology, it is not enough to think of political and economic transformation. Even more important is the *social* transformation of India. Without changing the social marginalization of the outcastes, pursuing political and economic goals will not bring about intended results. While Gandhi was concerned about rehabilitation of the untouchables within the Hindu fold, calling them *harijans* (people of God), and thus giving a religious sanction to their political marginalization and inequality, Ambedkar, on the other hand, himself a member of the untouchable community, realized the futility of religious solutions to what were and are deep-rooted social problems. He advocated strongly the need on the part of the outcastes to become politically strengthened and get actively involved in the political power (Gupta 1985). Nationalism for Ambedkar was not simply emancipation from the external colonial power but liberation from internal oppression as well, which entailed the exorcising of the caste-spirit. This ideological orientation is continued by the *dalit panthers,* who struggle for the emancipation of the untouchables today.

Finally, Marxist ideology has been an important force in Indian society, though the number of those openly belonging to the communist or Marxist party or followers of the ideology in its entirety may not be impressive. The Marxist analysis of Indian socioeconomic life with the study of the root causes of poverty has found much response among the downtrodden and those who support them in the struggle, especially wherever this analysis is coupled with the commitment of the Marxists in the task of liberation. Further, Marxism has brought to traditional Indian thinking and culture, which has the tendency to move on the transphenomenal sphere, a new and complementary dimension of the historical, social, and the collective; it has infused into India the importance of human responsibility in shaping the world, history, and the future. On the other hand, the limitations and inadequacies of Marxian ideology, especially its failure to take adequate account of the role of culture, the subjective dimensions of life and history, and its devaluation of religion have kept this idelogy from having a mass appeal.

None of these ideologies can be dismissed. They complement each other by their different foci and emphases. But none of these four major ideologies at work in India has proved capable of responding fully to the complexity of the Indian task of liberation. This is realized by many groups and organizations working at the grassroots. Hopes are that a distinctive ideology of integral Indian humanism will slowly emerge out of the encounter of these and various other streams of thought, and above all out of the concrete praxis of liberation.

This complex Indian world of ideologies is also a challenge to the church. The church can be a partner in the Indian search for a vision of liberation as well as a very resourceful contributor.

I shall confine my reflections to only four points:

1. I believe that Christianity can play a crucial role in strengthening the democratic and secular vision in India at a time when the political system and institutions deriving from it are utilized more for oppression than for liberation. Though the democratic and secular ideals emerged in Europe independent of the church, and even in opposition to it, yet the spiritual roots behind this vision stemmed from Christianity. If these institutions are to survive and realize their professsed goals, they must be constantly nourished by principles of moral and spiritual order. Christianity could be an active agent in promoting genuine freedom of people, their self-hood, equality, and justice at all levels of social and political life. In the face of growing communalism in India, there is a great need to evolve a true secular vision and practice. The church can help to generate from below new and fresh forces for the upholding of democracy and secular goals. The vision and practice of the church should not be communal, even when it is provoked to be so by the Hindu communal and fundamentalist forces. One communalism cannot be tackled by another of the same kind.

Most secular ideologies, even though they are known as secular, stem from a deep spiritual matrix insofar as they affirm the human, freedom, truth, and justice. On their part, the great reformers of modern India, from Raja Rammohan Roy down to Swami Agnivesh have lead the people to live the secular implications of religion going beyond a fundamentalist and alienating type of religiosity that glosses over the material basis of life. They find no opposition between secular and spiritual, but rather a mutual interpenetration. What we have then is a "sacred secularity," where secular ideologies and religions can meet and dialogue on the project of liberation. If dialogue with other religions is of crucial importance today for the Indian church in the project of liberation, of no less importance is the encounter with the humanist and secular ideologies for the same goal.

2. That Christianity can be a potent source of liberative vision is attested by its influence on the nineteenth-century Bengal Renaissance movement, *Brahmo Samaj* and Ramakrishna-Vivekananda movements, social reform movements, and others, which all contributed to the regeneration of Indian society (Thomas 1976a and 1976b). The whole present Indian situation is a pressing invitation to the church to play a similar role today. This means the church should interact with the various ideologies, with the vision, interpretation, and strategies they present. It should not be afraid of the powerful challenges these ideologies present to the Christian vision and practice in India.

3. It has been widely recognized that in India no significant social transformation can take place without reference to religion and its motivational force. Any ideology in India, therefore, has to reckon with the force religion represents in Indian society and has to take a stand. On the other hand, to be relevant the various religions are obliged to make a contribution to clarify and deepen the vision on humanity and society. The church can dialogue with other faiths in India in evolving a new vision imbued with spiritual, moral, and humanistic sense for the reconstruction of the country.

4. In the Indian situation, the contribution which Christianity and Marxism can make, interestingly, lies in the same direction. And this is understandable against the background of their common Judeo-Christian origin. In fact, the strong emphasis in both Christianity and Marxism on history, on human involvement, assuming responsibility for the future, strong affirmation of the human and the social are very helpful elements to reshape Indian cultural and religious vision and perspectives. This implies, then, that the relationship between Marxism and Christianity cannot be, in India, a simple extension of the debate in the West or in other parts of the world. Their relationship has to be viewed in the light of the many common contributions they can make to the liberation of the downtrodden and the transformation of Indian society.

CONCLUSION

The church is challenged to bring to bear upon the present dehumanizing Indian situation the force of a liberating humanism. In the words of J.P. Naik, a Hindu:

Hinduism has learnt one great thing from Christianity. I do not attach much importance to how many people accept Christianity as a religion. But the ideal that Hinduism got from Christianity was that the way of God lies through the service of man.... The emphasis on *seva*, the service of man as a method of realising God came through our contact with Christianity (Naik 1967, 134).

To be the church is to be with the people as Jesus was, manifesting the human face of the Divine. This implies that the church be truly incarnate, rooted among the people, enfleshing itself with the broken and tortured flesh of India's oppressed and suffering millions and becoming truly "flesh of India's flesh" (Rayan 1976, 257-67). The liberating mission of the church is, then, a process of deep immersion and inculturation. The church cannot exercise a liberative role as long as it keeps aloof from the struggles of the people and is engrossed in building up a narrow identity. The liberating mission of the church has to be exercised jointly with those forces and movements that are committed to the humanization of Indian society and with the brothers and sisters of other faiths engaged in the same cause.

Immersion, participation, dialogue, liberation, and inculturation are challenges to the church which cannot be faced by declarations, but have to be lived out. To quote Ashok Mehta, "If it is the claim of the Christians that even to this day they feel the agony of Christ on the cross whenever humanity suffers, as it were, it has to be proved in action, not by any statement" (Mehta 1974, 197). This is what liberation theology is all about.

REFERENCES

Asian bishops. 1975. In *For All the Peoples of Asia*, vol. 1, IMC Publications, Manila, 1984.
Augustine, P. A. 1981. "Conversion as a Social Protest," *Religion and Society*, vol. 28, no. 4.
Beteille, Andre. 1971. *Caste and Power: Changing Patterns of Stratification in a Tanjore Village*, University of California Press, Berkeley.
CBCI (Catholic Bishops' Conference of India). 1982. *Report of the Catholic Bishops' Conference of India (CBCI) General Meeting*, Tiruchirapalli, New Delhi.
Chatterjee, Margaret. 1983. *Gandhi's Religious Thought*, Macmillan, London.
D'Cruz, Emil. 1987. "Indian Secularism and Communalism: A Theoretical Framework," *Social Action* 37.
Engineer, Asghar Ali. 1989. *Communalism and Communal Violence in India*, Ajanta Publications, Delhi.
Forrester, D. B. 1980. *Caste and Christianity*, London.
Gupta, S. K. 1985. *The Scheduled Castes in Modern Indian Politics: Their Emergence as a Political Power*. Munshiram Manoharlal Publishers, New Delhi.
Iyer, Raghavan. 1973. *The Moral and Political Thought of Mahatma Gandhi*, Oxford University Press, Oxford/New York.
Kananaikil, Jose, ed. 1983. *Scheduled Castes and the Struggle Against Inequality*. Indian Social Institute, Delhi.

Koilparampil, G. 1982. *Caste in the Catholic Community in Kerala*, Cochin.
Kothari, Rajni. 1986. "Masses, Classes and the State," *Economic and Political Weekly* 21 (February 1, 1986).
Lambino, Antonio B. 1982. "Ideology, Social Change and the Christian Conscience." In *Faith, Ideologies and Christian Options*, Loyola Papers 7/8, Manila.
Mehta, Ashok. 1974. Quoted in S. J. Samartha, *The Hindu Response to the Unbound Christ*, CLS, Madras.
Naik, J. P. 1967. "The Role and Problems of Private Enterprise in Education." In *The Christian College and National Development*, CLS, Madras.
Oddie, G. A. 1979. *Social Protest in India: British Protestant Missionaries and Social Reform 1850-1890*, Manohar, New Delhi.
Panikkar, K. M. 1953. *Asia and Western Dominance*, London.
Puthanagady, Paul, ed. 1986. *Towards an Indian Theology of Liberation: The Statement, Papers and Proceedings of the Ninth Annual Meeting of the Indian Theological Association.* Bangalore.
Raj, S. Alboes. 1981. "Mass Religious Conversion as Protest Movement: A Framework," *Religion and Society*, vol. 28, no. 4.
Raj, Sebasti L. 1986. *Total Revolution: The Final Phase of Jayaprakash Narayan's Political Philosophy*, Satya Nilayam Publications, Madras.
Rayan, Samuel. 1976. "Flesh of India's Flesh," *Jeevadhara* 6.
Religion and Society, vol. 24, nos. 2 and 3 (June-September 1977). These issues were dedicated to the response of Christians and churches to the Emergency.
Roekaerts, M. 1980. *Christians and the Emergency in India* (May), Pro Mundi Vita, Dossiers.
Sa, Fidelis de. 1975. *Crisis in Chota Nagpur: The Juridical Conflict Between Jesuit Missionaries and British Government Officials, November 1889-March 1890*, Bangalore.
Sacred Congregation for the Doctrine of the Faith. 1986. *Instruction on Christian Freedom and Liberation*, TPI, Bangalore.
Saint, Kishore. 1987. Incident reported at a meeting sponsored by Caritas India in Delhi, May 1987. Saint is a Gandhian intellectual and grassroots activist in Rajasthan.
Schurhammer. 1977. *St.Francis Xavier: His Life, His Times*, vol. 2, Rome.
Shourie, Arun. 1982. "Reasons for Hope," *New Quest*, no. 34 (July-August 1982).
Tagore, Rabindranath. 1918. *Gitanjali*, Macmillan, New Delhi/New York.
Thomas, M. M. 1976a. *The Acknowledged Christ of Indian Renaissance*, CLS, Madras.
———. 1976b. *The Secular Ideologies of India and the Secular Meaning of Christ*, CLS, Madras.
———. 1978a. "Change in the Function and Understanding of the State in the Modern World," *Church and State, Opening a New Ecumenical Discussion*, WCC, Geneva.
———. 1978b. *Revolution in India and Christian Humanism*, New Delhi.
———. 1980. "Spiritual Penetration: Revolts of the Poor and the Oppressed," *Religion and Society*, vol. 27, no. 1, 10-20.
WCC. 1978. *Separation Without Hope? Essays on the Relation between the Church and the Poor During the Industrial Revolution and the Western Colonial Expansion*, Geneva.
Wilfred, Felix. 1983. "Temptations of the Church in India Today," *Vidyajyoti* 47.
———. 1988. *The Emergent Church in a New India*, Tiruchirapalli, New Delhi.

Contributors

Yvon Ambroise: Doctor in Sociology, and executive director of Caritas India, New Delhi.

Walter Fernandes: Former Director of Indian Social Institute, New Delhi.

T. K. John: Professor at the Theological Faculty of *Vidyajyoti*, New Delhi.

George M. Soares-Prabhu: Professor of New Testament at the theological faculty of *Jnana Deepa Vidyapeeth,* Pune.

Xavier Irudayaraj: Professor at *Arul Kadal,* Regional Theologate of the Jesuits, Madras.

Sebastian Kappen: Doctor in Theology; thinker, writer, and activist based in Bangalore.

Ignatius Puthiadam: Actively involved in interreligious dialogue and research at Varanasi (Banares); formerly professor of philosophy at *Satya Nilayam,* Madras.

Samuel Rayan: Former Principal of The School of Ecumenical Theology, Bangalore, and now professor emeritus at the Theological Faculty of *Vidyajyoti,* New Delhi.

Michael Amaladoss: General Assistant at the Jesuit Curia, Rome; formerly professor in St. Paul's Seminary, Tiruchirapalli, and dean at *Vidyajyoti,* New Delhi.

Felix Wilfred: Professor of Theology in St. Paul's Seminary, Tiruchirapalli; formerly president of the Indian Theological Association.

www.ingramcontent.com/pod-product-compliance
Lightning Source LLC
Chambersburg PA
CBHW062038220426
43662CB00010B/1552